Triumph GT6, Vitesse 2 litre 1969-73 Autobook

By Kenneth Ball
and the Autobooks Team of Technical Writers

Triumph GT6 Mk 2, 3 1969-73
Triumph Vitesse 2 litre Mk 2 1969-71

Autobooks Ltd. Golden Lane Brighton BN1 2QJ England

The AUTOBOOK series of Workshop Manuals is the largest in the world and covers the majority of British and Continental motor cars, as well as all major Japanese and Australian models. For a full list see the back of this manual.

CONTENTS

Introduction

Acknowledgement

Chapter 1	The Engine	9
Chapter 2	The Fuel System	27
Chapter 3	The Ignition System	41
Chapter 4	The Cooling System	51
Chapter 5	The Clutch	57
Chapter 6	The Gearbox and Overdrive	63
Chapter 7	Propeller Shaft, Rear Axle and Rear Suspension	75
Chapter 8	Front Suspension and Hubs	87
Chapter 9	The Steering System	93
Chapter 10	The Braking System	101
Chapter 11	The Electrical System	113
Chapter 12	The Bodywork	129
Appendix		147

ISBN 0 85147 389 X

First Edition   1970
Reprinted   1971
Reprinted   1972
Second Edition, fully revised   1972
Third Edition, fully revised   1973
Reprinted   1975
Reprinted   1975

© Autobooks Ltd 1975

723

Printed and bound in Brighton England for Autobooks Ltd by G. Beard & Son Ltd   A

ACKNOWLEDGEMENT

We wish to thank Standard-Triumph Ltd. for their co-operation and also for supplying data and illustrations. Considerable assistance has also been given by owners, who have discussed their cars in detail, and we would like to express our gratitude for this invaluable advice and help.

INTRODUCTION

This do-it-yourself Workshop Manual has been specially written for the owner who wishes to maintain his car in first class condition and to carry out his own servicing and repairs. Considerable savings on garage charges can be made, and one can drive in safety and confidence knowing the work has been done properly.

Comprehensive step-by-step instructions and illustrations are given on all dismantling, overhauling and assembling operations. Certain assemblies require the use of expensive special tools, the purchase of which would be unjustified. In these cases information is included but the reader is recommended to hand the unit to the agent for attention.

Throughout the Manual hints and tips are included which will be found invaluable, and there is an easy to follow fault diagnosis at the end of each chapter.

Whilst every care has been taken to ensure correctness of information it is obviously not possible to guarantee complete freedom from errors or to accept liability arising from such errors or omissions.

Instructions may refer to the righthand or lefthand sides of the vehicle or the components. These are the same as the righthand or lefthand of an observer standing behind the car and looking forward.

CHAPTER 1

THE ENGINE

1:1 Description
1:2 Removing the engine and gearbox
1:3 Removing and replacing the cylinder head
1:4 Servicing the head and valve gear
1:5 Servicing the valve timing gear
1:6 The camshaft and distributor drive gear
1:7 The clutch and flywheel
1:8 The sump

1:9   The oil pump
1:10 Lubrication, oil filter and relief valve
1:11 Pistons and connecting rods
1:12 Crankshaft and main bearings
1:13 Reassembling a stripped engine
1:14 Valve rocker adjustment
1:15 Emission control
1:16 Fault diagnosis

1:1 Description

The gearbox, though it is bolted to the engine, will be dealt with separately in **Chapter 6.** Apart from removing the engine and gearbox as a unit, this chapter will deal only with the engine.

The engine is similar in all models of cars covered by this manual but a version, differing only in detail, is produced for the U.S. market and is therefore built to produce the minimum exhaust pollution.

The usual features of Standard-Triumph design are again quite distinctive. **FIG 1:1** shows the fixed parts of the engine and **FIG 1:2** shows the moving parts. The keys to these two figures run consecutively, and throughout this chapter parts will be referred to using the part numbers from these keys, unless otherwise specifically stated. It will be seen that the engine is a six-cylinder unit, with the pistons in line, and that the overhead valves are operated by rockers moved by pushrods and cam followers from a camshaft mounted in the cylinder block. Details of bore and stroke, together with an extensive coverage of further technical information, are given in Technical Data at the end of this volume.

The crankshaft is supported in four main bearings. The main bearings and big-ends use renewable steel-backed alloy shells for the crankshaft to run in. Keyed to the front of the crankshaft are a sprocket and a pulley. A timing chain transmits the drive from the crankshaft sprocket to turn the camshaft sprocket and the camshaft. A fan belt round the crankshaft pulley drives the alternator, or generator, and water pump. The flywheel is bolted directly to the rear end of the crankshaft.

The camshaft runs in five bearings. A gear on the camshaft turns another gear which supplies the drive to the oil pump and to the distributor. The tachometer drive is embodied in the distributor. An extra cam on the camshaft operates the mechanical fuel pump mounted on the engine.

The lubricating oil is contained in the sump, from where it is drawn by the oil pump. The pressurized oil is fed first to a non-adjustable relief valve where excess oil is bled off back to the sump to limit the maximum oil pressure. The oil then passes through an external fullflow oil filter before reaching the fore and aft oil gallery running along the lefthand side of the engine. By internal

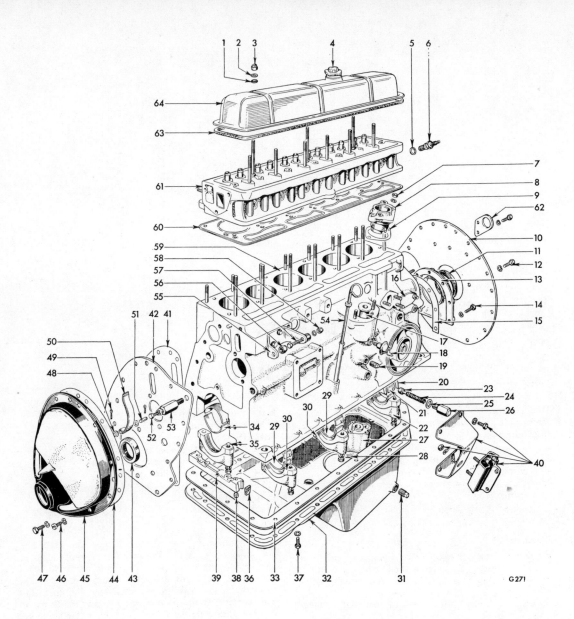

FIG 1:1 Engine details, fixed parts

Key to Fig 1:1   1 Fibre washer   2 Plain washer   3 Nyloc nut   4 Filler cap   5 Copper/asbestos washer
6 Sparking plug   7 Nut   8 Adaptor   9 Gasket   10 Rear engine plate   11 Rear oil seal   12 Bolt
13 Rear oil seal housing   14 Bolt   15 Gasket   16 Blanking plate   17 Oil pump drive shaft bush
18 Oil pressure switch   19 Plug   20 Crankshaft thrust washer   21 Rear bearing shell   22 Rear bearing cap
23 Relief valve   24 Spring   25 Copper washer   26 Cap nut   27 Oil pump body   28 Oil pump end plate
29 Centre bearing shell   30 Centre main bearing cap   31 Sump plug   32 Sump   33 Sump gasket
34 Front bearing shell   35 Front main bearing cap   36 Sealing wedges   37 Sump bolt   38 Slotted screw
39 Front sealing block   40 Front engine mounting   41 Gasket   42 Front engine plate   43 Oil seal   44 Gasket
45 Front timing cover   46 Slotted setscrew   47 Bolt   48 Plain washer   49 Splitpin   50 Chain tensioner
51 Pivot pin   52 Bolt   53 Generator pedestal   54 Dipstick   55 Bracket   56 Nyloc nut   57 Bolt
58 Nyloc nut   59 Cylinder block   60 Cylinder head gasket   61 Cylinder head   62 Lifting eye
63 Rocker cover gasket   64 Rocker cover

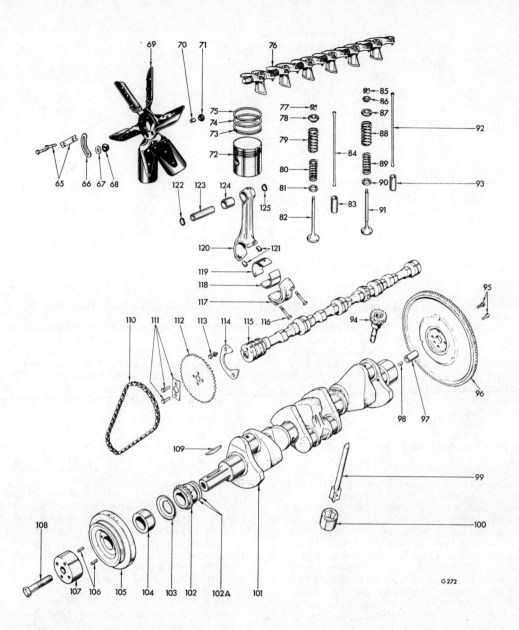

FIG 1:2 Engine details, moving parts

Key to Fig 1:2
65 Bolts and lock tabs   66 Balance weight   67 Washer   68 Rubber bush   69 Fan assembly
70 Steel bush   71 Rubber bush   72 Piston   73 Oil control ring   74 Tapered compression ring
75 Plain compression ring   76 Rocker shaft assembly (see FIG 1:6)   77 Split collets   78 Collar   79 Spring (outer)
80 Spring (inner)   81 Lower collar   82 Inlet valve   83 Cam follower   84 Pushrod   85 Split collets
86 Inner collar (exhaust)   87 Outer collar (exhaust)   88 Spring (outer)   89 Spring (inner)   90 Lower collar
91 Exhaust valve   92 Pushrod   93 Cam follower   94 Distributor and oil pump drive gear   95 Bolts
96 Flywheel   97 Bush   98 Dowel   99 Inner rotor and spindle   100 Outer rotor   101 Crankshaft
102 Sprocket   102A Shim   103 Flinger   104 Seal extension   105 Crankshaft pulley   106 Dowels
107 Fan boss   108 Bolt   109 Key   110 Timing chain   111 Bolts and lock plate   112 Camshaft sprocket
113 Bolt   114 Keeper plate   115 Camshaft   116 Bolt   117 Connecting rod cap
118 Connecting rod bearing shell (lower)   119 Connecting rod bearing shell (upper)   120 Connecting rod   121 Dowels
122 Circlip   123 Gudgeon pin   124 Gudgeon pin bush   125 Circlip

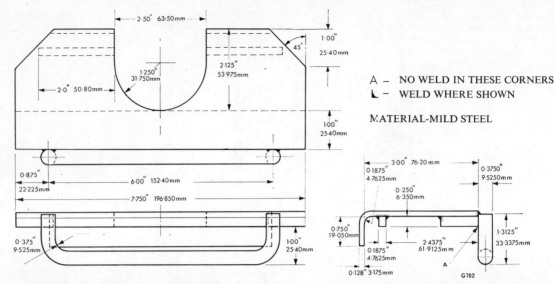

A – NO WELD IN THESE CORNERS
L – WELD WHERE SHOWN

MATERIAL-MILD STEEL

FIG 1:3 Details of tool for protecting the brake pipe when removing or refitting the engine

passages the oil is fed directly to the main bearings and the camshaft bearings. Drillings in the crankshaft lead the oil from the main bearings to the big-end bearings. Splash from the crankshaft lubricates the cylinder bores, pistons and small-end bearings. Seepage oil from the front camshaft bearing as well as the oil mist in the crankcase lubricate the timing chain and sprockets. A scroll and two flats on the rear end of the camshaft supply a metered quantity of oil to the valve rocker assembly. This oil runs down the pushrod tubes to lubricate the cam followers before finally returning to the sump.

Crankcase fumes are led from the engine through an emission valve to the induction manifold where they mix with the fuel and air mixture to become burnt in the engine. On standard engines the air enters through a filter in the filler cap, but on emission controlled engines this filler cap is sealed and crankcase ventilating air is drawn through a restrictor hole on the clean air side of the air filters. The emission valve contains a diaphragm which partially closes the valve when the vacuum in the induction manifold is high. This prevents excessive fumes and air being drawn through and upsetting the slow-running.

1:2 Removing the engine and gearbox

Removing the crankshaft from the engine is the only operation for which it is essential to have the engine removed from the car, though if major work is being carried out it will be found more convenient to have the engine on a bench rather than in the car. The front brake pipe lies along the top of the chassis crossmember and if the pipe is not protected it will be damaged when the engine is removed. **FIG 1:3** gives sufficient detail to make a protecting plate, and this plate is shown fitted in **FIG 1:4.**

If the operator is not a skilled automobile engineer, it is suggested that he will find much useful information in

'Hints on Maintenance and Overhaul' at the end of this manual, and that he should read it before starting work.

The engine and gearbox are removed from above, but to gain access underneath the car the front needs to be raised. **It should be stressed that any supports used must be firmly based and not likely to collapse during the operation, or serious injury could result.**

1 Isolate the battery. Remove the bonnet and engine bay side valances (see **Chapter 12**). Disconnect the radiator hoses and remove the radiator (see **Chapter 4**).

2 Remove the air cleaners and disconnect the throttle rod and choke cables from the carburetters. Disconnect the fuel pipe from the fuel pump at the carburetters. Remove the carburetters (see **Chapter 2**). Disconnect the heater hoses and heater controls to the water valve. Disconnect the exhaust pipe from the exhaust manifold. On the Vitesse the exhaust pipe is also held by a clip at the rear of the sump, so remove this clip.

3 Instead of removing the carburetters individually they may be removed with the inlet manifold. The inlet and exhaust manifolds are shown in **FIG 1:5.** Disconnect the water hoses to the manifold, and the hoses for the exhaust emission valve. Disconnect the vacuum pipe between the carburetters and distributor at the carburetter. Progressively slacken the securing nuts and bolts, and when they are removed, carefully ease the manifolds off the studs.

4 Disconnect the fuel pipe from the fuel pump. Either drain the fuel tank or plug the pipe to prevent fuel draining out. Disconnect electrical cables from distributor, generator or alternator, starter motor, temperature transmitter and oil pressure transmitter. Disconnect the tachometer drive from the distributor.

5 Remove the front seats and carpets (facia support and tunnel trim if fitted), the gearbox cover and then remove the gearbox top cover extension housing and gearbox top cover. Disconnect the overdrive wires on the GT6 Mk 3. Remove the clutch slave cylinder. Disconnect the speedometer drive and the front end

of the propeller shaft. Attach a sling to the engine lifting eyes and support the weight of the unit. Remove the gearbox rear mounting. These operations are covered in greater detail in **Chapter 6.**

6 Remove the bolts which secure the front engine mountings to the chassis. **Check that all connections from the engine and gearbox unit to the car are disconnected.** Raise the engine, tilting the gearbox downwards and pulling the unit forwards out of the car as it is raised. Stand the engine on old tyres or something similar to protect it from damage.

7 The engine is replaced in the reverse order of removal. The cooling system, gearbox, engine sump and clutch hydraulics will all have to be refilled and the clutch hydraulic system bled as soon as the engine has been refitted. Check all systems for leaks both before and after starting the engine.

1 : 3 Removing and replacing the cylinder head

The cylinder head and its associated components are shown in **FIG 1 : 6.** It is essential that, whenever the cylinder head securing nuts are removed or replaced, they are tightened or slackened progressively and evenly in the order shown in FIG 1 : 7. Failure to observe this precaution can easily result in the cylinder head becoming distorted, causing the head gasket to fail prematurely.

The cylinder head may be removed with the engine still fitted in the car.

1 Isolate the battery. Drain the cooling system and disconnect the radiator hoses, heater hoses and manifold hoses. Label the sparking plug leads, to ensure that they will be replaced in the correct order, and disconnect them from the sparking plugs.

2 Remove the air cleaners. Disconnect the exhaust pipe from the manifold flange. Disconnect all the carburetter controls including fuel supply pipe, vacuum pipe and breather pipe. Disconnect the control cable to the heater valve. Progressively slacken the six retaining clips and four bolts which secure the manifolds to the cylinder head and withdraw the manifolds complete with carburetters.

3 Slacken the generator (or alternator) mounting bolts and press the generator (or alternator) towards the cylinder block to slacken the fan belt. Take out the three bolts securing the water pump assembly in place and remove the water pump.

4 Remove the nuts 5, plain washers 4 and fibre washers 3. Lift off the rocker cover 2 with its gasket 1. Progressively slacken and remove the six nuts 29. Remove the washers 30 and lift off the complete rocker gear assembly.

5 Progressively slacken the cylinder head nuts in the order shown in **FIG 1 : 7** and when they are all loose remove them and the washers. Lift out the twelve pushrods 13 and store them in the correct order for reassembly.

6 Lift the cylinder head squarely up the studs to remove it. If the head is difficult to free, try tapping on the sides using a wooden block to hammer on. If the head is particularly obstinate, put the car in top gear and

FIG 1:4   Tool fitted on front chassis crossmember

push it slowly forwards so that the cylinder compression will break the seal and free the head.

7 Lift out the cam followers 12, using a magnet on a piece of string if they are difficult to grasp, and store them in the correct order for replacement. It is essential that cam followers and pushrods are replaced in the position from which they were removed.

Refitting the cylinder head is the reversal of the removal procedure but note the following points:

1 Examine the cam followers 12 to ensure that they are not chipped or worn. Replace them in their respective bores and check that they both rotate and slide freely in the bore.

2 Clean the mating faces of the cylinder head and block. Use a new gasket 11, and smear it lightly with clean grease as a seal. Replace the cylinder head and progressively tighten the securing nuts, in the correct order, until they are all at a torque of 65 to 70 lb ft (9 to 9.7 kg m). Replace the pushrods 13 in their correct positions.

3 Before refitting the rocker gear slacken the locknuts 34 and partially unscrew the adjusters 33 to make sure they will allow plenty of clearance and not bend the pushrods. Reset the valve clearance (see **Section 1 : 14**), after tightening the nuts 29 to a torque of 24 to 26 lb ft (3.3 to 3.6 kg m).

4 After replacing the remainder of the parts and filling the cooling system, run the car for 500 miles and then retighten the cylinder head securing nuts. The valve clearance must then also be reset, as this will alter every time the cylinder head nuts are tightened.

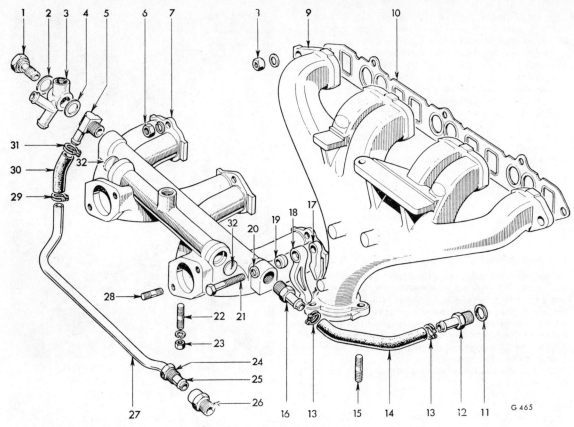

FIG 1:5   Manifold details

Key to Fig 1:5   1 Banjo bolt   2 Washer   3 Housing   4 Washer   5 Adaptor   6 Nut   7 Inlet manifold
8 Nut   9 Exhaust manifold   10 Gasket   11 Washer   12 Union   13 Clip   14 Hose   15 Stud
16 Union   17 Clamp   18 Clamp   19 Washer   20 Washer   21 Bolt   22 Stud   23 Bolt
24 Union nut   25 Olive   26 Union   27 Delivery tube   28 Stud   29 Clip   30 Hose   31 Clip   32 Seal

1:4 Servicing the head and valve gear

Remove the cylinder head as described in the previous section. To prevent dirt and chips from falling into the engine, block off the oil and water passages with bits of clean non-fluffy rags. Make sure the rags are large enough to prevent them falling through or being forgotten when the cylinder head is refitted.

Scrape the carbon from the combustion chambers in the head before removing the valves, so as to avoid damaging the valve seats. Use a blunt tool to remove the carbon. A rotary wire brush mounted in an electric drill is excellent for cleaning out the inlet and exhaust ports, but take great care not to damage the valve seats or guides. The combustion chambers and ports may be polished using emerycloth but the cylinder head must be cleaned very thoroughly in order to remove all abrasive particles, otherwise these will work their way into the bores causing scoring and damage.

Use a long metal straightedge, or better still a surface table and engineers blue, to check that the mating surfaces of the head and block are flat and undistorted. High-spots may be removed by careful use of a scraper,

but grinding on a surface grinder is the only cure for distortion.

Before removing the carbon from the tops of the pistons smear a little grease around the top of each bore. Set one pair of pistons nearly at TDC and use a soft tool, such as a sharpened stick of solder, to remove the carbon from the tops of the pistons. Leave the carbon around the periphery of the piston and the top of the bore as this protects the piston rings from heat as well as acting as an oil seal. An old piston ring laid on top of the piston will prevent this carbon being removed. **Never use abrasives on the pistons as particles can easily be left in the engine.** Turn the engine to bring another pair of pistons nearly to TDC and clean these before turning the engine again and bringing the final pair of pistons nearly to TDC. When all the pistons have been cleaned wipe away the grease from the bores. Turning the engine will raise the dirt to the top of the bores where it will stick to the grease and so can easily be cleaned away with it.

1 Refer to **FIG 1:6**. Use a valve spring compressor to remove the valves. The valve heads are held in place and the valve caps forced downwards to compress the valve springs 16 and 17. The valve collets 20

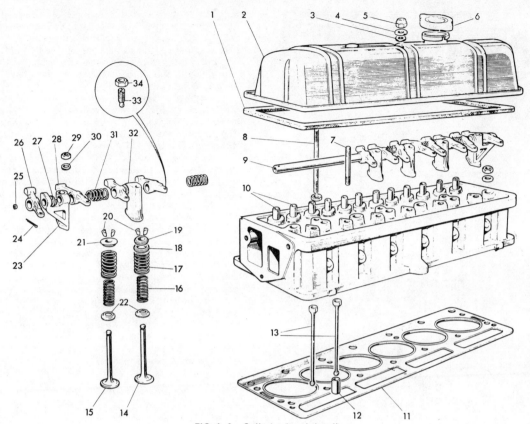

FIG 1:6   Cylinder head details

Key to Fig 1:6   1 Gasket (rocker cover)   2 Rocker cover   3 Fibre washer   4 Plain washer   5 Nyloc nut
6 Oil filter cap   7 Stud (rocker pedestal)   8 Stud (rocker cover)   9 Rocker shaft   10 Valve guides
11 Gasket (cylinder head)   12 Cam follower   13 Pushrods   14 Valve (exhaust)   15 Valve (inlet)
16 Valve spring (inner)   17 Valve spring (outer)   18 Upper spring seat (exhaust valve)   19 Valve cap (exhaust valve)
20 Valve collets   21 Valve cap (inlet valve)   22 Valve spring seats   23 Rocker pedestal (outer)   24 Splitpin
25 End plug (rocker shaft)   26 Rocker   27 Double spring washer (end rocker pedestal)   28 Rocker   29 Nut
30 Washer   31 Spring (rocker shaft)   32 Rocker pedestal (intermediate)   33 Tappet adjuster   34 Locknut (tappet adjuster)

are removed and the spring allowed to expand again. Note that the inlet valve has only one valve cap 21 and that the exhaust valves are fitted with valve cap 19 and a spring seat 18. Remove the caps and springs, and slide the valve out underneath the head. Mark the valves and store them, with their associated parts, in the correct order for reassembly. Note that later engines have single valve springs only.

2 Clean away carbon and deposits from the valve head, taking care not to damage the seat. Valve stems must be straight (check with a metal straightedge) and they must show no signs of wear or 'picking up'. If satisfactory, but the valve seats show signs of excessive pitting, have the valve seats reground at a garage. Do not attempt to remove excessive pitting using grinding paste as this will only remove metal from the seat in the head as well. Recut the seats in the head if they are badly worn or pitted. If the seats are then too wide they may be reduced using a 15 deg. facing cutter. Seats which are beyond recutting can be restored by having inserts fitted.

3 To grind-in valves put a light spring under the head and use medium-grade grinding paste, unless the seats are in good condition in which case fine-grade paste may be used immediately. Use a suction-cup tool to hold the valve head and grind with a semi-rotary movement, letting the valve rise off the seat occasionally by the pressure of the spring under the valve head. Use grinding paste sparingly and when the pitting has been removed, clean away the old paste and start using fine-grade paste. When the seats have a matt, grey, even finish clean away all traces of grinding paste from the valves and ports. If the thickness of the valve head above the ground seat A (see **FIG 1:8**) is less than $\frac{1}{32}$ inch (.8 mm) then the valve should be renewed.

4 Insert a new valve into each valve guide in turn. Raise the valve slightly and check that the diametric movement on the valve head does not exceed .020 inch (.508 mm). If this movement exceeds the dimension given then the valve guide is excessively worn and will have to be replaced. **FIG 1:9** shows the method of renewing the valve guides using Special Tool No. S.60A. The distance collar 6 ensures that the protrusion of the

FIG 1:7   Cylinder head nut tightening sequence

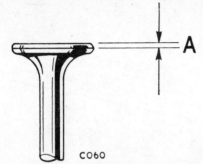

FIG 1:8   Renew the valve if the thickness **A** is less than $\frac{1}{32}$ inch (.8 mm)

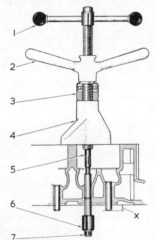

FIG 1:9   Renewing the valve guides using Special Tool No. S.60A

Key to Fig 1:9

	1 Tommy bar	2 Wingnut
3 Bearing assembly	4 Tool body	5 Centre spindle
6 Distance piece	7 Knurled nut	**X** .749 to .751 inch
(19.03 to 19.07 mm)		

valve guide above the face of the cylinder head is correct at .75 inch. If the special tool is not obtainable, use a stepped drift, of which the bottom inch fits snugly inside the guide, to drive the old guide downwards into the combustion chamber and then to drive the new guide, chamfered end leading, back into the cylinder head until from .749 to .751 inch (19.03 to 19.07 mm) is left protruding. After fitting new valve guides have the cylinder head seats recut, using garage equipment, to ensure concentricity with the guides.

5 Check the free lengths of the valve springs against the dimensions given in Technical Data. A rig can easily

be made up so that when the springs are compressed to their fitted lengths the compression can be measured using a spring balance, though measuring the springs' free length is an adequate check on their condition. If any springs are shorter than the dimension given the complete set should be renewed as they have all weakened with use.

6 The rocker gear assembly, also shown in **FIG 1:6**, is easily dismantled by removing the splitpins 24 and end plugs 25 from both ends of the rocker shaft 9. The parts can then be slid off the shaft and laid out in the order of removal. The rear outer pedestal 23 is secured to the rocker shaft 9 by a screw. Examine the faces of the rockers 26 and 28. If they are slightly worn the damage may be cleaned up using a fine carborundum stone, but if they are deeply pitted the rockers will have to be renewed.

7 Before reassembling and refitting the cylinder head clean all the parts with petrol or paraffin. Blow through oilways using paraffin under pressure or compressed air. Use rags or newspaper to wipe the sludge out of the rocker cover 2. If the cork gasket 1 is damaged, hardened, or permanently flattened, remove the old one and stick a new gasket to the rocker cover using jointing compound. Lay the rocker cover on a flat surface until the jointing compound is dry.

8 Reassemble the parts in the reverse order of dismantling and refit the cylinder head to the engine as previously instructed. Lubricate the valve stems and rocker assembly with clean engine oil.

1:5 Servicing the valve timing gear

The components are shown in **FIGS 1:1** and **1:2**. If the engine is still fitted to the car, drain the cooling system, and remove the radiator and the lefthand side engine valance (see **Chapter 4**). Isolate the battery by disconnecting the terminals. Remove the rocker cover.

1 Scribe a line across the fan assembly 69 and the balance weight 66 to ensure that they will be replaced in the same relative positions. Take out the bolts and lock tabs 65 and remove the fan assembly 69, washers 67, steel bushes 70 and rubber bushes 68 and 71. Slacken the generator mounting bolts and nuts 56 to 58 and remove the fan belt. Select first gear and apply the handbrake to prevent the crankshaft rotating. If the engine is out of the car, a clean piece of wood between a crankpin and the side of the crankcase will stop the crankshaft rotating. Remove the large bolt 108. Use an extractor, or a pair of levers, and withdraw the crankshaft pulley complete with the fan boss 107 and dowels 106 between them.

2 The timing cover 45 is held in place by nuts, bolts and screws as shown in **FIG 1:10**. Remove all these and withdraw the timing cover 45 and gasket 44. Withdraw from the crankshaft the seal extension 104 and the oil flinger 103.

3 Lay a straightedge tangentially across the sprockets along the chain, and pull the chain tightly away from the straightedge. If the maximum gap between the straightedge and the chain exceeds .4 inch (10 mm) the chain and sprockets are excessively worn and will have to be renewed. Never renew the timing chain alone as the teeth of the sprockets will have worn to hooks and will damage a new chain. **Renew chain**

and sprockets as a set. If the timing chain is noisy, but still within the wear limits, renew the timing chain tensioner 50. Remove the old tensioner by parting the blades sufficiently to slip them off the pivot pin 51. Replace a new tensioner in the same manner.

4 Remove the bolts and lock plates 111 and free the camshaft sprocket 112 from the camshaft. Remove the timing chain 110. Use an extractor or a pair of levers and remove the crankshaft sprocket 102 from the crankshaft. Carefully tap and lever out the key 109 and then remove the shims 102A from the crankshaft. Replace both sprockets, without the other parts, in their respective positions and lay a straightedge across the sides of the teeth. Press the straightedge firmly onto the camshaft sprocket 112 and measure, with feeler gauges, the gap between it and the teeth on the crankshaft sprocket 102. Make up shims 102A equal in thickness to the dimension measured and fit them to the crankshaft behind the crankshaft sprocket 102. This ensures that when they are refitted the two sprockets are level.

5 Wipe out the sludge using newspapers and old rags. Wash away any remaining dirt with petrol. Make sure that the correct shims 102A are fitted to the crankshaft and refit the key 109. If the original sprockets are to be refitted they are marked with scribed lines A and a pop mark B on the camshaft sprocket 112. When correctly set, another pop mark B on the camshaft aligns with the pop mark on the sprocket. Turn the camshaft until its pop mark B is approximately in the position shown in **FIG 1:11.** Now turn the crankshaft until Nos. 1 and 6 pistons are at TDC. The key 109 will be vertically upwards at TDC for Nos. 1 and 6 pistons. Fit the timing chain 110 to the two sprockets so that the scribed lines A are in line and ease both sprockets into place. Turn the camshaft until the securing holes exactly align with the threaded holes in the camshaft. Secure the camshaft sprocket in place with the bolts and lock plate 111. Before finally locking the securing bolts, press on the timing chain to simulate the tensioner pressure and check that the scribed lines A still align.

6 New sprockets will be unmarked so the valve timing will have to be set afresh. Turn the crankshaft so that it is approximately 45 deg. before TDC. This is to prevent the valves hitting the pistons when the camshaft is turned. Loosely attach the camshaft sprocket and turn the camshaft until No. 12 (rearmost) pushrod has reached its highest point of travel. Adjust the valve clearance on No. 1 (foremost) valve to .040 inch (1 mm). Again turn the camshaft until No. 11 (rear cylinder inlet valve) is at its highest point, and set the valve clearance on No. 2 valve to .040 inch. Keep turning the camshaft until Nos. 1 and 2 valves are on the point of balance, with one valve just about to open and the other just about to close. The position of the cams at this point is shown in **FIG 1:12.** Use feeler gauges and turn the camshaft until the valve clearances ar exactly equal on Nos. 1 and 2 valves. **Do not turn the camshaft from this position.** Turn the crankshaft until Nos. 1 and 6 pistons are at TDC and **do not turn the crankshaft from this position.**

The camshaft sprocket 112 is provided with four holes arranged in equally spaced pairs, but set so that the pairs are offset from the tooth centre. Lay the timing chain 110 around the two sprockets 102 and

FIG 1:10 Timing cover attachments

FIG 1:11 Timing sprocket markings, showing their relative positions when No. 1 cylinder is at TDC on the compression stroke

Key to Fig 1:11 **A** Scribed lines on sprockets
B Pop mark on sprocket opposite camshaft groove (or pop mark)

112 and fit the three back to the engine so that a pair of holes in the camshaft sprocket 112 exactly align with the threaded holes in the camshaft 115 when the chain and crankshaft sprocket are in place. Half-tooth adjustment is obtained by rotating the camshaft sprocket 90 deg. from its original position and quarter-tooth adjustment is made by turning the sprocket

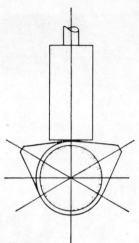

FIG 1:12   Position of cams at point of balance

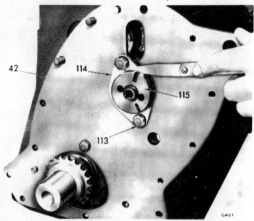

FIG 1:13   Measuring camshaft end float. Figure also shows the attachment of the engine front plate

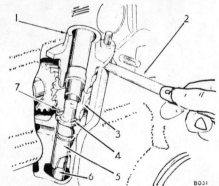

FIG 1:14   Method of measuring distributor pedestal and driving gear end float

Key to Fig 1:14   1 Distributor adaptor pedestal
2 Feeler gauges   3 Driving gear   4 Washer of ½ inch ID and
known thickness   5 Oil pump drive shaft bush   6 Oil pump
drive shaft   7 Securing pin

back to front. A combination of both these movements produces a three-quarter adjustment. Simulate the pressure of the chain tensioner with a finger, and check that the valve clearances on No. 1 piston are still equal before finally locking the camshaft sprocket in place. Oil the timing chain.

7 Examine the timing cover oil seal 43. If it is damaged or has leaked, carefully, so as to avoid distorting the cover, drive out the old seal and fit a new one in its place, with the lips facing the engine. Fit the oil-flinger 103 back to the crankshaft, concave side facing forwards. Fit a new gasket 44 onto the studs of the front plate of the engine. Use an Allen key or bent, stiff piece of wire to hold back the blades of the tensioner 50 and carefully slide the cover 45 back into place. When the blades of the tensioner are over the timing chain, remove the Allen key, taking care not to damage the gasket 44. Push the cover home and secure it with the bolts, screws and nuts as shown in FIG 1:10. Lightly oil the seal extension 104, and push it into place on the crankshaft through the oil seal 43, tapered end leading. If the seal extension 104 is scored or worn it should be renewed otherwise oil will leak past it.

8 Reset all the rocker clearances to .010 inch and replace the rocker cover. Replace the fan boss and crankshaft pulley. Refit the fan assembly and then the radiator. Fill the cooling system before starting the engine.

1:6 The camshaft and distributor drive gear

1 Remove the cylinder head (see Section 1:3). Remove the timing cover, chain and sprockets (see Section 1:5). Remove the two bolts securing the distributor clamp plate to the adaptor 8. Do not slacken the pinch bolt on the clamp or the ignition timing will be lost. Lift out the distributor. Undo the two nuts securing the adaptor to the crankcase, remove the adaptor and lift out the distributor drive gear 94. Disconnect both fuel pipes from the fuel pump, plugging the inlet pipe to prevent fuel syphoning out. Undo the nuts securing the fuel pump and remove it together with any shims or gaskets fitted.

2 Use feeler gauges to measure the camshaft end float as shown in FIG 1:13. The end float should be .004 to .008 inch (.1016 to .2032 mm) and if these dimensions are exceeded a new keeper plate 114 will have to be fitted.

3 Undo the bolts and washers 113 and slide the keeper plate 114 out of the annular groove on the camshaft 115. Very carefully, so as to avoid damaging the journals or cams, withdraw the camshaft from the engine.

4 Examine the camshaft for wear or damage to the cams, journals and distributor driving gear. If a new camshaft is to be fitted note that the exhaust emission controlled engine is fitted with a camshaft of different timing characteristics from the one fitted to standard engines.

5 Replace the camshaft in the reverse order of dismantling. Refit the distributor driving gear as described next.

Meshing distributor drive gear:

To ensure the correct positioning of the distributor it is essential that the driving gear 94 is correctly meshed with the camshaft gear. The driving gear and adaptor pedestal must also be refitted with the correct amount of end float otherwise the rate of wear throughout the valve timing mechanism will be excessive. As the parts are hidden inside the crankcase it is impossible to measure the end float directly and the following method, using a packing washer of known thickness, allows the amount of shimming required to be calculated.

1 Refer to **FIG 1:14**. Use a micrometer to measure the thickness of a plain $\frac{1}{2}$ inch ID washer 4 and then place it over the shaft of the distributor driving gear 3. Fit the gear 3 and washer 4 back into the engine so that the gear meshes with the gear on the camshaft and the dogs on the oil pump drive shaft 6 are properly engaged. Replace the adaptor pedestal 1 and measure, with feeler gauges, the gap between the pedestal and the crankcase.

2 Subtract the width of the gap, as measured, from the thickness of the washer 4. A negative answer will indicate that there is preload and that sufficient shims will have to be added to bring the preload to zero before adding further shims to give the correct amount of end float. If the answer is positive, then the difference between the answer and .005 inch (.12 mm) is the total thickness of shims required for the correct end float.

3 Lift off the adaptor pedestal 1, leaving the gear 3 and washer 4 in place. Make up a shim pack equal in thickness to the dimension calculated and refit the adaptor pedestal 1 with the shim pack between it and the crankcase. Again measure the gap 2 and, provided the shims are correct, the gap should be within .003 to .007 inch (.076 to .178 mm) less than the thickness of the washer 4. Adjust the shims if necessary to bring the end float within the limits and then remove the parts and discard the washer 4.

4 Turn the engine until No. 1 piston is at TDC with the cylinder on the compression stroke (both valves fully closed). Lower the gear 3 back into place, turning it slightly to allow it to mesh both with the gear on the camshaft and the oil pump driving dog, until it rests on top of the bush. When properly fitted the offset on the gear must be as shown in **FIG 1:15**. Fit the shims and then the adaptor pedestal. Secure the pedestal in place with two nuts and washers. Lower the distributor down the pedestal, turning the rotor arm so that the dogs engage with the slot in the driving gear. Secure the distributor in place with two bolts. If the pinch bolt on the distributor clamping plate has been slackened, then the ignition timing will have been been lost. Refer to **Chapter 3** for instructions on retiming the ignition.

1:7 The clutch and flywheel

Full instructions on servicing the clutch and its associated mechanism are given in **Chapter 5**. This section will only deal with removing and replacing the clutch. If the clutch and flywheel are to be examined while the engine is still in the car, then the gearbox will have to be removed (see **Chapter 6, Section 6:2**).

1 To make it easier to replace the flywheel in the correct position turn the engine so that Nos. 1 and 6 pistons are at TDC. Progressively slacken the ring of bolts

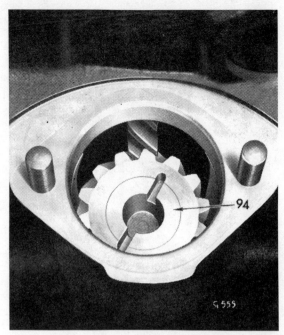

FIG 1:15 Position of the distributor drive gear when No. 1 piston is at TDC on the compression stroke

securing the clutch cover to the flywheel. Remove the clutch assembly and clutch driven plate.

2 Remove the four bolts 95 securing the flywheel to the crankshaft. Pull the flywheel back to clear it from the dowel 98.

3 If the flywheel is lightly scored the damage may be skimmed off in a lathe, but if the damage is deep the flywheel will have to be renewed. Renew the crankshaft spigot bush 97 if it is worn or shows chatter marks.

4 Replacing the parts is the reversal of the removal procedure. Make sure the mating faces of the flywheel and crankshaft are scrupulously clean. Mount a DTI on the engine backplate and check that the flywheel runout does not exceed .003 inch at a radius of 5 inches from the spigot bush centre. Press the crankshaft firmly forwards during this operation to ensure that the crankshaft end float does not falsify the reading. The clutch driven plate is refitted with the longer boss of the splined hub towards the gearbox. **It is essential that the driven plate is centralized, using a mandrel, while the securing bolts holding the clutch cover are tightened.**

Starter ring gear:

If teeth on the ring gear are worn or damaged the ring should be renewed. Lay the flywheel on hardwood blocks so that the clutch face is upwards. Tap the ring gear from the flywheel, using a copper drift, driving it off evenly all round and moving it in small stages.

Thoroughly clean the periphery of the flywheel, using a wire brush to remove all traces of rust or dirt. Lay the flywheel back on the hardwood blocks, clutch face downwards. Heat the new ring gear in boiling water.

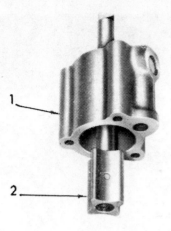

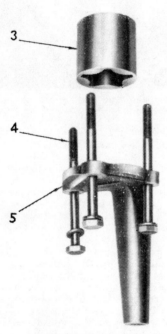

FIG 1:16 Oil pump details

Key to Fig 1:16   1 Housing   2 Inner rotor
3 Outer rotor   4 Bolt   5 End plate

Never heat it in a flame. When it is hot, refit it to the flywheel. The operation will be made easier by using four G-clamps spaced evenly around the flywheel and assisting these with light taps from a copper drift.

1:8 The sump

It is possible to remove the sump 32 while the engine is still in the car. Take the car for a sufficiently long run to heat the engine oil, so that it will flow more easily. Remove the drain plug 31 and let the oil drain into a suitable container. Drain the cooling system. Disconnect the hoses from the top of the thermostat housing.

Isolate the battery. Use a hoist and sling on the engine lifting eyes to support the engine. Slacken the righthand engine mounting bolts and remove the lefthand engine mounting bolts. Remove the sump securing bolts 37. Raise the engine on the hoist and lever it rearwards so that the sump can clear the front chassis crossmember. Remove the sump.

Refitting the sump is the reversal of the removal procedure. Since the task is fairly complicated, always fit a new gasket 33 to ensure that the sump will not leak after it is refitted. Clean away old oil and use a little grease or non-setting jointing compound to hold the gasket in place when refitting the sump. The sump bolts should be tightened to a torque of 16 to 18 lb ft (2.2 to 2.5 kg m) and once the gasket has settled they should be tightened to a minimum of 8 lb ft (1.1 kg m).

Fill the sump to the correct level with fresh oil and renew the oil filter element if required.

1:9 The oil pump

The components of the oil pump are shown in **FIG 1:16.** To take out the pump first remove the sump as described previously and then remove the pump by undoing the three bolts 4.

Clean the parts of the pump in petrol, then reassemble them dry, leaving off the end plate 5. Measure the clearance between the rotors as shown in **FIG 1:17,** and similarly measure the clearance between the outer rotor 3 and the housing 1. The clearance in both cases must not exceed .010 inch (.254 mm), though it is unlikely that it will do so, as the pump is continuously lubricated and should last throughout the life of the engine. Lay a straightedge across the base of the housing 1 and measure the end float of both rotors. This should not exceed .004 inch (.102 mm).

Reassemble the pump and lubricate it with clean engine oil. The pump is self-priming and requires no special precautions to be taken when the engine is first started, other than ensuring that the sump is filled to the correct level.

1:10 Lubrication, oil filter and relief valve

The oil circulation through the engine has already been discussed in **Section 1:1.** The oil filter and the circulation through it are shown in **FIG 1:18.** The relief valve is shown as parts 23 to 26 in **FIG 1:1.**

The oil filter is fitted to the lefthand side of the engine at the rear. A relief valve 5 is fitted into the assembly to allow oil to be passed to the engine if the filter element 3 becomes blocked with dirt. The element 3 should be renewed regularly and well before it has a chance of becoming blocked. Use rags or a drip tray to catch oil spilt when the unit is removed. Unscrew the centre bolt 8 and remove the filter from the engine. Take out and discard the old element 3. **Do not attempt to clean the element as nothing useful can be done with it.** Separate the internal parts of the casing and wash out with petrol. Renew the seal 7 if required. Use a small pointed tool to remove the seal 1 from the recess in the crankcase. Fit a new seal 1 back into the crankcase, taking great care to ensure that it is squarely and properly seated. Fit a new element into the casing, checking to make sure that it is a correct replacement. Do not omit the washer 2 which centralizes the element. Replace the filter, making sure that the casing 4 seats fully onto the seal 1 in the crankcase. Tighten the securing bolt 8 to a torque load of 15 to 18 lb ft (2.07 to 2.49 kg m). Wipe away any oil spillage from around the filter and start the engine. Check for oil leaks immediately. After the engine has been stopped and the oil level has settled, top up with clean oil to replace any lost in changing the filter.

Check the oil level in the engine when the car has not been run for some time and is standing on level ground. Failure to do this can result in the sump being overfilled with consequent oil wastage.

Low oil pressure can occasionally be caused by the relief valve. Unscrew the cap nut 26 and remove the parts. Wash them in petrol and use a piece of non-fluffy rag to clean the seating in the crankcase. Check the spring 24 to ensure that it is within the tolerances given in Technical Data and renew it if it is weak. Replace the parts using a new copper washer 25.

1:11 Pistons and connecting rods

These can be removed with the engine still fitted to the car, but the sump has to be removed to gain access to the big-ends, and the cylinder head must be removed in order to take out the pistons and connecting rods. It is probably easier to remove the engine from the car in order to withdraw the pistons and connecting rods (see also **Section 1:8**). The engine should be left in the car if the big-end bearings only are to be renewed. Depending on his ability, the owner should decide for himself which way to tackle the task.

Big-end bearings:

The big-end bearing caps 117 should already be marked for position and order, but if they are not marked do so with light pop marks.

1 Remove the bolts 116 from each bearing cap 117 in turn. Pull off the caps and lay them out in the order in which they were removed. Separate the shells 118 from the caps 117, still keeping the parts in order.
2 Push the connecting rods 120 and pistons 72 up the bores of the cylinders to clear the connecting rods from the crankpins. If the cylinder head has been removed the pistons and connecting rods can be pushed out through the top of the cylinder block.
3 Slide out the top bearing shells 119 from the connecting rods and lay these in order together with the appropriate bearing caps. Examine all the bearing shells 118 and 119. Renew the complete set if any show signs of pitting, scoring or wear.
4 Examine the crankpins and measure them with a micrometer. If they are excessively worn, tapered or oval, the crankshaft will have to be removed from the engine and reground down to the next suitable diameter then fitted with undersize bearings. **Never file the caps 117 or the connecting rods 120 in an attempt to take up wear.** Do not scrape or bore new bearing shells.
5 Clean away dirt using petrol and non-fluffy rags. Refit the bearing shells 118 and 119 into their respective positions, making sure that the tags are properly seated into the recesses in the bearing cap or the connecting rod. Squirt clean engine oil onto the crankpins and pull the connecting rod down the bore so that it locates in position over the crankpin. Refit

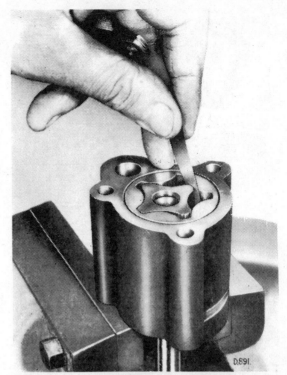

FIG 1:17   Measuring the clearance between the inner and outer rotors

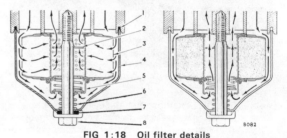

FIG 1:18   Oil filter details

Key to Fig 1:18   1 Rubber seal   2 Locating washer
3 Filter element   4 Container   5 Relief valve   6 Spring
7 Seal   8 Attachment bolt

the bearing caps 117 to their correct connecting rods, and secure them in place with the bolts 116 tightened to a torque of 38 to 42 lb ft (5.3 to 5.8 kg m). Refit the sump and fill to the correct level with fresh engine oil.

Cylinder bores:

When the pistons and connecting rods have been removed, examine the bores of the cylinders for wear. Ideally a Mercer dial gauge should be used to measure the bore, but by using judgement and a set of feeler gauges as a guide the wear can be estimated fairly accurately. The maximum wear will occur near the top of the bore across its thrust axis. If the bore wear exceeds .010 inch (.254 mm) the cylinders must be rebored to take +.020 inch (+.508 mm) oversize pistons. If the

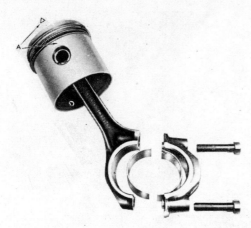

FIG 1:19   Piston and connecting rod assembly

FIG 1:20   Measuring the crankshaft end float

wear is such that, after reboring, the cylinders will be too large for +.020 inch pistons, then the cylinders must be bored out to take dry liners. The liners are then bored to take standard pistons.

If the wear is not sufficient to warrant reboring, but new piston rings are to be fitted, the unworn ridge around the top of the bore must be removed, using garage equipment. A new top ring will hit this ridge if it is left, and cause early failure of the ring.

Pistons:

The piston and connecting rod assembly is shown in **FIG 1:19**. The triangular mark A must face the front of the engine when the piston is fitted. The offset of the connecting rod must be fitted to face the camshaft side of the engine. Pistons will also have a grade letter F, G, or H stamped on the crown, and the piston must be fitted to a similar grade of bore. The dimensions of the three grades of piston are given in Technical Data. The dimension A is measured at the very bottom of the skirt, at right angles to the gudgeon pin axis, while the dimension B is similarly measured immediately below the piston ring grooves.

To separate the pistons from the connecting rods, remove the circlips 122 and 125 and, by hand, press out the gudgeon pin 123. Heat the piston in boiling water to ease a stiff gudgeon pin.

Piston rings:

Three rings are fitted to each piston; a plain compression ring at the top, tapered compression ring in the middle groove and an oil control ring at the bottom. Lacquering on the sides of the piston is an indication that gases have been blowing past the piston rings.

A piston ring expanding tool will greatly facilitate removing and replacing piston rings, but it is not essential. Remove the rings from the top of the piston by sliding a thin piece of metal, such as a discarded .020 inch feeler gauge, under one end and passing it around the ring, at the same time pressing the raised part onto the land above. Use three equi-spaced shims to protect the piston when sliding rings on or off.

Clean carbon and dirt from the ring grooves using a piece of broken ring, but taking great care not to remove metal otherwise the oil consumption will be increased. Carefully clean out the oil drain holes behind the oil control ring.

Before fitting new rings check that the gaps between the ends are correct. Fit the ring into the bore and press it down, about $\frac{1}{4}$ inch from the top, using a piston. Measure the gap between the ends with feeler gauges and, if need be, carefully file the ends until the gap is between .008 and .013 inch (.203 and .327 mm).

Fit the oil control ring first. The corrugated spacer is fitted and then the scrapers, one above the spacer and the other below it. The second ring is fitted with the narrowest diameter of the taper uppermost, and the marking T or TOP also uppermost.

The connecting rods:

The big-end bearings are renewable as already instructed. The gudgeon pin 123 runs in a renewable phosphor/bronze bush 124. Wipe out any oil and dry the gudgeon pin. At room temperature it should be possible to push the gudgeon pin through the bush by hand. If the gudgeon pin falls through under its own weight the bush is too slack and should be renewed. As the bushes must be jig reamed to very accurate tolerances after fitting, this operation is best left to a service station.

The connecting rods should be checked for twist and bend, but as this operation also calls for accurate jigs this too is best left to a service station.

Refitting the pistons and connecting rods:

Assemble the matching pistons to their connecting rods so that when the triangular mark is forwards the offset of the connecting rod faces the camshaft. Press the gudgeon pins into place by hand, heating the pistons in boiling water if required. Secure the gudgeon pins in place with the two circlips. Turn the piston rings so that the gaps are evenly spaced around the piston. Lightly oil the rings and gudgeon pin. Use a piston ring clamp to compress the rings. With the offset of the connecting rod facing the camshaft, lower the assembly down the correct cylinder bore. Enter the skirt of the piston and gently press down, allowing the clamp to slide off the rings as they enter. Do not force the piston down and carefully check that no rings are jammed, otherwise they will snap. Reconnect the big-ends as described earlier.

1:12 Crankshaft and main bearings

1 Remove the engine from the car (see **Section 1:2**) and separate the gearbox from the engine. Remove the clutch and flywheel (see **Section 1:7**) and take off the rear engine plate 10. Remove the valve timing gear (see **Section 1:5**). Take off the camshaft keeper plate 114. If the engine is to be completely dismantled then the cylinder head should be removed and the camshaft withdrawn, but this is not necessary provided that the keeper plate 114 is removed and the camshaft prevented from moving about. Remove the front engine plate 42 and its gasket 41. Turn the engine over and support it securely in place. Remove the sump (see **Section 1:8**) and disconnect the big-ends (see **Section 1:11**). Push the connecting rods down the bore to clear them from the crankshaft and loosely replace the bearing caps 117 to their correct connecting rods.

2 Mount a DTI on the crankcase as shown in **FIG 1:20**. Lever the crankshaft backwards and forwards to measure the end float, which should be .006 to .008 inch (.152 to .203 mm). If the limit is exceeded, oversize thrust washers will have to be fitted on reassembly and the end float rechecked.

3 Check that the bearing caps 35, 30 and 22 are all numbered as shown in **FIG 1:21**. Undo the two screws 38 and remove the front sealing block 39. Undo the seven screws 14 and remove the rear oil seal housing 13 complete with the oil seal 11 and the gasket 15. Progressively slacken the bolts securing the main bearing caps. When the bolts are loose, remove them and the main bearing caps, laying out the parts in order. Lift out the crankshaft 101. Slide out the bearing shells 34, 29 and 21 and lay these beside their respective bearing caps.

4 Examine and measure the crankshaft journals. If they are excessively scored, worn, tapered or oval the crankshaft must be reground to the next suitable size down and undersize bearings fitted. Examine the shell bearings. If any of these are pitted, scored or worn the complete set should be renewed. Similarly examine the four thrust washers 20 fitted on either side of the rear main bearing.

Refitting the crankshaft:

1 Clean all the parts. Clean the crankshaft with paraffin or petrol. Blow through all the oilways with paraffin under pressure and then with compressed air. This is particularly important if the crankshaft has been reground or a bearing has run, as particles of swarf or whitemetal may remain to cause early failure of the new bearings.

2 Lay the top row of bearing shells into their correct recesses in the crankcase, making sure that the tags on the shells are properly seated. If new bearing shells are being fitted, they only need to have the protective cleaned off and should not be bored or scraped.

FIG 1:21 The position and the order of the markings on the main bearing caps

FIG 1:22 Inserting the thrust washers

Similarly replace the bottom row of bearing shells into their respective main bearing caps.

3 Lay the crankshaft in place and replace the bearing caps in their correct positions, after lubricating the crankshaft journals with clean engine oil. Refit the thrust washers 20 so that the whitemetal faces the crankshaft, as shown in **FIG 1:22**. Tighten the securing bolts finger tight to hold the bearing caps in place. Progressively tighten all the securing bolts to a torque load of 55 to 60 lb ft (7.604 to 8.295 kg m). Recheck the crankshaft end float as described in operation 2 of removal.

4 Examine the oil seal 11 in the housing 13. The housing has two small holes for driving out a worn or damaged oil seal. A new oil seal 11 should be fitted so that its lips face into the engine. Smear both sides of a new paper gasket 15 thinly with jointing compound and place the gasket in position on the crankcase. Carefully, so as to avoid damage to the oil seal, slide the housing into position on the engine. Churchill tool No. S.335 should then be fitted to the crankshaft, and the housing moved until the tool seats in the bore of the housing,

FIG 1:23 Driving the sealing wedges into position on the front sealing block

after which the housing should be secured with the seven bolts 14. If no tool is available to centralize the housing, lightly secure it in place with the securing bolts and use feeler gauges to equalize the gap around the crankshaft before finally tightening the securing bolts to a torque of 16 to 18 lb ft (2.2 to 2.5 kg m).

5 Remove the old sealing wedges 36 and all traces of old jointing compound from the front sealing block 39. Secure the block lightly in place with the two screws 38. Smear two new sealing wedges 36 with jointing compound and tap them into place on the front sealing block as shown in **FIG 1:23**. Lay a straightedge across the front of the crankcase and align the sealing block front face to the straightedge. Fully tighten the two securing screws 38. Use a sharp knife to trim the protruding ends of the wedges 36 flush with the bottom face of the sealing block.

6 Fit a new paper gasket 41 to the front of the engine and replace the front engine plate 42. The rear engine plate 10 is fitted without any gasket. Reassemble the engine in the reverse order of dismantling and refit it to the car. It should be noted that the rear oil seal 11 can be replaced without removing the engine from the car, though the gearbox and flywheel must be removed to gain acess to it.

1:13 Reassembling a stripped engine

All dismantling and reassembling operations have been dealt with in detail in the various sections, so that it is simply a matter of tackling the tasks in the correct sequence. **Absolute cleanliness is essential.** All metal parts should be thoroughly cleaned and degreased. If a trichlorethylene degreasing bath is available use this to clean the components. Carefully scrape off all remains of old gaskets or jointing compound, and use new seals and gaskets. Blow through oilways with paraffin followed by dry compressed air. Lubricate all running surfaces with clean engine oil.

Start by fitting the crankshaft, followed by the pistons, connecting rods and big-end bearings. Completely refit the camshaft and valve timing gear. This is only possible if the original sprockets are being refitted, otherwise

the timing geat will have to be refitted after the cylinder head has been replaced. Refit the oil pump, sump, flywheel and clutch. The engine can then be turned the right way up for refitting the cylinder head. Leave accessories such as water pump, generator, fuel pump, oil filter and carburetters to the last as they will only be in the way and possibly get damaged if fitted earlier. Refit the engine to the car after mating it up with the gearbox. Torque wrench loads for all important fixings are either given in the relevant sections or in Technical Data.

It will be found easier to adjust the valve clearances before mating the gearbox to the engine, as the engine can easily be turned using the flywheel.

1:14 Valve rocker adjustment

No starting handle is provided so some other means of turning the engine will have to be found. Remove all the sparking plugs and turn the engine by the crankshaft mounted cooling fan. If the engine is too stiff to turn by this method, engage a gear and jack-up a rear wheel. Turn the engine by turning the rear jacked-up road wheel.

1 All valve adjustments should be carried out with a cold engine. Remove the rocker cover 64.

2 Turn the engine over until the valves of any cylinder are at the point of balance, as described in **Section 1:5**. Note the number of the cylinder (counting from the front of the engine) and turn the engine one more complete revolution. This will ensure that the cam followers for that particular cylinder will be resting on the concentric bases and that both valves are fully shut.

3 The valve operating details are shown in **FIG 1:24**. Hold the adjuster 3 with a screwdriver and use a spanner to slacken the locknut 4. Press down on the screwdriver and rotate the adjuster anticlockwise (when viewed from above) until a .010 inch (.25 mm) feeler gauge will slide easily into the gap between the valve stem and the face of the rocker 2. Still firmly pressing down on the screwdriver turn the adjuster 3 clockwise to decrease the gap, until resistance is just felt on the feeler gauge when it is moved. Hold the adjuster 3 so that it does not turn, and tighten the locknut 4. Recheck the valve clearance after tightening the locknut in case it has changed. Repeat the operation on the other valve of the cylinder. If the faces of the rockers 2 are badly pitted the feeler gauge will only bridge the depression, giving a false reading, so worn rockers should be renewed. A more accurate method is to use a DTI to measure the movement on the end of the rocker.

4 Turn the engine through one-third of a revolution and then the next cylinder in the firing order (1–5–3–6–2–4) will be in position for adjusting the valve rocker clearances. Carry on until all six cylinders have been adjusted, and replace the rocker cover.

1:15 Emission control

Engines destined for the American market have been modified to meet the Federal regulations governing the emission of contaminants from the exhaust and engine. A modified cylinder head with a lower compression ratio of 8.5:1, and a camshaft with 10–50–50–10 timing are both fitted. The exhaust valve seating faces are Stellited to ensure that the valve seating will be effective between overhauls. Apart from these differences the engine is the same as the standard engine and may be treated in the same way, though an additional check is required every 6000 miles.

With the engine at normal working temperature, remove all six sparking plugs. Screw a compression tester into each plug hole in turn. Depress the accelerator and turn the engine over by the starter motor for 2 to 3 seconds, and note the compression pressure. The readings should all be within 5 lb/sq in of each other. A greater difference indicates that that cylinder is leaking and attention is required on the condition of the bore, piston rings, valves or valve guides.

The crankcase breathing has already been discussed in **Section 1:1**, and other differences are in the fuel and ignition systems.

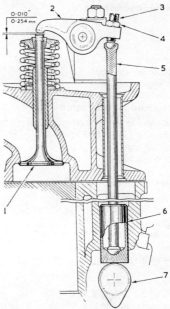

FIG 1:24 Valve operating details, showing the position for adjusting the valve rocker clearance

Key to Fig 1:24 1 Valve 2 Rocker 3 Adjuster 4 Locknut 5 Pushrod 6 Tappet 7 Camshaft

1:16 Fault diagnosis

(a) Engine will not start

1 Defective coil
2 Water on sparking plug leads
3 Ignition wires loose or faulty
4 Dirty, pitted or incorrectly set contact breaker points
5 Faulty distributor capacitor (condenser)
6 Too much choke
7 Too little choke
8 Faulty or jammed starter
9 Sparking plug leads wrongly connected
10 Vapour lock in fuel pipes (hot weather only)
11 Defective fuel pump
12 Blocked petrol filter or carburetter jets
13 Leaking valves
14 Sticking valves
15 Valve timing incorrect
16 Ignition timing incorrect
17 Defective fuel pump

(b) Engine stalls

1 Check 1, 3, 4, 5, 6, 7, 10, 11, 12, 13, 14 and 17 in (a)
2 Sparking plugs defective or gaps incorrectly set
3 Retarded ignition
4 Mixture too weak
5 Water in fuel system
6 Petrol tank vent blocked
7 Incorrect valve clearance
8 Sticking air valve in carburetter

(c) Engine idles badly

1 Check 2 and 7 in (b)
2 Air leak at manifold joints
3 Jet blocked or out of adjustment
4 Air leak in carburetter
5 Over-rich mixture
6 Worn piston rings
7 Worn valve stems or guides
8 Weak exhaust valve springs

(d) Engine misfires

1 Check all of (a) except for 6, 7, 8 and 10. Also check 2, 3, 4 and 7 in (b)

(e) Engine overheats (see Chapter 4)

(f) Compression low

1 Check 13 and 14 in (a); 6 and 7 in (c); and 2 in (d)
2 Worn piston ring grooves
3 Scored or worn cylinder bores

(g) Engine lacks power

1 Check 4, 6, 12, 13, 14, 15, 16 and 17 in (a); 2, 3, 4 and 7 in (b); 6 and 7 in (c); and 2 in (d). Also check (e) and (f)
2 Leaking cylinder head gasket
3 Fouled sparking plugs
4 Automatic advance not operating
5 Sticking air valve in carburetter

(h) Burnt valves or seats

1 Check 13 and 14 in (a); 7 in (b); and 2 in (d). Also check (e)
2 Excessive carbon around valve seat and head

(j) Sticking valves

1 Check 2 in (d)
2 Bent valve stem
3 Scored valve stem or guide
4 Incorrect valve clearance
5 Gummy deposits on valve stem

(k) Excessive cylinder wear

1 Check 6 in (a) and see Chapter 4
2 Lack of oil
3 Dirty oil
4 Piston rings gummed up or broken
5 Badly fitted piston rings
6 Connecting rods bent

(l) Excessive oil consumption

1 Check 6 and 7 in (c); and check (k). Also check 3 in (f)
2 Oil return holes in pistons choked with carbon
3 Oil level too high
4 External oil leaks

(m) Crankshaft and connecting rod bearing failure

1 Check 2 and 3 in (k)
2 Restricted oilways
3 Worn journals or crankpins
4 Loose bearing caps
5 Extremely low oil pressure
6 Bent connecting rod

(n) Low oil pressure

1 Check 2 and 3 in (k); 2, 3 and 4 in (m)
2 Oil pressure gauge and its connections faulty

(o) Internal water leakage (see Chapter 4)

(p) Poor circulation (see Chapter 4)

(q) Corrosion (see Chapter 4)

(r) High fuel consumption (see Chapter 2)

(s) Engine vibration

1 Loose generator bolts
2 Fan blades out of balance, or rubber bushes worn out
3 Exhaust pipe mountings too tight

(t) 'Pinking'

1 Using too low a grade of fuel
2 Ignition too far advanced
3 Excessive carbon in the cylinder head

(u) Engine 'knocks'

1 Worn big-end bearings
2 Worn main bearings
3 Piston knock (slap)
4 Excessive crankshaft end float
5 Worn small-end bushes
6 Incorrectly adjusted rocker clearances

CHAPTER 2

THE FUEL SYSTEM

2:1 Description
2:2 Routine maintenance
2:3 The fuel pump
2:4 Operation of Stromberg carburetter
2:5 Servicing the standard carburetters
2:6 Adjusting the standard carburetters
2:7 Exhaust emission control carburetters

2:8 Servicing emission control carburetters
2:9 Adjusting emission control carburetters
2:10 Air cleaner
2:11 Crankcase emission control valve
2:12 Stromberg carburetters type CDSEV
2:13 Emission control systems
2:14 Fault diagnosis

2:1 Description

An engine-driven AC mechanical fuel pump and twin Stromberg carburetters are fitted as standard equipment to all the models covered by this manual. Two air filter elements inside a single case are fitted, to clean the incoming air and remove the microscopic particles of dust which would otherwise cause excessive wear to the carburetters and engine.

On all models the fuel tank is at the rear of the car. On the Vitesse the fuel tank is in the lefthand side of the luggage compartment and a drain plug is fitted under the car, behind the lefthand side of the rear wheel arch. Fuel can be prevented from syphoning out of the fuel tank, when the supplying pipe at the fuel pump is disconnected, by disconnecting the supply pipe from the top of the fuel tank. A reserve tap is fitted to the Vitesse to allow a quantity of fuel to be kept in reserve, and unless the reserve is actually in use the tap should always be kept in the normal position, not on reserve. The fuel tank on the GT6 is fitted under the luggage floor at the rear of the car. No reserve tap is fitted, neither is there a separate drain plug. The tank must be drained by disconnecting the supply fuel pipe from underneath the fuel tank.

The carburetters fitted to the exhaust emission controlled engine are designed and made to a very high specification, ensuring that they meet the requirements of the US Federal law concerning pollution emission by internal combustion engines. Exhaust gas analyzers and special test equipment are essential for setting these carburetters and unauthorized tampering can easily result in the car failing to meet the requirements of the law.

The principles of operation of the fuel pump and carburetters will be dealt with in the relevant sections.

2:2 Routine maintenance

1 At periodic intervals remove the hexagon nuts from the tops of the carburetters and top the oil well up with engine oil. The correct level is when the oil is within $\frac{1}{4}$ inch of the end of the rod in which the damper operates.

2 Check the carburetter controls and linkages for freedom of movement and lightly oil the pivot points and cables.

3 At regular intervals clean out the sediment bowl and the gauze filter on the fuel pump. If water contaminated fuel has been used, or if there is an excess of dirt in the pump sediment bowl, drain the fuel tank and use an

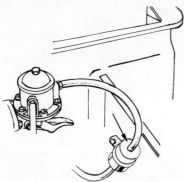

FIG 2:1 Position of fuel line filter on emission controlled engines

airline to blow through the fuel pipes. In particularly bad cases the fuel tank will have to be removed and cleaned internally.

4 At regular intervals, depending on the climatic conditions, clean the air cleaner elements or renew them as required.

Emission control system:

In addition to the routine maintenance described just previously, certain extra maintenance is required.

1 At 6000 miles, as well as checking the damper oil level, the slow-running speed and the idle trim screw should be reset. **The proper equipment must be used for these operations,** as the ear alone cannot detect the minor differences between accurate and inaccurate settings.

2 A fuel filter is fitted into the supply line to the fuel pump. The filter is shown in **FIG 2:1**. Every 12,000 miles the filter must be renewed, ensuring that the new filter is fitted so that the inlet side is facing downwards into the direction of fuel flow. The filter is a sealed unit and cannot be cleaned.

3 At every 24000 miles renew the parts of the carburetters supplied in a Red Emission Pack 'B'. Detailed instructions for these operations will be given later in the chapter.

4 Every 50,000 miles the carburetters should be completely stripped and reconditioned, otherwise fit new or reconditioned carburetters in their place. To tie in with the normal servicing schedules it is suggested that this operation be carried out at 48,000 miles.

2:3 The fuel pump

This is an AC mechanical fuel pump driven from a cam on the engine camshaft. The details of the pump are shown in **FIG 2:2**. The foot of the rocker arm 18 follows the movement of the cam in the engine, being held against it by the pressure of the return spring 21. The rocker 18 is connected, through a link arm, to the diaphragm assembly 12. The link arm is so made, with a step acting against the rocker arm 18, that it is only driven downwards by the rocker arm and once in the down position it can stay there. As the link moves downwards it draws with it the diaphragm assembly 12 creating a suction in the pump chamber. This suction draws fuel from the sediment chamber and through the filter gauze 3. When the foot of the rocker 18 is released

by the cam it frees the link and diaphragm, allowing them to rise under the action of the diaphragm spring 13. The inlet valve closes and the outlet valve opens, allowing the fuel to be pumped to the carburetter float chamber. This sequence continues until the carburetter float chamber is full and the float chamber needle valve closes preventing any more fuel entering. The fuel pressure rises and holds the diaphragm down against the

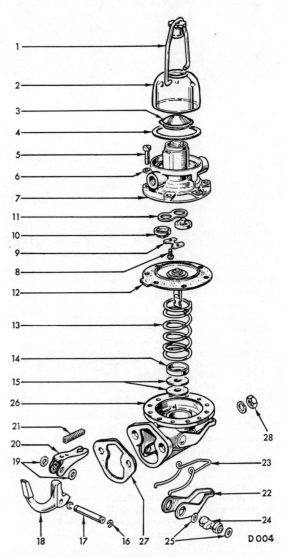

FIG 2:2 Fuel pump details

Key to Fig 2:2   1 Stirrup   2 Sediment bowl
3 Filter gauze   4 Cork seal   5 Screw   6 Spring washer
7 Upper body   8 Retaining plate screw   9 Retaining plate
10 Valve assemblies 11 Valve gasket 12 Diaphragm assembly
13 Diaphragm spring   14 Cup   15 Washers   16 Circlip
17 Rocker arm pin   18 Rocker arm   19 Distance washers
20 Link lever   21 Rocker arm spring   22 Primer lever
23 Primer lever spring   24 Primer lever shaft
25 Cork seals   26 Lower body   27 Pump gasket
28 Pump retainer nut

spring, and no more fuel is pumped until the level in the float chamber drops. When the fuel pressure drops again the diaphragm rises and the pumping action continues until the float chamber is again filled.

Cleaning the sediment chamber:

This operation is carried out with the pump still fitted to the engine. Disconnect and plug the fuel inlet pipe, to prevent fuel syphoning out. Remove, from the top of the pump, the stirrup 1 sediment bowl 2 and filter gauze 3. Use a thin screwdriver to scrape the sediment loose from the sediment bowl. Wash the bowl, cover and filter gauze in clean fuel and blow out any sediment with a airline. Take care not to damage valves. Renew the gauze if the mesh is broken, and renew the sealing ring 4 if it is damaged or flattened. Replace the parts in the reverse order of removal, hand prime the carburetters, using the primer lever 22, and check for fuel leaks. Again check for leaks after starting the engine.

Removing the fuel pump:

The pump is mounted on the lefthand side rear of the engine. Disconnect both fuel lines at the pump and plug the supply pipe to prevent fuel draining out. Unscrew the two securing nuts 28 and withdraw the pump from the engine complete with the gasket 27.

Before replacing the pump check that the flange on the body is flat and undamaged. True it up by careful filing if required. Use a new gasket 27, smearing both sides with a little non-setting jointing compound, and do not overtighten the nuts 28 otherwise the flange will be distorted and cause oil leaks.

Dismantling the fuel pump:

The pump is dismantled by removing the parts in the sequence shown in **FIG 2:2,** but noting the following points.
1 Clean the outside of the pump with clean fuel and an old toothbrush. Lightly file a mark across the flanges of the body 7 and the lower body 26 to ensure that they will be replaced in the same relative position on reassembly.
2 The valves 10 are pressed into the body 7 and then held in place by peening the body over them.
3 Remove the diaphragm 12 from the link lever by pressing the diaphragm lightly down and turning it through 90 degrees, then lifting it out of engagement with the link lever.

Reassembling the pump is the reversal of the dismantling procedure. **The inlet and outlet valves must be replaced pointing in the directions shown in FIG 2:2.** Test the fuel pump by operating the primer lever 22 with the pipe to the carburetter float chamber disconnected. When the pump is full, every stroke of the primer lever should produce a good jet of fuel from the pipe. If a pressure gauge is available, check that the pump produces, and holds for a reasonable time, 1.5 to 2.5 lb/sq in (.1 to .18 kg/sq cm).

2:4 Operation of Stromberg carburetter

The Stromberg carburetter uses a constant-vacuum variable choke orifice controlled by a vacuum-operated air valve. This method of design and construction requires a single jet only, which is sufficient for all running and starting conditions of the engine.

The valve is in the form of a piston attached to a diaphragm operating in a suction chamber in the top of the carburetter. The suction in the inlet is fed to the suction chamber by internal passages and this causes the air valve to rise. As the air valve rises the vacuum will drop and the height of the air valve will be such that the weight of the piston and pressure of the return spring will be balanced by the vacuum. The engine is controlled by a butterfly valve downstream of the air valve assembly.

To control the fuel a tapered needle, working in a fixed area jet, is attached underneath the air valve. As the air valve rises it draws the needle out of the jet. As the needle is tapered the effective area of the jet assembly is increased and a larger amount of fuel is drawn out by the constant vacuum.

An oil filled damper is fitted to the top of the air valve assembly. This damper serves the dual purpose of damping out rapid fluctuations of the air valve as well as acting as an accelerator pump. On acceleration the damper causes the air valve to lag behind the instantaneous demands made by the engine, causing the choke area to be smaller than required. The speed of the airflow through the choke is increased above the normal standard and consequently the suction is also increased. The increased suction draws extra fuel through the jet to enrich the mixture for acceleration.

Operating the choke knob in the car rotates a starter bar which mechanically lifts the air valve, enriching the mixture for cold starts. The starter bar is connected by a cam to the throttle so the engine idling speed is also increased for cold starts.

2:5 Servicing the standard carburetters

The carburetter details and linkages are shown in **FIG 2:3,** and the adjustment points, when fitted to the engine are shown in **FIG 2:4.**

To remove the carburetters disconnect the fuel pipe, vacuum pipe choke control and throttle control. Unscrew the nuts holding the carburetter flanges to the inlet manifold and remove both carburetters together, still connected by the linkage.

Dismantling the carburetters:

Slacken the clamp bolts 34 and 65 to separate the carburetters. It is advisable to dismantle and reassemble one carburetter at a time. This not only ensures that the parts are not mixed but also gives an assembled unit from which the correct assembly of the parts can be checked.
1 Clean the outside of the carburetter with fuel, using rags and an old toothbrush. Lightly file a mark across the flanges of the top cover 5 and body 61 to facilitate reassembly in the correct position. Unscrew and remove the damper assembly 12 and drain the oil out of the oil well.
2 Remove the four screws 3 and their washers. Carefully lift off the top cover 5. The diaphragm 8 may stick to the cover, so care is needed. Withdraw the piston 9 and diaphragm assembly, **taking great care not to drop the parts, rest the weight on the needle or otherwise bend or damage the needle 11.**

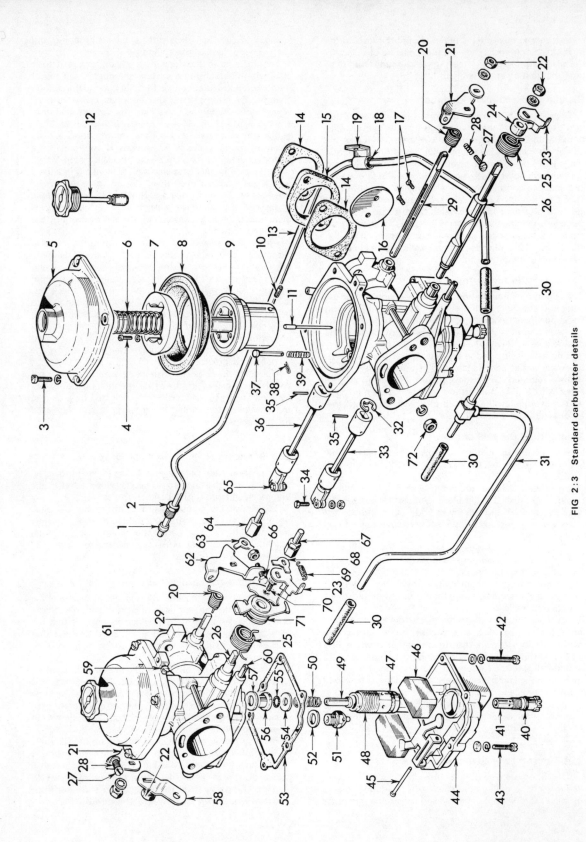

FIG 2:3   Standard carburetter details

Key to Figs 2:3, 2:4, 2:5, 2:6 and 2:7

1 Sleeve
2 Nut
3 Top cover screw
4 Screw
5 Top cover
6 Coil spring
7 Retaining ring
8 Diaphragm
9 Air valve
10 Locking screw
11 Needle
12 Damper
13 Pipe
14 Gasket
15 Insulator
16 Butterfly throttle valve
17 Screws
18 Grommet
19 Bracket
20 Spring
21 Throttle stop lever
22 Nuts
23 Lever
24 Bush
25 Return spring
26 Starter bar spindle
27 Throttle stop screw
28 Spring
29 Throttle spindle
30 Fuel pipe connector
31 Pipe
32 Circlip
33 Coupling
34 Clamping bolt
35 Pin
36 Coupling
37 Air valve lifting pin
38 Spring clip
39 Spring
40 O-ring
41 Orifice adjusting screw
42 Screw (long)
43 Screw (short)
44 Float chamber cover
45 Fulcrum pin
46 Float assembly
47 O-ring
48 Bushing screw
49 Jet
50 Spring
51 Needle valve
52 Washer
53 Gasket
54 Washer
55 O-ring
56 Bushing
57 Washer
58 Connecting link
59 Screw
60 Petrol inlet
61 Body
62 Stop lever
63 Lockplate
64 Coupling nut
65 Clamping bolt
66 Cam screw
67 Coupling nut
68 Lockplate
69 Spring
70 Cam screw
71 Choke cam lever
72 Nut

3 Turn the carburetter over and remove the float chamber 44 by undoing the screws 42 and 43. Withdraw the pin 45 and lift out the floats 46. Unscrew and remove the needle valve assembly 51 and the washer 52.

4 Using a spanner on the hexagonal portion remove the bushing screw assembly. Unscrew the adjusting screw 41 from the bushing screw 48 and remove the seals 40 and 47. Lift out the remainder of the jet parts from the carburetter. These parts are all shown in greater detail in **FIG 2:5**.

5 The throttle spindle can be removed if required. On the front carburetter undo the nut 22 and remove the stop lever 21 and spring 20. On the rear carburetter free the locktab 63 and unscrew the coupling nut 64. The stop lever 62 and spring 20 can then be removed. Remove the two screws 17 securing the throttle butterfly 16 and slide the butterfly out of the slot in the spindle 29. The throttle spindle 29 can then be slid out of the carburetter.

6 The starter bar 26 can be removed by undoing the nut 22 or 67, removing the linkage and sliding the bar out of the carburetter.

Cleaning and examining the parts:

1 Wash all the metal parts in petrol using a toothbrush to scrub away any dirt and sediment in the crevices. Sediment which is difficult to remove should first be loosened with a thin screwdriver.

2 Examine the air valve assembly. If the diaphragm 8 is damaged renew it. The diaphragm is secured to the pistons by the screws 4 and retaining ring 7. The diaphragm has a tab which fits into the slot in the body of the carburetter, so ensure that the new diaphragm is fitted to the piston in the same relative position as the old diaphragm. Check the needle 11. If it is bent or scored it should be renewed. Slacken the screw 10 and if the needle is stiff to remove tap it lightly inwards before pulling it out. The new needle must be of the correct size and fitted so that the bottom of the shoulder on the needle is flush with the face of the piston.

3 Examine the needle of the needle valve assembly 51. If the tapered seat on the needle is worn to a step renew the assembly.

4 Check the wear around the throttle spindle 29 and starter bar 26. Excessive wear will cause poor idling and difficulty in setting the carburetters. Renew the spindles if they are worn, and if there is still excessive wear the whole carburetter will have to be renewed.

5 If the needle 11 was bent or scored check the jet 49 as this too may be damaged. Renew if it is worn or if the orifice is not truly circular.

Reassembling the carburetters:

Use new seals and gaskets throughout. These are available in kits. Reassembly is the reversal of the dismantling procedure but note the following points:

1 Leave the bushing screw 48 slack by half a turn. The jet assembly will have to be recentred after assembly is completed.

2 Make sure that the tag on the diaphragm 8 is located in its slot in the body, and take care to enter the needle 11 into the jet 49 when refitting the air valve assembly.

3 Before fitting the float chamber cover 44 check that the fuel level in the float chamber is correct.

FIG 2:4   Standard carburetter adjustment points
(For Key see Fig 2:3)

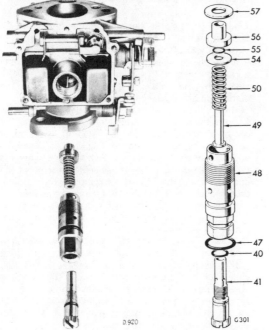

FIG 2:5   Standard carburetter jet details
(For Key see Fig 2:3)

Float chamber fuel level:

This operation must be carried out with the carburetter removed from the car. Invert the carburetter and remove the float chamber cover 44. Check that the highest point of the floats 46 is .71 inch (18 mm) above the bottom face of the body 61, as shown in **FIG 2:6**. If required, reset the level by carefully bending the tag on the floats 46 which contacts the needle of the valve assembly 51. An additional thin washer under the assembly 51 will lower the fuel level.

Centralizing the jet:

This operation must be carried out every time the bushing screw 48 is slackened or a new needle 11 is fitted. Remove the air cleaner and the damper 12. Raise the air valve assembly and let it fall under its own weight. It should fall freely and the piston 9 should hit the bridge in the air intake with an audible click. Dirty or sticky oil on the piston rod can be a cause of the air valve failing to fall freely. Remove the top cover 5 and the air valve assembly. Clean out with clean fuel or methylated spirits, lightly oil the piston rod and refit the assembly and cover, after checking that the needle 11 is straight. A bent needle can be a cause of the air valve sticking. If the air valve still fails to fall freely centralize the jet as follows:

1 Raise the air valve to prevent the needle fouling in the jet. Screw the adjusting screw 41 up until the top of the jet 49 is flush with the bridge in the air intake. Slacken the bushing screw 48 by half a turn. Lower the air valve and press it firmly down using a pencil through the damper hole in the top cover.

2 Slowly tighten the bushing screw 48 while checking that the needle 11 remains free in the jet orifice. Check by raising the piston $\frac{1}{4}$ inch and letting it fall. The piston should stop firmly on the bridge. When satisfied replace the damper, after checking the oil level, and replace the air cleaner.

2:6 Adjusting the standard carburetters

Provided the correct needle and jets are fitted, setting the carburetter for slow-running sets the carburetters for all running conditions. To satisfactorily adjust and tune the carburetters the rest of the engine must be in good condition and the ignition timing correctly set.

If the carburetters have been dismantled set them both to an approximate running position, with the throttle clamping bolt 65 slack. Turn the adjusting screws 40 up until the top of the jet 49 is level with the bridge in the air intake. Unscrew each adjusting screw 40 three complete turns. This roughly sets the mixture strength. Slacken the idle-speed adjusting screws 27, shown also in **FIG 2:7**, until with the throttle butterflies closed the screws are just off their stops. Check that the screw 66 is clear of the cam 71. Open the throttles by screwing in the adjusting screws 27 by one and a half turns. This sets the idling speed.

1 Remove the air cleaners and slacken the clamp bolts 65 and 34 after the engine has been run long enough to reach its normal working temperature. Check that the screw 66 is well clear of the cam 71.

2 Adjust both idling screws 27 to give a slow-running speed of 600 to 650 rev/min. Use a length of $\frac{3}{4}$ inch bore tube to balance the airflow through the carburetters. Use the tube to listen to the hiss in each intake and adjust the screws 27 until the hiss in each is equal and the engine is running at the correct idling speed. If a balance meter is available this should be used in preference to tuning by ear.

3 If the mixture is correct the engine will idle with a smooth regular beat. Check by lifting each air valve in turn $\frac{1}{32}$ inch. If the mixture on that carburetter is too rich the engine speed will rise, and if the mixture is too weak the engine will falter or stop. A rich mixture is further indicated by an uneven beat and black smoke

from the exhaust. A weak, splashy misfire with colourless exhaust means that the mixture is too weak

4 Adjust the mixture strength on each carburetter by turning the adjusting screw 41. Viewed from underneath, turning the screw clockwise weakens the mixture and turning it anticlockwise (down) enriches the mixture. As the mixture is adjusted the engine speed may vary so adjust it but still keeping the airflow through the carburetters balanced. The carburetters are partially interdependent so when the mixture on one is correct the other should be rechecked. When satisfied tighten the clamping screw 65 to lock the throttles together.

5 Switch off the engine and operate the choke control knob until the lifting edge of the starter bar 26 on the rear carburetter just contacts the underside of the piston 9. Turn the starter bar lever 23 on the front carburetter until the starter bar just contacts the front carburetter piston. Tighten the clamp nut 34 to lock the starter bars together.

6 Adjust the fast idle screw 66 until its head is $\frac{1}{16}$ inch (1.6 mm) from the face of the cam 71, as shown in **FIG 2:7**. Refit the air cleaner assembly.

2:7 Exhaust emission control carburetters

Twin Stromberg CDSE carburetters are fitted. These should not be tampered with and only adjusted using the correct equipment. The details of a CDSE carburetter are shown in **FIG 2:8**. Though they function on the same principle as the standard carburetters they vary in many details. The jet assembly is fixed and mixture control is effected by a separate trimming screw 3. A temperature compensating device which progressively opens as the engine temperature increases ensures even idling at all engine temperatures. A redesigned accelerator linkage, shown in **FIG 2:9**, incorporates a 'lost motion' linkage to operate a vacuum control valve when the throttle is closed. A throttle bypass valve is set to open at a predetermined manifold depression to admit extra air during deceleration. A redesigned choke cable operates each carburetter individually.

It must be stressed that unauthorized tampering, or failure to use the correct equipment will most likely cause the car to fail to meet the requirements of the US Federal antipollution laws.

2:8 Servicing emission control carburetters

This service should be carried out at 24,000 miles and all the parts required are supplied in one Red Emission Pack 'B'.

1 Remove the carburetters from the car and separate them. Remove each damper assembly in turn and drain the oil out of the damper oil well. Loosely replace the dampers. Undo each plug 70 in turn and drain the fuel out of the float chamber. Service one carburetter at a time to ensure that parts are not interchanged between them.

2 Unscrew the plug 70 and discard the seal 71. A new seal is provided. Remove the float chamber cover 65 and discard the gasket 62. Check the floats 64 for damage and withdraw the pin 61 to free them. Remove and discard the needle valve assembly 63. Thoroughly clean all the parts and remove any sediment. Refit the new needle valve assembly 63 with its

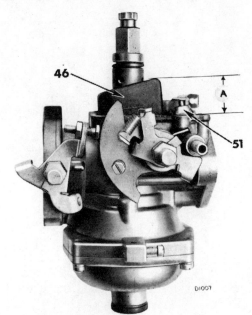

FIG 2:6   Checking float chamber fuel level
(For Key see Fig 2:3)

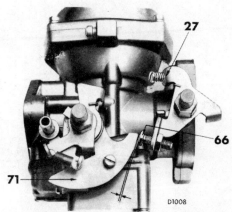

FIG 2:7   Standard carburetter fast-idle adjustment
(For Key see Fig 2:3)

washer. Replace the floats and check that their highest point, when inverted, is 16.0 to 17.0 mm above the face of the carburetter body. Adjust if required by carefully bending the tag on the floats. Refit the float chamber cover and plug using new gaskets and seals.

3 Remove the damper assembly. Take off the top cover 19 and remove the air valve assembly. Remove the screws 23 and the ring 22 to free the diaphragm 24 from the piston 25. Discard the old diaphragm. Refit the new diaphragm so that its tag locates in the piston. Take care not to damage the needle 27.

4 Slacken the screw 26, carefully, and remove and discard the needle 27. Insert the new needle partially into the base of the piston so that the flat portion on the needle faces the securing screw 26. Use a narrow

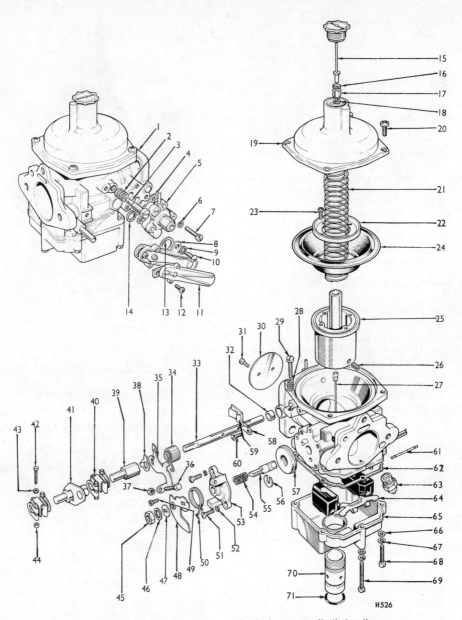

FIG 2:8 CDSE carburetter (emission controlled) details

Key to Fig 2:8   1 Carburetter   2 Spring--idle trimming screw   3 Idle trimming screw   4 Gasket--bypass valve
5 Bypass valve.   6 Lockwasher under (7)   7 Screw--securing (5)   8 Temperature compensator unit
9 Lockwasher under (10)   10 Screw--securing (8)   11 Cover--temperature compensator   12 Screw--securing (11)
13 Seal--on compensator body   14 Seal--inside carburetter   15 Damper rod--damper assembly   16 Washer--
damper assembly   17 Distance sleeve--damper assembly   18 Circlip--damper assembly   19 Cover--air valve
20 Screws--securing (19)   21 Spring--air valve return   22 Ring--diaphragm attachment   23 Screw--securing (22) (24)
24 Diaphragm   25 Air valve   26 Screw--securing (27)   27 Needle assembly   28 Spring--idle adjusting screw
29 Idle adjusting screw   30 Throttle disc   31 Screw--securing (30)   32 Seal--throttle spindle   33 Throttle spindle
34 Spring--throttle return   35 Lever--throttle   36 Screw--fast idle   37 Locknut--securing (36)   38 Lockwasher--
retaining (39)   39 Nut--throttle spindle   40 Coupling--throttle spindles   41 Connecting lever assembly
42 Clamping bolt   43 Washer--under (42)   44 Nut--securing (42)   45 Nut*   46 Shakeproof washer*
47 Washer*   48 Lever*   49 Screw--cable attachment*   50 Return spring*   51 Screw*   52 Shakeproof washer*
53 Starter box cover*   54 Spring*   55 Spindle*   56 Retainer*   57 Valve plate*   58 Cable abutment bracket
59 Spring clip   60 Screw--securing (58)   61 Float pivot pin   62 Gasket--float chamber   63 Needle valve
64 Float assembly   65 Float chamber cover   66 Washer--under (68/69)   67 Spring washer--under (68/69)
68 Screw--securing (65)   69 Screw--securing (65)   70 Plug   71 Rubber O-ring--for (70)   *Starter box assembly

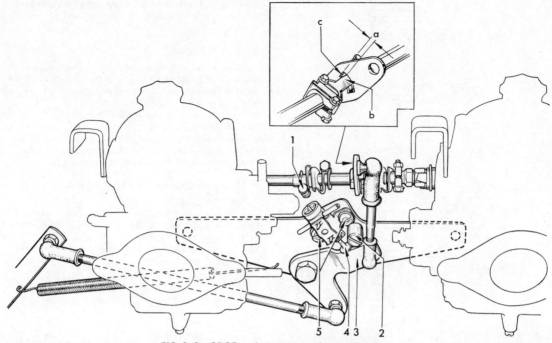

FIG 2:9 CDSE carburetter accelerator linkage

Key to Fig 2:9   a Insert a $\frac{1}{16}$ inch drill shank in this space when adjusting accelerator controls   b Driving tongue integral with operating shaft   c Driving edge of lower slot   1 Spring coupling clamp bolts   2 Throttle stop   3 Relay lever   4 Vacuum valve plunger   5 Vacuum valve securing screws

straightedge, about 1 inch wide, against the needle shoulder to press the needle into place. Keep pressing until the straightedge aligns the shoulder of the needle with the face of the piston. Lightly tighten the securing screw 26 to avoid crushing the needle biasing spring housing. If the operation has been performed correctly then the needle shoulder should be flush with the piston and the needle biased towards the throttle. **This position is extremely critical and must be accurately set.** Refit the air valve assembly, guiding the needle with a finger through the air intake, and ensuring that the tag on the diaphragm seats in the slot in the body. Replace the top cover and damper assembly.

5 Take out the screws 10 and remove the temperature compensator 8. Release the cover 11 by removing the two screw 12 and check the valve for freedom of movement by lifting it from its seat. **Do not strain, bend or alter the bi-metal blade.** Check that the clearance all round the valve is even to allow it to expand with heat. If the valve is offset, slacken the securing screw and move the blade laterally to centralize the valve. Replace the cover 11 if the valve is satisfactory. Secure the temperature compensator back onto the body using new seals 13 and 14.

6 Remove the bypass valve assembly 5 and its gasket 4, by undoing the three screws 7. Unscrew the throttle spindle nut 39 and remove the lever 35 and spring 34. A small hole is provided in the spindle seals 32 to facilitate prizing or pulling them out. Replace them with the new seals. Refit the lever, spring and nut to

the spindle. Refit the bypass valve assembly 5 using a new gasket 4.

7 Refit the carburetters to the manifold using new flange gaskets.

2:9 Adjusting emission control carburetters

These carburetters cannot be tuned by ear and the correct equipment must be used.
Accelerator linkage:

Refer to **FIG 2:9**.

1 Slacken both clamp bolts 1. Ensure that the fast-idle screw 3 is clear of the cam 6, as shown in **FIG 2:10**. Unscrew the idling screw on each carburetter until the throttle butterfly is shut. Screw in each screw $1\frac{1}{2}$ complete turns to open the throttles.

2 Start the engine and run it until it reaches its normal operating temperature. Check that the choke knob is fully in and that neither cold start lever is operated. Adjust the cables if necessary. Use a balance meter to balance the airflow through the carburetters, adjusting the idling screws to suit and setting the engine to idle at 800/850 rev/min. Stop the engine.

3 Insert the shank of a $\frac{1}{16}$ inch drill into the slot **a** formed between the lever tongue **b** and the edge of the slot **c**. Press the relay lever 3 against the stop cam 2 and tighten both clamping bolts 1. Remove the drill.

4 Slacken the screw 5 and move the vacuum valve body towards the relay lever 3 until the plunger 4 is fully depressed. Tighten the securing screws 5. Check the valve position. Slowly operate the accelerator linkage

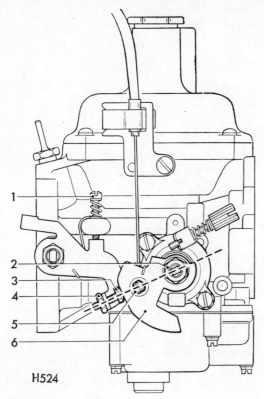

H524

FIG 2:10 Position of choke-cam lever when setting fast-idle speed

Key to Fig 2:10
1 Idling screw
2 Starter box
3 Fast-idle screw
4 Locknut
5 Cable trunnion
6 Choke cam-lever

while watching the valve plunger 4. It should have reached the end of its stroke when **b** touches **c** and the throttle is about to open.

Setting the fast idling:

1 Adjust the cables to ensure that each cam 6 is against its stop when the choke control in the car is pushed fully in.
2 Pull the choke knob until the fast-idle screw 3, trunnion 5 and centre of the cam are all in line as shown in **FIG 2:10**. Slacken the locknut 4 on each carburetter and adjust the fast-idle screws until they just contact the cams 6.
3 Start the engine, and with it cold (68 to 86°F) adjust each screw 3 equally to give an engine speed of 1100 rev/min. Tighten the locknuts and recheck the engine speed. Stop the engine.

Setting the mixture strength:

This is carried out by adjusting the trim screw. **It is essential that exhaust gas analyzer equipment is used** to give a CO level, when warm, of 2.5 to 3.5 percent or an air/fuel ratio of 13.5:1 when idling. The difference between the screw fully in and fully out cannot be detected by ear. The trim screw should also be used, **in conjunction with analyzer equipment,** to set the mixture for different engine conditions such as after running-in.

2:10 Air cleaner

These differ slightly between the emission controlled engine and the standard engine. In all cases the vent holes must be lined up with the matching holes in the carburetters.

The assembly is shown in **FIG 2:11**. At periodic intervals, depending on climatic conditions, the air cleaner case should be dismantled, loose dirt brushed off the filter elements and the inside of the casing cleaned out. Once dirty the elements have to be renewed.

2:11 Exhaust emission control valve

The details of the assembly are shown in **FIG 2:12** and the parts are held together by a spring clip over the top. At regular intervals the valve should be dismantled and cleaned in methylated spirits (denatured alcohol). Stubborn deposits can be loosened from the metal parts by boiling them in water.

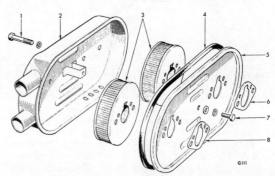

FIG 2:11 Air cleaner details

Key to Fig 2:11
1 Attachment bolts
2 Coverplate
3 Cleaner elements
4 Gasket
5 Backplate
6 Flange gasket
7 Centre bolt
8 Flange gasket

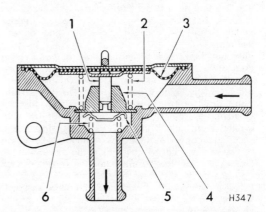

FIG 2:12 Emission control valve details

Key to Fig 2:12
1 Valve
2 Spring
3 Diaphragm
4 Orifice plate
5 Plate valve
6 Spring

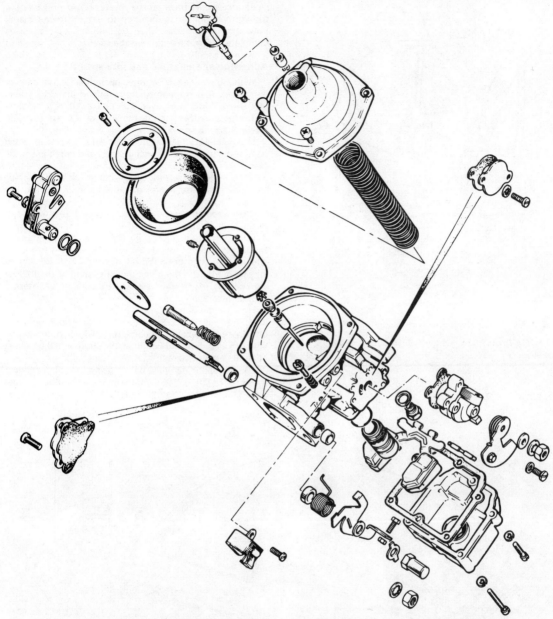

FIG 2:13 Exploded view of the components of Stromberg carburetter type CDSEV

2:12 Stromberg carburetters type CDSEV

This type of carburetter is fitted to later models of the GT6 and has certain points of difference from those described earlier. One feature is the method of venting the float chamber in order to comply with certain evaporative control regulations. A preset valve allows fuel vapours to be drawn into the engine under all running conditions except when the throttle is closed, when the vapours are led through an external pipe to a vapour trap. No adjustment needs to be made from the preset position. The components of the CDSEV carburetter are shown in the exploded view of **FIG 2:13**.

Idle trimming screw:

This device, fitted to USA cars only, can be seen in the exploded diagram lying parallel to the throttle spindle together with its retaining spring. The purpose of this screw is to give a very fine adjustment to compensate for the difference between a new engine and one that is fully run-in.

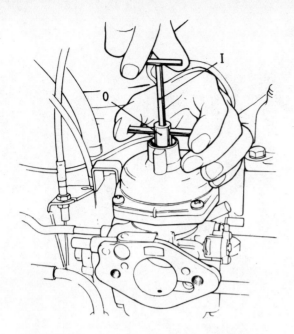

FIG 2:14 Adjusting the mixture using tool No. S353

Key to Fig 2:14   I Inner tool   O Outer tool body

As the engine frees off the screw should be gradually turned in a clockwise direction to reduce the air bleed, until it is fully home when the running-in process is complete. Do not overtighten the screw.

Adjusting the mixture and idle speed:

With the engine fully warmed up, remove the air cleaner and check that the dampers are topped up. Check also that the fast-idle cam lever, 6 in **FIG 2:10**, is against its stop and that there is clearance between the fast-idle screw 3 and the cam.

Using a thin screwdriver lift the piston in each carburetter in turn by $\frac{1}{32}$ inch (.8 mm) and note the engine response.

If the engine speed increases, the mixture is too rich.

If the speed decreases or the engine stalls, it is too weak.

If the speed increases momentarily and then returns to normal, the mixture is correct.

If the mixture requires adjustment, remove the damper from the top of the air valve cover and carefully insert the special adjusting tool S353 into the hollow piston rod, as shown in **FIG 2:14**, so that the inner shaft of the tool (I) engages in the hexagon shaped cavity in the needle adjusting screw.

Hold the outer part O of the tool and carefully turn the inner part as necessary, clockwise to enrich or anti-clockwise to weaken the mixture. Check the mixture strength as before and continue adjusting until the correct mixture is obtained.

The idle speed can now be set, using the idling screw 1 (see **FIG 2:10**), to 700–750 rev/min or 800–850 rev/min on USA emission controlled models.

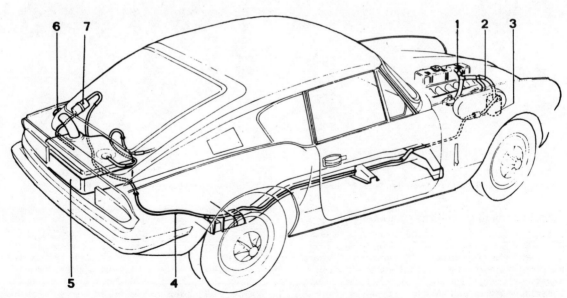

FIG 2:15 Showing a typical evaporation system

Key to Fig 2:15   1 Pipe, engine to carburetter   2 Canister purge pipe   3 Charcoal canister   4 Pipe from fuel evaporation tank to canister   5 Fuel tank   6 Sealed filler cap   7 Separator tank

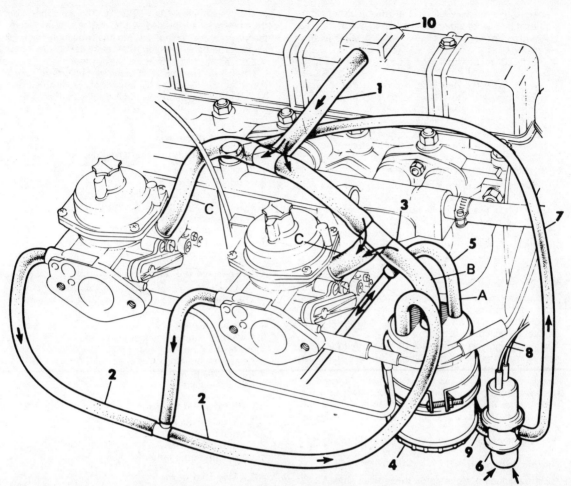

FIG 2:16   Crankcase breathing system layout

Key to Fig 2:16   1 Crankcase breather pipe   2 Vent valve connecting pipes   3 Canister purge pipe   4 Charcoal canister
5 Pipe to fuel tank   6 Anti-run-on valve   7 Vacuum control pipe   8 Solenoid connection   9 Canister to run-on control pipe
10 Flame arrestor   A, B $\frac{1}{32}$ inch restrictors   C $\frac{3}{16}$ inch restrictors

Setting the fast-idle:

Check that the two mixture control/fast-idle cam levers return correctly to their stops and that the mixture control cables are correctly adjusted. Pull out the mixture control knob and insert a $\frac{5}{16}$ inch (7.937 mm) diameter bar between each cam and its square-shaped stop in turn.

Release the locknut 4 on each fast-idle screw 3 and adjust the screws so that they just touch their cams. Remove the bar, push the control knob in and then check that the engine speed is 1100 rev/min when it is pulled out again. If the engine is hot at the time, the speed should be between 1100 and 1300 rev/min.

Make any necessary adjustments to the fast-idle screw to obtain this engine speed, whilst using a balance meter, or a rubber tube as described in **Section 2:6**, to maintain synchronisation of the two throttles.

Tighten the locknuts and refit the air cleaner.

2:13 Emission control systems

In order to comply with anti-pollution legislation in force in various market areas a number of components have been introduced to ensure that these cars comply with the regulations in the appropriate countries. All relevant technical data will be found on the plate under the bonnet for a particular model year and servicing schedules are given in the 'Passport to Service' booklet.

Evaporation control systems:

A typical layout for a later type system is shown in **FIG 2:15** and the main components operate as follows:
1 The carburetter float chambers are vented to the engine during open throttle running and to the carbon canister at closed throttle.
2 The carbon canister, in which vapours from the fuel tank are adsorbed, is vented to atmosphere (on

later models by way of an anti-run-on valve) and purged by way of piping to the carburetter.

3 A separator tank prevents liquid fuel from reaching the canister.

4 The fuel filler cap is sealed to prevent evaporative loss.

5 On early models a pipe from each corner of the fuel storage tank leads to an expansion tank to prevent a fuel overflow to the evaporative system.

6 On later cars the fuel tank filler tube extends down into the tank to prevent complete filling and so provides room for expansion in hot weather.

Adsorption canister filter renewal:

Unscrew the retaining clamp nut and bolt and lift out the canister without disturbing the hoses.

Unscrew the base of the canister and lift out the filter element. Clean out any carbon particles.

Insert a new filter and screw on the canister base. Check that the hose connections are in order.

From 1973 a non-replaceable filter is fitted.

Anti-running-on valve:

This device, mounted on the carbon canister from 1973 on, prevents the engine from continuing to run after the ignition has been switched off due to heat causing compression ignition.

When the ignition is switched off, a solenoid operated valve seals off the inlet to the bottom of the canister and a connection to the inlet manifold applies a degree of vacuum to the canister and thence to the float chambers. This is sufficient to prevent fuel being drawn into the engine. When the engine has stopped and the oil pressure drops to zero, the solenoid is de-activated and the engine is again ready for use.

No maintenance is possible on the control valve.

Thermostatic switch:

This component, mounted on the radiator since 1973, is connected in the vacuum pipe from the carburetter to the distributor and opens the pipe to atmosphere at temperatures of above 105°C (220°F). This puts the vacuum retard out of action, the ignition timing is advanced and the engine speed increases. By this means more efficient cooling is achieved during prolonged periods of idling and overheating is prevented at high ambient temperatures.

Crankcase emission control:

Crankcase breathing and the disposal of blow-by gases is achieved on fully controlled engines by means of the system shown in **FIG 2:16**. The emissions from the crankcase are burned in the engine's normal combustion process, being led into the induction tracts as shown. The flame arrestor 10 incorporates a wire gauge strainer which also acts as an oil separator.

No extra maintenance is required, but it is of course important to ensure the soundness of the flexible hoses and their connections otherwise carburation will be upset.

2:14 Fault diagnosis

(a) Leakage or insufficient fuel delivered

1 Tank vent restricted
2 Petrol pipes blocked
3 Air leaks at pipe connections
4 Pump or carburetter filters blocked
5 Pump gaskets faulty
6 Pump diaphragm defective
7 Pump valves sticking or seating badly
8 Fuel vaporizing in pipelines due to heat

(b) Excessive fuel consumption

1 Carburetters need adjusting
2 Fuel leakage
3 Sticking controls or choke linkage
4 Dirty air cleaners
5 Excessive engine temperature
6 Brakes binding
7 Tyres underinflated
8 Idling speed too high
9 Car overloaded

(c) Idling speed too high

1 Rich fuel mixture
2 Carburetter controls sticking
3 Slow-running screws incorrectly adjusted
4 Worn carburetter butterfly valve

(d) Noisy fuel pump

1 Loose mountings
2 Air leaks on suction side and at diaphragm
3 Obstruction in fuel pipe
4 Clogged pump filter

(e) No fuel delivery

1 Float needle stuck
2 Tank vent obstructed
3 Pipeline obstructed
4 Pump diaphragm stiff or damaged
5 Inlet valve in pump stuck open
6 Bad air leak on suction side of pump

CHAPTER 3

THE IGNITION SYSTEM

3:1 Description
3:2 Routine maintenance
3:3 Ignition faults
3:4 Servicing the Delco Remy type distributor
3:5 Servicing the Lucas type distributor

3:6 Setting the ignition timing
3:7 Sparking plugs
3:8 Ignition coil
3:9 Fault diagnosis

3:1 Description

The distributor is mounted on the engine and is driven by gears from the camshaft at half engine speed (each cylinder only firing once for every two revolutions of the engine). The distributor contains a shaft, driven from the engine, and a cam at the top of this shaft opens, and then allows to close, the contact points mounted on the body of the distributor. A rotor arm on top of the shaft and a distributor cap fixed to the body direct the HT voltage to the firing cylinder sparking plug. When the contact points are closed, an LT current flows through the ignition coil primary coil and contact points. There are six lobes on the rotating cam and the distributor position is set so that a lobe is just opening the contacts when the appropriate cylinder is in the exact firing position. As the contacts open the current is sharply cut off, assisted by the action of the capacitor, and the magnetic field in the ignition coil collapses rapidly, inducing a high voltage in the secondary turns of the ignition coil. This high voltage is taken by an HT lead to the carbon brush in the centre of the distributor cap, and as the carbon brush contacts the rotor arm the high voltage is then directed to the correct sparking plug.

A centrifugal advance mechanism is fitted to the distributor shaft. As the engine speed increases, two weights are flung further out against the restraint exercised by two springs. The movement of the weights turns the cam in relation to the shaft in the direction of rotation, thus advancing the ignition point as the engine speed rises.

A vacuum unit is connected to the inlet manifold. The vacuum unit is also connected to the baseplate of the contacts and, by rotating the plate in relation to the distributor body, the ignition point is set to comply with the engine load and throttle opening conditions.

On the standard engines the vacuum unit is fitted with a vernier adjustment so that the ignition point can be accurately and manually set for different grades of fuel or adjusted to suit the engine condition.

The emission controlled engine has a distributor which is fitted with a double-acting vacuum unit. Under running conditions it acts normally to set the ignition point, but when the throttle is closed, on deceleration or idling, a valve on the throttle linkage opens, allowing full manifold pressure to be exerted on the reverse side of the unit. At the same time air valves open on the manifold, allowing excess air to pass to the engine. The mixture is thus

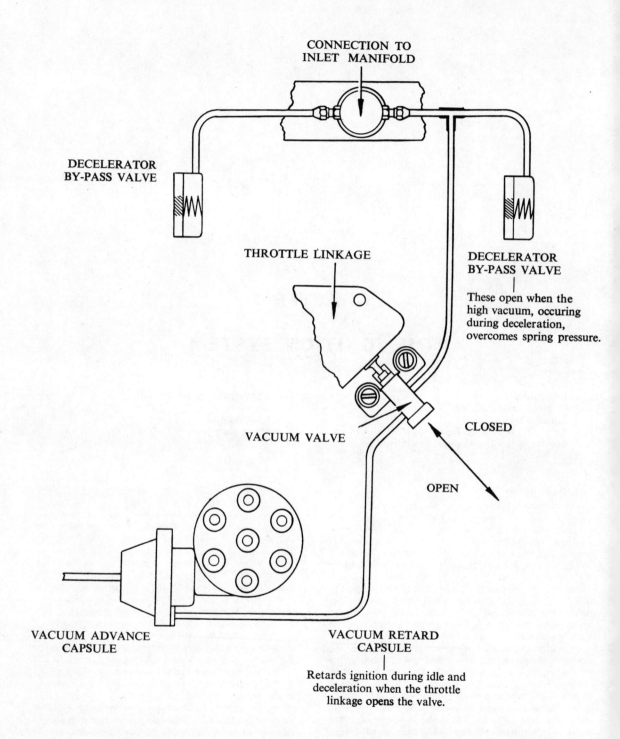

CONNECTION TO
INLET MANIFOLD

DECELERATOR
BY-PASS VALVE

THROTTLE LINKAGE

DECELERATOR
BY-PASS VALVE

These open when the
high vacuum, occuring
during deceleration,
overcomes spring pressure.

CLOSED

VACUUM VALVE

OPEN

VACUUM ADVANCE
CAPSULE

VACUUM RETARD
CAPSULE

Retards ignition during idle and
deceleration when the throttle
linkage opens the valve.

FIG 3:1   Vacuum circuit for deceleration and idling control weakened and the ignition fully retarded to prevent exhaust emission on deceleration. The layout is illustrated in **FIG 3:1**.

The GT6 models are fitted with Delco Remy 200 or 204 series type distributors, of which the details of a typical one are shown in **FIG 3:2**. The Vitesse models are fitted with Lucas 22D6 distributors and the details of these are shown in **FIG 3:3**.

3:2 Routine maintenance

Ensure that the outside of the distributor, the HT leads and top of the ignition coil are always kept clean and dry. Wipe away moisture or oil with a clean, dry cloth, paying particular attention to the crevices between the HT leads on the distributor cap.

Remove the distributor cap 5 and pull off the rotor arm 1, shown in both **FIG 3:2** and **FIG 3:3**. The lubrication points for the Delco Remy distributor are shown in **FIG 3:4** and those for the Lucas distributor are shown in **FIG 3:5**. Pour a few drops of engine oil into the top of the cam at 1. Put a single drop of oil onto the contact pivot 2. Work the moving contact to and fro to ensure that it is free and to allow the oil to spread evenly. If the contact sticks the points will have to be removed and the pivot lightly polished with a piece of fine emerycloth. Pour a few drops of oil through the point marked 3 to lubricate the centrifugal timing control. On the Delco Remy type (see **FIG 3:4**) pour about 5 cc of oil through the hole 4 to soak the felt pad at the base of the distributor. On all types lightly grease the face of the cam, with petroleum jelly or Mobilegrease No. 2. This point is shown as item 5 in **FIG 3:4** and item 4 in **FIG 3:5**. Wipe off any surplus oil. Wipe out the distributor cap and the rotor arm before replacing them.

Adjusting the Delco Remy contact breaker points:

The method is shown in **FIG 3:6**. Make sure the points are clean before adjusting them. Turn the engine so that a lobe of the cam is under the foot of the moving contact and that the points are at their widest gap. (The engine can be turned by rotating the cooling fan). Slacken the securing screw 1 and turn the eccentric screw 2 as shown until the gap between the points is .015 inch (.38 mm) as measured with feeler gauges. Tighten the securing screw 1 and check that the gap has not altered. Replace the rotor arm and distributor cap.

Adjusting the Lucas contact breaker points:

The method is shown in **FIG 3:7**. Make sure the points are clean and rotate the engine until the points gap is widest. Slacken the securing screw 1. Insert the screwdriver into the slots 4 and by twisting it adjust the gap until it is .014 to .016 inch (.36 to .41 mm) as measured with feeler gauges. Tighten the securing screw and check that the gap has not altered. Replace the rotor arm and distributor cap.

Cleaning the contact breaker points:

The surfaces should have a clean, grey, frosted appearance. If they are dirty or partially worn they should be cleaned, but if they are excessively pitted or worn they must be renewed. Use a fine contact file to remove dirt, and face the contacts so that they meet squarely and

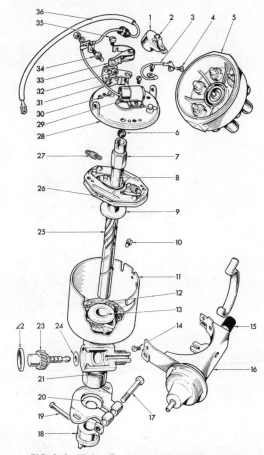

FIG 3:2   Delco Remy type distributor details

Key to Fig 3:2   1 Rotor   2 Rotor contact
3 Mounting plate earth lead   4 Side screw   5 Cap
6 Oil retaining felt   7 Cam   8 Cam spindle
9 Upper thrust washer   10 Short side screw   11 Housing
12 Oil retaining felt   13 Upper sintered iron bearing
14 Side screw   15 Vernier adjustment knob
16 Vacuum advance mechanism   17 Clamp bolt
18 Coupling   19 Coupling pin   20 Lower thrust washer
21 Rubber O-ring   22 Staked plug
23 Tachometer drive gear   24 Thrust washer
25 Shaft and centrifugal advance mechanism unit 26 Weight
27 Control spring   28 Mounting plate   29 Condenser
30 Eccentric screw   31 Fixed contact
32 Terminal stud inner nut   33 Moving contact
34 Terminal stud   35 Lock screw   36 Low-tension wire

evenly. The points should not be dressed smooth. The use of emerycloth or sandpaper is liable to leave particles imbedded in the points, which will cause arcing.

The points are removed by taking off the nut securing the moving contact spring and removing the cable terminals. The moving contact can then be lifted out and the fixed contact removed after taking out the securing screw. The capacitor is secured to the baseplate by one cross-headed screw. Take great care to reassemble the parts in the reverse order of dismantling and ensure that all insulating washers and cable terminals are fitted in their correct places. Use methylated spirits to remove any protective from new contact breaker sets.

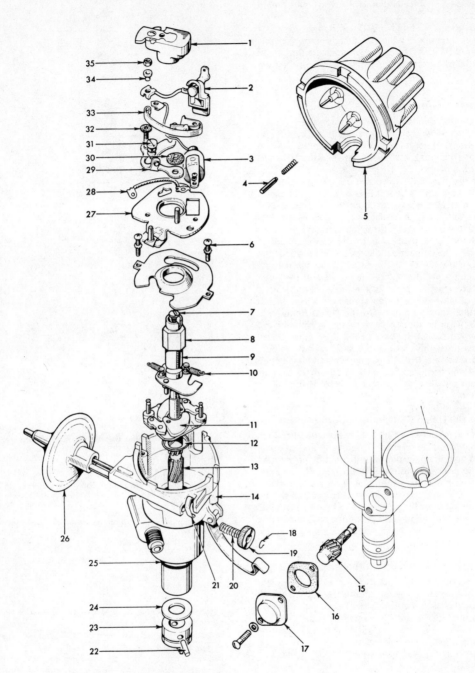

FIG 3:3 Lucas type distributor details

Key to Fig 3:3   1 Rotor   2 Terminal block   3 Capacitor   4 High-tension carbon brush   5 Cover   6 Side screw
7 Cam spindle screw   8 Cam   9 Cam spindle   10 Control spring   11 Weight   12 Distance collar
13 Shaft and action plate   14 Body   15 Tachometer drive gear   16 Gasket   17 Cover   18 Circlip
19 Micrometer adjustment nut   20 Spring   21 Ratchet spring   22 Driving dog pin   23 Driving dog
24 Thrust washer   25 Rubber O-ring   26 Vacuum timing control   27 Moving plate   28 Moving plate earth lead
29 Fixed contact   30 Large insulation washer   31 Lock screw   32 Small insulation washer   33 Moving contact
34 Insulation piece   35 Nut

3:3 Ignition faults

If the engine runs unevenly, and the carburetters are correctly adjusted, set the engine to idle at a fast speed. Taking care not to touch any metal parts of the HT leads, short out or disconnect each plug lead in turn. Use an insulated handle screwdriver between the plug top and the cylinder head to short the plug. Shorting or disconnecting a sparking plug that is firing properly will make the uneven running more pronounced, while shorting a sparking plug that is not firing will make no difference.

Having located the faulty cylinder stop the engine and remove any insulator or shroud fitted to that HT lead. Start the engine, and taking care to avoid shocks, hold the metal end of the lead about $\frac{3}{16}$ inch (5 mm) away from a clean metal part of the engine (but not near the carburetter). A strong regular spark shows that the fault might lie with the sparking plug. Remember that a sticking valve in the engine will cause similar symptoms. Stop the engine, remove the sparking plug and either clean it, as described in **Section 3:7**, or else substitute it with a new sparking plug.

If the spark is weak or irregular check that the HT lead is not cracked or perished. If the lead is found to be faulty renew it and repeat the test. If there is no improvement, remove the distributor cap and wipe the inside with a clean soft cloth. Check that the carbon brush protrudes from the moulding and moves freely against the pressure of the internal spring. Examine the inside surface of the distributor cap for cracks or 'tracking'. 'Tracking' can be seen as a thin black line between the electrodes or to some metal part in contact with the cap. Scraping away the tracking with a sharp knife may effect a temporary cure. **Renewing the cap is the only permanent cure for cracks or tracking.**

Testing the low-tension circuit:

Before carrying out any electrical tests, confirm that the contact points are clean and correctly set.

1 Disconnect the LT cable between the distributor and the coil at the CB terminal on the coil. Connect a low-wattage 12-volt test bulb between the cable and the terminal. Switch on the ignition and turn the engine slowly over by hand. The bulb should light when the contacts close and extinguish as they open. If the lamp stays on continuously there is a shortcircuit in the distributor. Check for faulty insulation or incorrect assembly. If these are correct suspect the capacitor. The light failing to come on at all indicates that no current is reaching the distributor, provided the points are correct.

2 If the lamp does not light, remove it and reconnect the cable to the CB terminal on the coil. Disconnect the other cable to the coil at the SW terminal. Connect the test lamp between this cable and a good earth point on the car. When the ignition is switched on the lamp should light and stay lit continuously. The lamp now lighting indicates a fault in the ignition coil. The lamp still failing to light shows that the circuit is faulty and this should then be checked through.

3 If, with the ignition on, the fuel and temperature gauges register and the ignition warning light comes on, then the fault will lie between the ignition switch and the distributor. If the gauges do not register and the light does not come on, them the fault lies in the

FIG 3:4 Delco Remy type distributor lubrication points

FIG 3:5 Lucas type distributor lubrication points

FIG 3:6 Delco Remy type distributor contact breaker adjustment

FIG 3:7 Lucas type distributor contact breaker adjustment

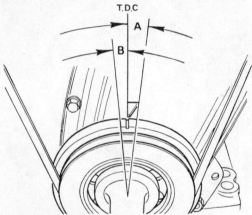

FIG 3:8 Timing marks on crankshaft pulley fitted to earlier engines

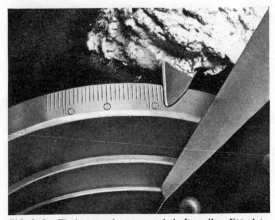

FIG 3:9 Timing marks on crankshaft pulley fitted to later engines

battery and ignition switch part of the circuit. First check the battery terminals for security and cleanliness and see that the battery is charged. Use a 0—20 voltmeter, or a low-wattage test bulb, to test the connections and wires. A wiring diagram is given in Technical Data and this should be used to help identify the correct circuit.

The capacitor:

The capacitor (condenser) is made up of metal foil insulated with paper. If the insulation breaks down the sparks tend to erode away the metal foil in the area, preventing a shortcircuit. However, if a voltmeter connected across the open points shows no reading or the test lamp stays on continuously in test 1, with the ignition switched on, then the capacitor is suspect.

An open circuit capacitor is more difficult to diagnose, but it may be suspected if the points are badly burned or 'blued' and starting is difficult.

Specialized equipment is necessary for testing the capacitor so it is best to check a suspect capacitor by substituting a known satisfactory one.

3:4 Servicing the Delco Remy type distributor

Turn the engine until No. 1 (front) piston is at TDC on the compression stroke. TDC will be indicated by the pointer on the timing cover aligning with the marks on the crankshaft pulley, shown either in **FIG 3:8** or **3:9** depending on type. The compression stroke is found by removing the sparking plug from No. 1 cylinder and having a second operator slowly turn the engine over by rotating the fan blades. The first operator blocks the sparking plug hole with his thumb and as the piston approaches TDC on the compression stroke a rise in pressure will be felt in the cylinder. Remove the distributor cap and check that the rotor arm is pointing as shown in **FIG 3:10**. If the rotor arm position is incorrect the distributor driving gear will have to be remeshed as shown in **Chapter 1, Section 1:6**.

Removing the distributor:

1 Disconnect the vacuum pipe(s) to the vacuum control unit. Disconnect the low-tension cable from the CB terminal on the ignition coil. Disconnect the tachometer drive cable.

2 Remove the two setscrews securing the distributor clamp plate to the drive pedestal and withdraw the distributor. Do not slacken the clamp plate pinch bolt 17 or the ignition timing will be lost, and do not turn the engine after the distributor has been removed.

3 Replace the distributor in the reverse order of removal. Check that the rotor arm still points in the correct direction to ensure that the distributor has not been incorrectly reassembled. Provided the engine is still in its set position and the clamp pinch bolt has not been slackened, then the ignition timing will still be correct. **On emission controlled engines the setting must be checked using a stroboscopic light.**

Dismantling the distributor:

1 Undo the two screws 14 and 4 and slide out the vacuum control unit 16. The vacuum control unit, and its method of attachment, for the emission controlled

engine is shown in **FIG 3:11**. Remove the screw 10 and lift out the complete contact breaker assembly. This can be dismantled as described in 'cleaning contact points' in **Section 3:2**.

2 The springs 27 can be removed from the advance mechanism and these should be discarded and new springs fitted on reassembly. The centrifugal advance mechanism cannot be dismantled and if it is faulty it should be replaced with a new unit.

3 **The distributor should not be dismantled further unless a new staked plug 22 is available.** Use a thin chisel or screwdriver and prise out the old plug 22 after piercing a hole in it. Press out the tachometer drive gear 23 and thrust washer 24 using a twist-drill shank or similar thin tool.

4 **Note the relative positions of the rotor arm driving slot and the offset on the driving coupling 18.** File and tap out the pin 19 and remove the coupling 18 and thrust washer 20. The shaft 25 can now be withdrawn from the body and the top thrust washer 9 removed. Take the felt 12 out of the body after removing the securing clip.

Reassembling the distributor :

1 Wash all the metal parts and the two oil retaining felts 6 and 12 in clean petrol. Squeeze the felts out and allow them to dry, before soaking them in engine oil. If the sintered bearings are worn they should be renewed.

2 Replace the felt 12 and its clip. Fit the thrust washer 9 back onto the shaft 25 and slide the assembly back into the body. Fit new springs 27 to the advance mechanism and lubricate the pivots. Refit the thrust washer 20 and the driving coupling 18 so that it is in the correct relationship with the slot in the cam. If a new shaft is fitted it will be undrilled. Drill the shaft so that the coupling offset in relation to the rotor arm is as shown in **FIG 3:12** and the end float on the shaft is .002 to .005 inch (.0508 to .127 mm).

3 Smear the distributor drive gear 23 and thrust washer 24 all over with Shell Alvania No. 2 grease (or equivalent) and refit them into the body of the distributor. Press a new staked plug 22 into place and secure it by staking in six positions.

4 Refit the contact breaker assembly securing it with the screw 10. After refitting the vacuum control unit 16 replace the other two screws 14 and 4, noting that the earth lead 3 is held by screw 4.

3:5 Servicing the Lucas type distributor

Set the engine to TDC on No. 1 piston at compression, as described early in **Section 3:4**. Remove the distributor in a similar manner to the Delco Remy type as described earlier. Check that the distributor drive gear is positioned as shown in **Chapter 1, FIG 1:15**. Note the position of the rotor arm before removing the distributor.

Dismantling the distributor :

1 Remove the two screws 6, slide out the terminal 2 and lift out the complete contact breaker assembly after disconnecting the spring from the vacuum unit 26.

2 Remove the circlip 18 and unscrew the adjusting nut 19 to free the vacuum unit. Take care to lose neither the spring 20 or the ratchet spring 21.

FIG 3:10 Correct position of the rotor arm on the Delco Remy type distributor when No. 1 piston is at TDC on the compression stroke

FIG 3:11 Lubrication and adjustment points on the Delco Remy D.204 distributor (emission control engine). Note the method of attachment of the vacuum control unit

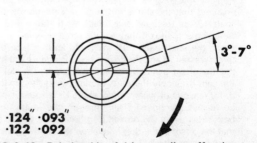

FIG 3:12 Relationship of drive coupling offset key to rotor arm on Delco Remy type distributor

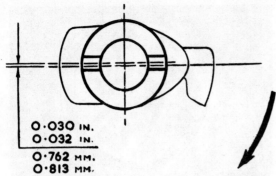

O·030 IN.
O·032 IN.
O·762 MM.
O·813 MM.

FIG 3:13   Relationship of driving dog offset tongue to rotor arm on Lucas type distributor

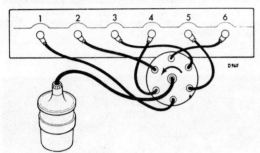

FIG 3:14   Correct positioning of HT leads

3 Remove the cover 17, gasket 16 and withdraw the tachometer drive 15. Note the relationship of the rotor arm driving slot in the cam, shaft 13 and driving dog 23. Tap out the pin 22 and remove the driving dog 23 and thrust washer 24. Withdraw the shaft assembly from the body of the distributor.

4 Carefully, without distorting or twisting them, remove the springs 10. Remove the screw 7 and separate the cam assembly from the shaft assembly 13.

Reassembling the distributor :

1 Clean all the parts in petrol. Examine them for wear and renew worn parts. If the shaft 13 end float is excessive, the washers 12 and 24 should be renewed. Lubricate all bearing surfaces and pivots with clean engine oil before reassembly. This includes the distributor driving gear 15.

2 Replace the weights 11 and refit the cam assembly, ensuring that the slot is in the correct relation to the shaft 13, and secure it in place with the screw 7. Renew the springs if they are distorted or weak.

3 Insert the shaft back into the body and replace the thrust washer 24 and the driving dog 23, again ensuring that the offset is in correct relationship with the slot in the cam 8. Secure the parts in place with the pin 22. If, for reasons of wear, a new shaft 13 is fitted it will be received undrilled. Drill through the shaft from both sides using the driving dog holes as a guide, so that the offset of the dog in relation to the rotor arm is as shown in **FIG 3:13**. Drill the hole so that the end float is correct at .002 to .006 inch (.0508 to .1524 mm).

4 Replace the tachometer drive using a new gasket 16. Refit the vacuum unit 26, spring 20, nut 19 and circlip 18 ensuring that the spring 21 is already in place. Connect the vacuum unit spring to its appropriate peg on the contact breaker assembly.

3:6 Setting the ignition timing

1 On some earlier engines the crankshaft pulley will have only one mark, as shown in **FIG 3:8**, and this mark indicates that the No. 1 and 6 pistons are at TDC. Later engines are fitted with a crankshaft pulley graduated in crankshaft degrees as shown in **FIG 3:9**. In the latter case Nos. 1 and 6 pistons are at TDC when the O-mark is aligned with the pointer on the timing cover. A mark distance A will have to be scribed on the earlier type of crankshaft pulley for the static ignition setting. 1 crankshaft degree is equal to .05 inch on the periphery of the crankshaft pulley. Set the required distance accurately on a pair of dividers and use these to mark the correct position on the pulley periphery. The distance and the correct setting for the models covered by this manual are as follows:

Model	Degrees BTDC	Distance A
GT6 Mk 2	10	.5 inch
GT6 Plus	6 (approx)	.3 inch
Vitesse Mk 2	10	.5 inch

The dimension B is for the stroboscopic setting of the GT6 Plus ignition at idling speed and the distance should be .2 inch giving 4 deg. ATDC.

2 Turn the engine by hand in a clockwise direction until No. 1 piston is on the compression stroke and the timing cover is exactly aligned with the correct mark on the crankshaft pulley. Disconnect the LT cable between the distributor and the ignition coil at the CB terminal on the coil. Reconnect the wire in series with a low-wattage 12-volt test bulb directly to the positive terminal of the battery.

3 Check that the rotor arm is pointing in the direction of the contact connected to No. 1 sparking plug. Slacken the clamp plate pinch bolt and turn the distributor until the points have just opened. This point will be indicated by the test bulb going out. Tighten the pinch bolt sufficiently to prevent the distributor rotating.

4 Turn the engine one complete turn in a clockwise direction and stop turning at the exact point that the test bulb goes out again. Check that the pointer on the timing cover is again aligned with the correct mark on the crankshaft pulley. Adjust the position of the distributor if necessary and rotate the engine in a clockwise direction for one more complete turn so that No. 1 cylinder is again firing. Check that the setting is correct.

5 Disconnect the test lamp and reconnect the wire to the ignition coil. Replace the distributor cap if it has been removed.

Stroboscopic method of setting the timing :

This method may be used on all models but it must be used on the emission controlled engine as the static setting is not sufficiently accurate. Usually it is normal to add 2 degrees of crankshaft movement to the static setting to allow for backlash and any advance in the distributor. On non-emission controlled engines mark this position on the crankshaft pulley with a thin white line. The emission controlled engine is different as the distributor is additionally retarded at idling speed. On this engine mark the 4 deg. ATDC point with a thin white line. On all engines put a thin white line on the edge of the timing cover pointer.

Set the static timing position of the engine as just described to allow the engine to be safely started. Run the engine until it reaches its normal working temperature. Run the engine at 800 to 850 rev/min.

Connect a stroboscopic light as directed by the instrument makers and set it to shine down on the crankshaft pulley. **The engine cooling fan is rotating at high speed and may be invisible. Take great care to keep hands, clothing and equipment well clear.**

Slacken the distributor clamp bolt and rotate the distributor until the white line on the crankshaft pulley appears exactly aligned with the white line on the pointer. Tighten the distributor clamp bolt.

The stroboscopic light can also be used to check that the advance and retard mechanism is functioning correctly.

3 : 7 Sparking plugs

Inspect, clean and adjust sparking plugs regularly. The inspection of the deposits on the electrodes is particularly useful because the type and colour of the deposit gives a clue to the conditions inside the combustion chamber, and is therefore most useful when tuning the engine.

Remove the sparking plugs by loosening them a couple of turns and blowing away loose dirt from the plug recesses with compressed air or a tyre pump, before removing them completely. Store the sparking plugs in in the order of removal. Examine the gaskets and renew them if they are less than half of their original thickness.

Examine the firing end of the sparking plug to note the type of deposit. Normally the deposit should be powdery and should range in colour from brown to greyish tan. There will also be light wear on the electrodes and the general effect is one which comes from mixed periods of high-speed and low-speed driving. Cleaning and re-setting the gaps is all that will be required. If the deposits are white or yellowish they will indicate long periods of constant speed or much low-speed city driving. Again the treatment is straightforward.

Black, wet deposits are caused by oil entering the combustion chamber past worn pistons, rings or down worn valve guides or worn valve stems. Hotter running sparking plugs may help to alleviate the problem, but the only cure is an engine overhaul.

Overheated electrodes have a white, blistered look about the centre electrode and the side electrode may be badly eroded. This may be caused by poor cooling, incorrect ignition, running with too weak a mixture, incorrect grade of sparking plugs or sustained high speeds with heavy loads.

Dry, black, fluffy deposits are usually the result of running with a rich mixture. Incomplete combustion may also be a cause and this might be traced to defective ignition or excessive idling.

Have the sparking plugs cleaned on an abrasive-blasting machine and then tested under pressure after attention to the electrodes. File these until they are clean, bright and parallel. Set the electrode gap to .025 inch

(.64 mm). **Do not bend the centre electrode.** Sparking plugs should be renewed after every 12,000 miles.

Before replacing the sparking plugs, clean the threads with a wire brush and smear the threads with a little graphite grease to prevent them from binding in the cylinder head. **Never use ordinary grease or oil as it will bake hard and jam the plug.** If it is found that the sparking plugs cannot be screwed into place by hand, run a tap down the threads in the cylinder head. Failing a tap, use an old sparking plug with cross-cuts down the threads. Grease the tool well so the chips and dirt stick to the grease instead of falling down the cylinder bore. Clean the insulator on the sparking plug with a petrol-moistened cloth to remove all dirt and grease. Screw the sparking plug in hand tight, by hand only, and finally tighten it to a torque of 14 to 16 lb ft (1.9 to 2.2 kg m). If a torque wrench is not available, tighten with a normal box spanner through half a turn.

HT cables :

These are neoprene covered and are of the resistive type for suppression of radio and television interference. **They should not be replaced by ordinary tinned copper HT cables** as the conductor consists of a special nylon or cotton thread impregnated with carbon. Their resistance is approximately 420 ohms per inch so a serviceable cable should give a reading of between 3000 and 12,000 ohms. In some cases a short length of tinned copper is inserted in the end of the cable to provide a suitable pick-up point, so do not be misled by this into thinking that the conductor is all tinned copper.

The HT cables are held in the distributor cap by spiked screws in the individual contact points. The positions of the HT leads, in the correct firing order of 1–5–3–6–2–4 and with the ignition correctly set, are shown in **FIG 3 : 14**.

3 : 8 Ignition coil

Early cars are fitted with a 12-volt Lucas coil, type HA12, later cars have a 6-volt coil and a ballast resistor in series in the electrical supply which reduces the battery 12-volts to 6-volts for normal engine operation. When the starter switch is operated, the ballast resistor is bypassed and the full battery voltage—slightly reduced by the starter load—is applied temporarily to the coil. This voltage overload provides a higher voltage at the sparking plugs and assists when starting a cold engine.

Early coils of this later type are Lucas 16C6 which has its resistor unit mounted on the coil, later versions are 15C6 and have a ballast resistor wire incorporated in the wire harness serving the coil.

3 : 9 Fault diagnosis

(a) Engine will not fire

1 Battery discharged
2 Distributor points dirty, pitted or out of adjustment
3 Distributor cap dirty, cracked or 'tracking'
4 Carbon brush inside distributor cap not in contact with rotor arm
5 Faulty cable or loose connection in low-tension circuit

6 Distributor rotor arm cracked
7 Faulty ignition coil
8 Broken contact breaker spring
9 Contact points stuck open
10 Faulty capacitor
11 Water on HT leads, distributor cap or ignition coil
12 Faulty ignition lead between ignition coil and distributor

(b) Engine misfires
1 Check 2, 3, 5 and 7 in (a)
2 Weak contact spring
3 HT leads cracked or perished
4 Sparking plug loose
5 Sparking plug insulation cracked
6 Sparking plug gap incorrect
7 Ignition timing too far advanced

CHAPTER 4

THE COOLING SYSTEM

4:1 Description
4:2 Protective maintenance
4:3 The radiator
4:4 Adjusting the fan belt

4:5 The water pump
4:6 The thermostat
4:7 Frost precautions
4:8 Fault diagnosis

4:1 Description

All the models covered by this manual have a pressurized no-loss cooling system. The inlet manifold is heated by hot water from the engine circulating around it, to ensure that the fuel is completely vaporized by the time it reaches the combustion chambers.

The natural thermo-syphon flow of the water is augmented by a centrifugal impeller-type pump driven by a belt from the crankshaft. A thermostat valve fitted integrally in the pump housing controls the flow of water to the radiator. The water circulation through the engine, with the thermostat valve open, is shown in **FIG 4:1**.

When the engine is cold the thermostat valve is shut and the water, instead of passing through the radiator, is bypassed back around the engine thus ensuring a shorter warm-up period. The thermostat does not shut off the supply of water to the inlet manifold so this is rapidly heated, allowing the choke control to be returned earlier than it would if the manifold were not heated. The bypass water is also available to the heater inside the car. When the water reaches a sufficient temperature the thermostat valve opens, allowing the hot water to pass through the radiator where it is cooled by the passage of air over the radiator fins. A cooling fan is fitted to the

front of the crankshaft to ensure that there is air circulation even when the car is stationary or travelling slowly.

The filler cap fitted to the radiator contains a valve which limits the pressure in the cooling system to 7 lb/sq inch (13 lb/sq inch on GT6 Mk 3), and above this pressure the valve opens allowing water to pass to an overflow bottle. When the temperature drops and the water contracts, a vacuum relief valve in the filler cap opens allowing the water to return from the overflow bottle.

Never remove a filler cap when the engine is hot or overheated. Scalding water will be forced out of the filler by the internal pressure.

4:2 Protective maintenance

A sealing plug (25 in **FIG 4:4**), is fitted to the water pump. Every 12,000 miles this plug should be removed and a grease nipple fitted in its place. Use a hand grease gun to inject a maximum of five strokes of grease into the pump. Remove the grease nipple and replace the sealing plug.

The cooling system should be flushed yearly. As antifreeze loses its inhibiting qualities after a year it is best to flush the system just before adding fresh antifreeze.

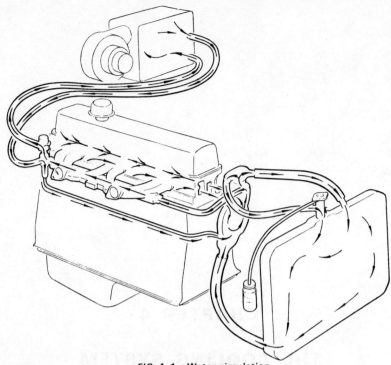

FIG 4:1 Water circulation

Draining:

Remove the filler cap from the radiator and set the heater control to hot. Open the tap on the bottom of the radiator and the tap on the righthand side of the cylinder block. If the antifreeze is less than a year old the coolant should be collected in a clean container for re-use.

Flushing:

Drain the cooling system and unscrew both drain taps to provide an unobstructed flow for the flushing water. Insert a hosepipe into the filler on the radiator and flush through until the water comes out clean from the drain holes.

Filling:

Replace the drain taps if they have been removed and make sure that they are closed. Leave the heater control on hot and fill the system through the filler on the radiator with soft clean water. Fill the system right up leaving no air gap above the water. Replace the filler cap and run the engine until it is hot. Allow the engine to cool and fill the overflow bottle half-full.

4:3 The radiator
GT6:

This radiator is shown in **FIG 4:2**. To remove the radiator drain the cooling system and remove the air duct 9. Disconnect the two top hoses 12 and 16, the bottom hose 22 and the overflow hose 6. Remove the four mounting bolts 20 and lift the radiator out of the car. Replace the radiator by reversing the removal operation, refilling the system after the radiator is replaced.

Vitesse:

This radiator is shown in **FIG 4:3**. To remove the radiator drain the cooling system and disconnect the top hose 13, bottom hose 15 and the overflow hose 23. Remove the nuts and washers 4. Undo and remove the nuts 9 and bolts 6, carefully noting the positions of the packing pieces 5 and washers 7 and 8. Lift the radiator out of the car.

Refill the cooling system after replacing the radiator in the reverse order of removal.

4:4 Adjusting the fan belt

Slacken the top adjusting bolt on the generator/alternator and the pivot bolt(s) underneath the generator/alternator. Ease the generator away from the cylinder block, using a wooden lever between the generator and the cylinder block to hold the generator in place. The belt tension is correct when it can be pressed inwards $\frac{3}{4}$ inch at its longest run, between the generator pulley and the crankshaft pulley. Tighten the pivot bolts and adjustment bolt.

The belt is adjusted in exactly the same way when an alternator is fitted, but **the wooden lever must only be used between the alternator front end bracket and cylinder block otherwise the alternator bearings will be damaged.**

Do not overtighten the belt otherwise the alternator/generator bearings will be damaged. The belt can be removed by slackening the bolts and pushing the alternator/generator towards the cylinder block to slacken the belt.

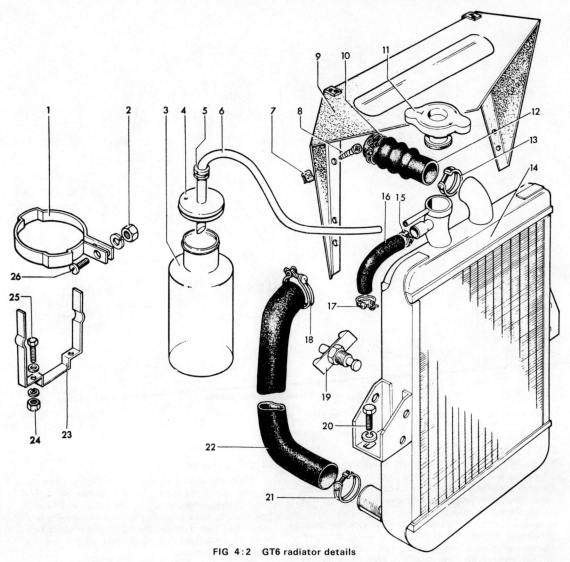

FIG 4:2   GT6 radiator details

Key to Fig 4:2   1 Bottle strap   2 Nut   3 Overflow bottle   4 Cap   5 Grommet   6 Overflow pipe   7 Spire fix nut
8 Spire screw   9 Air duct   10 Hose clip (top hose)   11 Radiator cap   12 Top hose (convoluted)   13 Hose clip (top hose)
14 Radiator   15 Hose clip   16 Top hose   17 Hose clip   18 Hose clip   19 Drain tap   20 Mounting bolt
21 Hose clip   22 Bottom hose   23 Bracket   24 Nut   25 Bolt   26 Screw

4:5 The water pump

Typical water pump details are shown in **FIG 4:4**. To service the pump the body 8 need not be removed from the engine. Drain the cooling system, undo the nuts and washers holding the bearing housing 13 to the body 8 and withdraw the bearing housing assembly.

To remove the complete pump, drain the cooling system and disconnect all the water hoses to the pump assembly. Disconnect the electrical cable to the temperature transmitter 5. Remove the three bolts 26, 27 and 28, noting their positions as they are all of different lengths. Lift off the pump and the gasket 7.

Replacing the pump, or bearing housing, is the reversal of the removal procedure. Clean away all traces of the old gasket 7 or 12 and any jointing compound. Use a new gasket and smear both sides lightly with non-setting jointing compound.

Dismantling the bearing housing:

1 Remove the nut 19 and washer 20 and withdraw the pulley 21. Extract the Woodruff key 24 from the spindle 14.
2 Use a suitable extractor to remove the impeller 9 from the spindle. Remove the seal 11 from the back of the impeller.

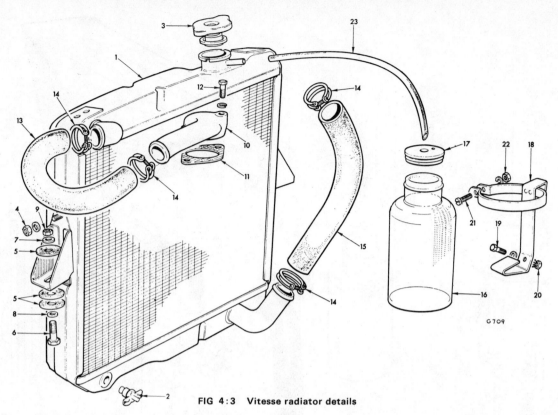

FIG 4:3 Vitesse radiator details

Key to Fig 4:3   1 Radiator   2 Tap   3 Filler cap   4 Nut   5 Packing piece   6 Bolt   7 Washer   8 Washer
9 Nut   10 Water elbow   11 Gasket   12 Bolt   13 Hose   14 Hose clips   15 Hose   16 Bottle   17 Cap
18 Bracket   19 Screw   20 Nut   21 Screw   22 Nut   23 Pipe

3 Remove the circlip 22 and gently tap out the spindle 14, complete with the bearings, from the housing 13.

4 Remove the spinner 15, circlip 23 and washer 16 from the spindle. Use a press to remove the bearings and spacer from the spindle.

5 Use clean water and a brush to remove sediment from the parts. Renew the impeller 9 if the blades are badly eroded or if it has lost its tight fit on the spindle 14. Wash the bearings 18 in clean fuel and renew them if they are worn or run roughly. It is permissible to use a special cutter to reface the sealing face of the housing 13 if it is lightly scored or worn. Renew the seal 11 if it shows signs of wear or has been leaking.

Reassembling the bearing housing :

This is the reversal of the dismantling procedure, but note the following points:

1 The ballbearings 18 must be refitted to the spindle so that their sealing faces are away from the spacer 17. Pack them with grease before refitting the spindle into the bearing housing.

2 Use a press to refit the impeller 9 and seal 11 assembly back onto the spindle 14. Fit a .030 inch (.762 mm) spacer between the impeller and housing and press the impeller on until the spacer is nipped. Remove the spacer and the clearance between the parts will be correct.

4:6 The thermostat

The thermostat 6 is secured in the water pump body 8 by the cover 2 and bolts 1 and 4, as shown in **FIG 4:4**. To remove the thermostat take off the bolts 1 and 4 and lift up the cover 2, still attached to the water hoses. The gasket 3 can then be lifted off and the thermostat 6 withdrawn. The cooling system should be drained so that the level is below the thermostat.

The thermostat is replaced in the reverse order of removal. Note that the gasket 3 is fitted after the thermostat has been replaced in its housing.

The thermostat may be tested by suspending it in water. Heat the water, measuring the temperature with a thermometer, and noting the temperature at which the valve starts to open. If the valve does not start to open between 79.5 and 83.5°C (175 and 183°F), or the valve sticks in the open position, the thermostat is defective and must be replaced with a new one.

4:7 Frost precautions

Antifreeze should always be used in very cold weather, otherwise there is a danger of the bottom half of the radiator freezing, even when the engine is running. **Draining the cooling system overnight is not an adequate frost precaution as some water will remain in the heater.**

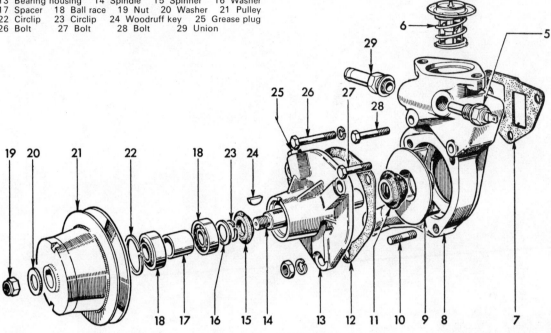

FIG 4:4 Water pump details (later models of the GT6 are slightly different)

Key to Fig 4:4 1 Bolt 2 Elbow 3 Gasket 4 Bolt
5 Temperature transmitter   6 Thermostat   7 Gasket
8 Body   9 Impeller   10 Stud   11 Seal   12 Gasket
13 Bearing housing   14 Spindle   15 Spinner   16 Washer
17 Spacer   18 Ball race   19 Nut   20 Washer   21 Pulley
22 Circlip   23 Circlip   24 Woodruff key   25 Grease plug
26 Bolt   27 Bolt   28 Bolt   29 Union

Most branded names of antifreeze are suitable but ensure that they meet BSI.3151 or 3152 specification. The total capacity of the cooling system on all models covered by this manual is 11 Imperial pints (13.2 US pints, 6.2 litres) and the proportion of antifreeze should be sufficient to give protection at the lowest temperatures expected.

Antifreeze	25%	30%	35%
Complete protection	10°F	3°F	—4°F
	—12°C	—16°C	—20°C
Safe limit*	0°F	—8°F	—18°F
	—17°C	—22°C	—28°C
Lower protection limit**	—14°F	—22°F	—28°F
	—26°C	—30°C	—33°C

*The coolant will be mushy but the engine can be started and the car driven after a short warm-up period.

**The engine and radiator will be protected from damage but the engine must not be started until it has been thawed out.

The cooling system should be flushed through before adding antifreeze. **Make sure the drain taps are closed** and pour in the correct quantity of antifreeze first and then fill the system with soft clean water. Run the engine until it is hot and when it has cooled down again half fill the overflow bottle with a mixture of antifreeze and water.

Never use antifreeze in the screenwasher. A mixture of one part methylated spirits to two parts of water should be used instead.

4:8 Fault diagnosis

(a) Internal water leakage

1 Cracked cylinder wall
2 Cracked cylinder head
3 Loose cylinder head nuts
4 Faulty gasket

(b) Poor circulation

1 Radiator core blocked
2 Engine water passages restricted by deposits
3 Low water level
4 Loose fan belt
5 Defective fan belt
6 Perished or collapsed water hoses

(c) Corrosion

1 Impurities in the water
2 Infrequent draining and flushing

(d) Overheating

1 Check (b)
2 Sludge in crankcase
3 Incorrect ignition timing
4 Weak mixture
5 Low oil level in sump
6 Tight engine
7 Choked exhaust system
8 Binding brakes
9 Slipping clutch
10 Incorrect valve timing

CHAPTER 5

THE CLUTCH

5:1 Description
5:2 Routine maintenance
5:3 The master cylinder
5:4 Servicing the slave cylinder

5:5 Bleeding the hydraulic system
5:6 Servicing the clutch
5:7 The clutch release mechanism
5:8 Fault diagnosis

5:1 Description

All the models covered by this manual are fitted with a diaphragm spring operated clutch. A sectioned view of the clutch is shown in **FIG 5:1**. The cover, which contains the parts, is bolted to the engine flywheel and revolves with it. The driven plate is splined to the gearbox input shaft so that they revolve together. In operation the diaphragm spring forces the pressure plate forwards to grip the driven plate between itself and the rear face of the flywheel, so that the driven plate revolves with the engine and drive is transmitted to the gearbox. When the clutch pedal is pressed, hydraulic and lever action moves the release bearing forwards to press on the centre of the fingers of the diaphragm spring. This pivots between the two rings held by the rivets, and the outer edge of the spring draws back the pressure plate to release the pressure on the driven plate. The driven plate and gearbox input shaft are then free to revolve independently, or come to a stop, without transmitting drive.

A hydrostatic type of slave cylinder is fitted to the clutch housing, so wear in the clutch is taken up automatically and no adjustment is required.

5:2 Routine maintenance

1 At regular intervals check the level in the master cylinder reservoir. The clutch master cylinder is the one with the reservoir of smaller diameter, otherwise on standard cars the two master cylinders are of similar design and construction. Wipe the top clean before removing the filler cap to prevent dirt from falling into the reservoir. If required, top up to the level of the marking on the side of the reservoir, using clean fresh Girling/Castrol Crimson Clutch and Brake Fluid to specification SAE.70.R3. **The use of an incorrect fluid is dangerous as it may attack the materials of the seals causing them to fail.** Excessive consumption of fluid indicates a leak which must be rectified. Check that the breather hole in the filler cap is clear before replacing the cap.

2 It is strongly recommended that the system be dismantled at three-yearly intervals and that old seals and fluid be discarded, and the components examined. Before dismantling the system pump the fluid out through the bleed nipple on the slave cylinder and flush it out by pumping at least a pint of methylated

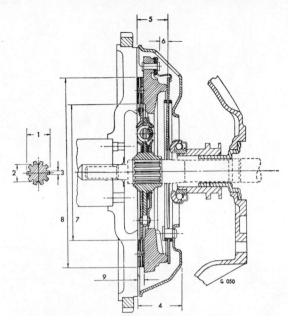

FIG 5:1 Sectioned view of the clutch

Key to Fig 5:1
1 Splines O/D   .998 inch (25.35 mm), .996 inch (25.30 mm)
2 Splines I/D   .870 inch (22.10 mm), .804 inch (20.42 mm)
3 Splines   1.00 inch (25.4 mm) x 10 SAE
4 Flywheel face to cover   2.05 inch (52.07 mm)
5 Flywheel face to spring tips (measured 1.92 inch (48.77 mm)
   diameter using .28 inch (7.1 mm) thickness gauge plate
   1.492 inch (35.35 mm), 1.376 inch (34.95 mm)
6 Maximum travel .290 inch (7.36 mm), .270 inch (6.86 mm)
7 Lining O/D   8.00 inch (203 mm)
8 Lining I/D   5.75 inch (146 mm)
9 Driven plate thickness (under 950 lb (431 kg) load)
   .290 inch (7.36 mm), .270 inch (6.86 mm)

spirits through the system. This will ensure that the
pipes are freed from dirt and any old gummy fluid.

5:3 The master cylinder

Apart from the size of the reservoir, the clutch master
cylinder and brake master cylinder on standard cars are of
exactly the same design and construction and are serviced
in the same manner.

Removal :

The details of the pedal, brackets and master cylinder
are shown in **FIG 5:2**.

1 Syphon the fluid out of the reservoir. **Use rags to
   prevent fluid from spilling onto the paintwork,
   as fluid is a very effective paint remover.**
2 Undo the union securing the pipe from the reservoir
   at the connection on the side of the master cylinder.
   Withdraw the metal pipe, taking care not to bend or
   distort it.
3 Pull back the rubber dust cover 11 and remove the
   clevis pin 14 securing the master cylinder pushrod to
   the pedal 7. Undo the two bolts 16 and remove the
   master cylinder from the car.

The master cylinder is replaced by reversing the order
of removal. After the master cylinder has been refitted the
reservoir must be refilled and the system bled as instructed
in **Section 5:5**.

Operation :

A sectioned view of the master cylinder is shown in
FIG 5:3. The view A is with no pressure applied to the
pushrod and the view B is with the brake pedal depressed
and pressure on the pushrod.

When the plunger 9 is pressed down the bore the seal
8 prevents leakage of fluid back past the plunger. The
pressure in the fluid in front of the plunger rises and is
passed out through the outlet to operate the slave cylinder.
The pressure also ensures that the valve seal 2 is kept
firmly shut. When the pedal is released the plunger moves
back up the bore under the action of the return spring 6
and the pressure in the system drops. As the plunger
reaches the end of its return stroke the head of the valve
shank 5 is caught up by the spring retainer 7 and the force
of the return spring overcomes the pressure of the spring
washer 3. Thus the valve seal 2 is drawn into the open
position opening the interconnection between the
reservoir and the cylinder proper. The pressures in the
reservoir and cylinder are then equalized. As soon as the
plunger starts to move on its pressure stroke the spring
washer 3 closes the valve seal 2, and pressure can then
build up in the cylinder damper.

Dismantling the master cylinder :

The details of the master cylinder are shown in **FIG 5:4**.
The key to this figure is the same as the key to **FIG 5:3**.

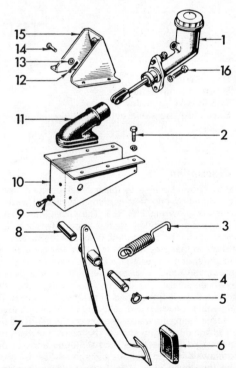

FIG 5:2 Master cylinder and pedal mounting details

Key to Fig 5:2   1 Master cylinder   2 Bolt   3 Spring
4 Fulcrum pin   5 Circlip   6 Pedal rubber   7 Pedal
8 Pivot bush   9 Bolt   10 Pedal bracket
11 Rubber dust excluder   12 Splitpin   13 Plain washer
14 Clevis pin   15 Master cylinder bracket   16 Bolt

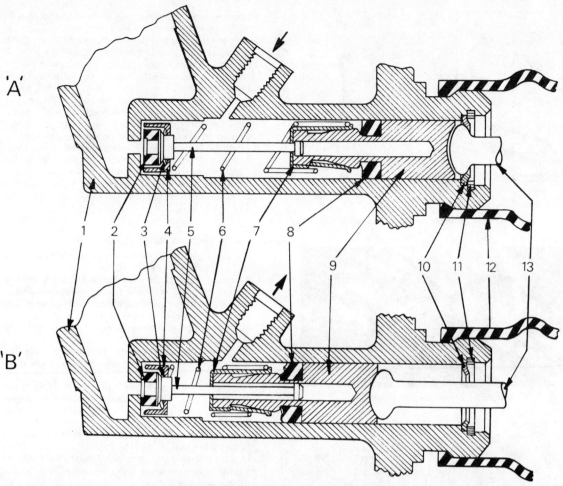

FIG 5:3 Sectioned view of master cylinder

Key to Figs 5:3 and 5:4   1 Master cylinder body   2 Seal (valve)   3 Spring (valve seal)   4 Distance piece   5 Valve
6 Plunger return spring   7 Retainer   8 Seal (plunger)   9 Plunger   10 Abutment plate   11 Circlip   12 Dust excluder
13 Pushrod

and the parts may be identified using either of these two figures, **FIG 5:3** showing the relationship of the parts when they are assembled.

1 If it is still fitted, remove the dust cover 12. Lightly press in the pushrod 13 to relieve the pressure of the return spring and use a pair of long-nosed pliers to remove the circlip 11. The pushrod 13 and its abutment plate 10 can now be removed.

2 Shake out the internal parts, or if they are difficult to remove apply gentle air pressure at the outlet to blow them out.

3 Part the coils of the return spring 6 and use a thin screwdriver to lift the leaf of the spring retainer 7 above the level of the shoulder on the plunger 9. Pull the spring retainer free from the plunger.

4 Lightly compress the return spring 6 and slide the stem of the valve 5 sideways into the larger offset hole in the spring retainer. When the spring is released the head of the valve will pass through the larger offset hole, allowing the spring retainer 7 to be freed from the

valve 5. Remove the spring 6, distance piece 4 and spring washer 3.

5 Use the fingers only to remove the two seals 2 and 8.

Examining the parts:

Cleanliness is absolutely essential when dealing with any parts in the hydraulic system. Lay parts out on clean sheets of paper to prevent them from picking up dirt or dust. Wash the parts in methylated spirits or clean hydraulic fluid. If any other solvent is used on the metal parts it must be dried off completely before reassembly, as any traces may affect the material of the seals causing them to fail.

The seals should be renewed so discard old seals automatically. There is little point in refitting the old seals only to find that they leak within a short time and that the whole operation will have to be repeated.

Examine the bore of the cylinder, which should be smooth and highly-polished. Pitting, wear or score marks mean that a new master cylinder assembly must be fitted.

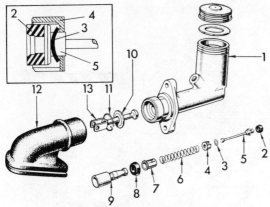

FIG 5:4   Master cylinder details

FIG 5:5   Slave cylinder mounting

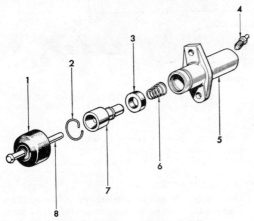

FIG 5:6   Slave cylinder details

Key to Figs 5:5 and 5:6   1 Dust cover   2 Circlip
3 Seal   4 Bleed nipple   5 Body   6 Spring   7 Piston
8 Pushrod   9 Mounting bolts

Reassembling the master cylinder:

1 Before each part is fitted dip it in clean hydraulic fluid
and fit it wet.
2 Use the fingers only to refit the two seals 2 and 8. Both
are fitted so that their lips face into the cylinder bore.
Once in place work the seals around so that they are
properly and squarely seated in position. Refit the

spring washer 3 and distance piece 4 so that they fit
as shown in the inset in **FIG 5:4**.
3 Refit the return spring 6. Slide the head of the valve 5
through the larger offset hole in the spring retainer 7
and fit the spring retainer so that it is in position in the
spring and the valve stem is in the central smaller hole.
4 Press the plunger 9 assembly back into the spring
retainer 7, making sure that the leaf on the retainer
seats squarely behind the shoulder on the plunger. If
required, part the coils of the spring and use a thin
screwdriver to press the leaf gently into position.
5 Again dip the completed internal assembly into clean
hydraulic fluid and fit it back into the bore of the
cylinder. **Take great care not to damage or bend
back the seal 8 as it enters the bore.** Hold the
parts in place with the pushrod 13 and refit the circlip
11.

5:4 Servicing the slave cylinder

The slave cylinder mounting is shown in **FIG 5:5** and
its details are shown in **FIG 5:6**.
1 Before attempting to remove the slave cylinder, remove
the trim and gearbox cover to gain access to the cylinder.
Attach a length of small-bore tube to the bleed nipple
4. Open the bleed nipple half a turn and pump the
fluid into a clean container, using full steady strokes of
the clutch pedal.
2 Disconnect the metal pipe at the slave cylinder and
remove the two mounting bolts 9 to free the slave
cylinder.
3 Remove the dust cover 1 and pushrod 8. Press in the
piston 7 and use a pair of long-nosed pliers to remove
the circlip 2. The internal parts of the cylinder can now
be shaken out.
4 Remove the seal 3 and discard it. Wash the parts in
methylated spirits or clean hydraulic fluid, laying them
on a clean sheet of paper to dry. If the bore of the body
5 is not highly-polished, with a smooth surface, renew
the complete assembly.
5 Dip a new seal 3 into clean hydraulic fluid and use only
the fingers to refit it squarely and securely onto the
piston 7. Fit the narrow diameter of the spring 6 onto the
piston and smear the assembly with clean hydraulic
fluid.
6 Refit the internal assembly back into the bore of the
cylinder. **Take great care not to damage or bend
back the lips of the seal 3 as it enters the bore.**
Secure the parts in place with the circlip 2.
7 Refit the pushrod 8 and dust cover 1. Smear the end
of the pushrod with a little zinc oxide grease and refit
the slave cylinder to the clutch housing.
8 Fill the master cylinder reservoir and bleed the system
as described in **Section 5:5**. Replace the gearbox
cover and trim.

5:5 Bleeding the hydraulic system

This is not routine maintenance and is only necessary
when air has entered the system. Air can enter either when
the system is dismantled or if the level in the reservoir is
allowed to fall so low the air is drawn into the master
cylinder.
Fill the reservoir up to within $\frac{1}{4}$ inch from the top and
ensure that it is kept topped up throughout the bleeding

operation, as fluid will be continuously used. If the level is allowed to fall too low then air might again be drawn into the system.

Always discard the first fluid bled through the system. The remainder of the fluid bled through should also be discarded unless it is perfectly clean. **Never return fluid that has just been bled through directly to the master cylinder reservoir.** Store it for at least 24 hours in a sealed clean container to allow the minute air bubbles to disperse.

1 Remove the dust cover fitted over the bleed nipple on the slave cylinder. Wipe the nipple clean and fit onto it a length of small-bore plastic or rubber hose. Dip the free end of the hose into a little clean hydraulic fluid in a clean glass container.

2 Open the bleed nipple one complete turn and have a second operator pump the clutch pedal with full strokes. Allow the pedal to return unassisted and leave a short pause between each stroke.

3 When air ceases to bubble out with the fluid from the pipe and only clear fluid is ejected, have the clutch pedal held down in its fully depressed position and tighten the bleed nipple.

4 Pump the pedal a few times to ensure that it has a solid feel and that all the sponginess due to air in the system is gone. Have the pedal held down with a firm pressure and examine the system for leaks, after removing the bleed hose.

5:6 Servicing the clutch

If the engine is still fitted to the car then the gearbox must be removed so as to gain access to the clutch. Remove the gearbox as instructed in **Chapter 6, Section 6:2**. Progressively and evenly slacken the ring of bolts securing the clutch to the flywheel. Remove the bolts when they are loose and lift off the clutch cover assembly and the driven plate.

The condition and rectification of the flywheel face has already been dealt with in **Chapter 1, Section 1:7**. If the clutch assembly is defective the unit must be renewed as it cannot be dismantled and rectified.

The driven plate is renewable on its own and it should be examined for defects. Check that there is still plenty of wear on the linings and that they stand well proud of their securing rivets. Check all rivets for security and see that the cushioning springs are secure in their mountings. Examine the splines in the hub to see that they are not worn or damaged. Renew the driven plate if the linings are excessively worn or if it shows any other defect.

For maximum efficiency the friction linings should have a polished light-coloured glaze through which the grain of the material is clearly visible. Any oil leaking into the clutch will show on the linings. Small quantities of oil will produce darker smears, while larger quantities of oil will be shown by a dark glaze, all over the friction linings, which is dark enough to hide the grain of the material. A large oil leak will be obvious from the free oil in the housing and the oil soaked appearance of the linings. The source of the oil leak will have to be traced and rectified before the clutch is refitted. Provided that the grain of the material is still visible the driven plate may be used again. Renew the driven plate if the grain is not visible otherwise the clutch will always have a tendency to drag, slip or be fierce.

FIG 5:7 Centralizing the driven plate

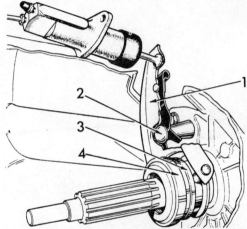

FIG 5:8 Clutch release mechanism details

Key to Fig 5:8 1 Release lever 2 Pivot pin
3 Throwout sleeve 4 Throwout bearing

The clutch is refitted in the reverse order of removal. Centralize the driven plate with a mandrel, as shown in **FIG 5:7**, while progressively tightening the bolts securing the clutch cover to the flywheel. An old gearbox input shaft is the most convenient mandrel. If the driven plate is not centralized it will be nearly impossible to refit the gearbox.

5:7 The clutch release mechanism

The details of the parts are shown in **FIG 5:8**. To gain access to the release bearing 4 the gearbox must be removed from the engine (see **Chapter 6, Section 6:2**). Unclip the release lever 1 from the spherical bearing pin 2 and withdraw the release lever. The bearing 4 and sleeve 3 can now be drawn off the gearbox input shaft. The bearing 4 is a sealed unit and must be renewed if it is worn, defective or noisy. Press the sleeve from the bearing to separate them.

Replace the parts in the reverse order of dismantling lubricating the pivot pins with a light smear of zinc oxide grease.

5:8 Fault diagnosis

(a) Drag or spin

1 Oil or grease on the driven plate linings
2 Leaking master cylinder, slave cylinder or interconnecting pipes
3 Driven plate hub binding on the splines of the gearbox input shaft
4 Distorted driven plate
5 Warped or damaged pressure plate
6 Broken driven plate linings
7 Air in the clutch hydraulic system

(b) Fierceness or snatch

1 Check 1, 2, 4 and 5 in (a)
2 Worn clutch linings

(c) Slip

1 Check 1 in (a) and 2 in (b)
2 Seized piston in slave cylinder

(d) Judder

1 Check 1 and 4 in (a)
2 Contact area of driven plate linings not evenly distributed
3 Faulty engine mountings

(e) Tick or knock

1 Badly worn driven plate splines
2 Worn release bearing

CHAPTER 6

THE GEARBOX AND OVERDRIVE

6:1 Description
6:2 Removing the gearbox
6:3 Dismantling the gearbox
6:4 Reassembling the gearbox

6:5 Gearchange extension and top cover assembly
6:6 The overdrive
6:7 Fault diagnosis

6:1 Description

The gearbox is fitted with four forward speeds and one reverse. All four forward speeds are fitted with synchromesh engagement and reverse is obtained by sliding into mesh an idler which reverses the direction of rotation of the mainshaft. The gearlever is mounted on a separate extension which brings it within easy reach of the driver's hand. Gear selection is by three selector shafts and forks mounted in the gearbox top cover. The three selector shafts are fitted with an interlock mechanism which allows only one shaft to be moved at a time and so prevents the inadvertent selection of two gears at the same time. Spring-operated plungers engage in detents in the selector shafts to prevent them moving from the selected position.

The mainshaft rotates in two ballbearings, the rear bearing being held in the removable rear extension. The input shaft also rotates in a ballbearing mounted in the front of the gearbox casing. A spigot on the mainshaft fits into a roller bearing in the input shaft and the countershaft gear cluster rotates about similar roller bearings on the countershaft. Thrust washers are fitted to take the end thrusts and to control the end float.

A drain plug is fitted underneath the gearbox casing and a combined level and filler plug is fitted to the right-hand side of the gearbox casing. The gearbox is filled with the correct grade of Hypoid oil so that the level is just at the bottom of the filler hole.

An overdrive may be fitted as an optional extra, in which case it takes the place of the rear extension. The overdrive is selected using an electric switch which is located on the steering column in early models and in the knob on the gearlever in 1971 cars, and operates only on the top two speeds. An isolator switch is fitted to prevent accidental operation in any other speeds. To prevent the engine from overspeeding the overdrive should not be disengaged above an engine speed of 4800 rev/min.

The overdrive is fitted with a separate drain plug but shares the same oil supply as the gearbox, and both are filled together through the gearbox filler. The overdrive always relies on the friction of a cone clutch for its satisfactory operation, either engaged or disengaged, and for this reason **no additives must be put into the gearbox oil when an overdrive is fitted.**

The gearchange extension, top cover, rear extension (or overdrive) and speedometer drive pinion parts can be removed without fully taking the gearbox out of the car.

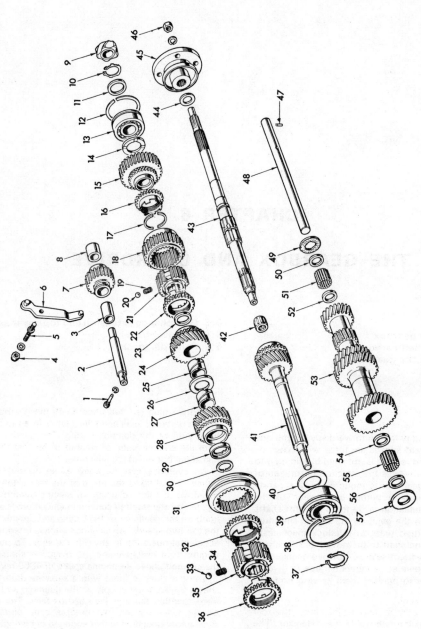

FIG 6:1 Gearbox moving parts

Key to Fig 6:1 1 Locating bolt   2 Reverse idler spindle   3 Reverse idler bush   4 Nyloc nut   5 Pivot pin   6 Reverse actuator   7 Reverse idler gear   8 Distance tube   9 Speedometer driven gear   10 Circlip   11 Washer   12 Snap ring   13 Centre ballrace   14 Thrust washer   15 1st speed gear   16 Baulk ring   17 Split collars   18 1st/2nd synchromesh sleeve   19 Spring   20 Ball   21 1st/2nd synchromesh hub   22 Baulk ring   23 Thrust washer   24 2nd speed gear   25 2nd gear bush   26 Thrust washer   27 3rd gear bush   28 3rd speed gear   29 Circlip washer   30 Circlip   31 3rd/Top synchromesh sleeve   32 Baulk ring   33 Ball   34 Spring   35 3rd/Top synchromesh hub   36 Baulk ring   37 Circlip   38 Snap ring   39 Front ballrace   40 Oil thrower   41 Input shaft   42 Roller bearing   43 Mainshaft   44 Thrust washer   45 Coupling flange   46 Nut   47 Pin   48 Countershaft spindle   49 Rear thrust washer   50 Retaining ring   51 Needle rollers   52 Retaining ring   53 Countershaft gear cluster   54 Retaining ring   55 Needle rollers   56 Retaining ring   57 Front thrust washer

6:2 Removing the gearbox

The details of the moving parts of the gearbox are shown in **FIG 6:1** and the details of the fixed parts are shown in **FIG 6:2**. Before starting to remove the gearbox, jack up the car and place it securely on stands or ramps so as to have sufficient room to work underneath the car. The actual gearboxes on all models covered by this manual are similar, but there are minor differences in the method of attachment between the GT6 and the Vitesse. Before removing any parts drain the oil out of the gearbox, and disconnect the battery.

GT6:

Remove the seats. Remove the facia support by first taking out the top pair of securing bolts and then the pair of bolts securing each leg to the floor. Remove the transmission side tunnel finishers by taking out the four screws and safety belt anchor bolts. Unscrew the gearlever knob and remove the carpets. From underneath the car disconnect the exhaust pipe attachment by taking out the bolt that holds the clip. This bolt is one of those securing the rear extension to the gearbox casing.

Vitesse:

Remove the front seats, unscrew the gearlever knob and remove the front carpets. Disconnect the exhaust pipe from the clip at the junction of the clutch housing and engine.

All the models are similar from here on so proceed as follows:

1 Remove the screws and plates that secure the gearbox cover and lift out the cover. The gearbox will then appear as shown in **FIG 6:3**. Referring to **FIG 6:2**, remove the top cover and gearchange extension assembly by taking out the bolts 104 and 88 and easing the cover off the dowels 115. Remove the gasket 106 and cover the gearbox aperture with a sheet of cardboard to prevent any dirt from falling into the gearbox.

2 Remove the two bolts N and lift the clutch slave cylinder out of the way, still attached to its supply pipe. Unscrew the knurled nut P and disconnect the speedometer cable. Remove the nuts and bolts connecting the propeller shaft to the drive flange on the gearbox.

3 Remove the nuts U securing the gearbox mounting rubbers to the bracket. Working from underneath the car, remove the bolts W, shown in **FIG 6:4**, securing the mounting bracket V to the chassis bracket. Place a jack under the rear of the engine sump, and using a block of wood to protect the sump, jack up the engine until the rear extension is clear of the mounting bracket V and the bracket can be taken out. Undo the ring of nuts securing the clutch housing to the rear of the engine. Support the weight of the gearbox and ease it back until the input shaft is clear of the clutch, **taking great care not to let the weight of the gearbox hang on the input shaft**. Raise the rear end of the gearbox and manoeuvre the clutch housing out from underneath the parcel shelf. The gearbox can then be removed from the car.

Refit the gearbox in the reverse order of removal, **again taking care not to let the weight of the gearbox hang on the input shaft**. Refill the gearbox with oil to the correct level before replacing the gearbox cover.

6:3 Dismantling the gearbox

Some special tools are required and the task will be much more difficult without these tools. If the owner doubts in any way his ability to perform satisfactory work he is strongly advised to take the unit to a suitably equipped garage.

1 Unscrew the peg bolt 127 and withdraw the speedometer driven gear parts as shown in **FIG 6:5**. Hold the driven flange 45 using the special peg spanner No. S.337 and remove the nut and washer 46. Withdraw the driving flange from the mainshaft 43. Unscrew all the bolts 120 and carefully drive the rear extension 119 off from the gearbox by tapping on the lugs using a soft-faced hammer. Eject the ballrace 118 and oil seal 17 from the extension.

2 Unclip the clutch release lever from the pivot post 136 and remove the lever complete with the clutch release bearing. Remove the four bolts 135, the single bolt 133 and copper washer 134. Remove the clutch cover 137 and take out the three springs 138 from underneath it. The oil seal 130 and oil seal housing 131 will be attached to the clutch housing.

3 Remove the reverse spindle securing bolt 1, as shown in **FIG 6:6**, and withdraw the spindle 2 and distance piece 8. Press out the countershaft by inserting a piece of tubing .655 inch (16.64 mm) in diameter and 6.5 inch (165 mm) long from the front of the gearbox. Leave the tubing in place in the countershaft gear cluster so as to retain the roller bearings in position, allowing the countershaft gears to fall clear of the mainshaft gears.

4 Attach the special tool No. S.4235A-2 to the front end of the input shaft, as shown in **FIG 6:7**, and, by sliding the moving weight smartly along the shaft so that it impacts on the handle, draw the input shaft assembly out of the gearbox. Shake out the roller bearing 42. Remove the circlip 37 and snap ring 38 then use an extractor to remove the bearing 39, thus also freeing the oil thrower 40.

5 Use a Churchill hand press and adaptors to remove the speedometer drive gear 9. Remove the circlip 10, distance washer 11 and snap ring 12. Use adaptor No. S.4221A-19/1 (which fits into the annular groove in the bearing 13) and the hand press to withdraw the bearing 13 while supporting the front end of the mainshaft with the abutment plate No. S.4221A-19, as shown in **FIG 6:8**. Remove the abutment plate, tilt the front end of the mainshaft assembly upwards and withdraw the complete mainshaft assembly out through the top aperture.

6 Slide off the parts as follows: third/top synchromesh unit, third gear baulk ring 32, thrust washer 14, first speed gear 15 and first gear baulk ring 16. Use tool No. S.144 to remove the mainshaft circlip 30. The circlip will probably be damaged on removal so a new circlip should always be fitted on reassembly, but retain the old circlip as, despite damage, it will still be needed later. Slide the remainder of the parts off the mainshaft, carefully noting their position and order

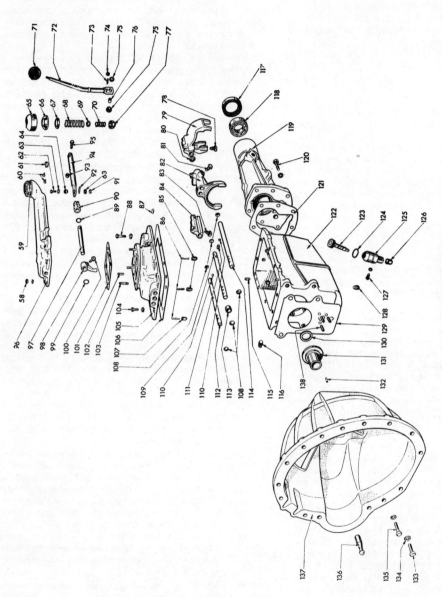

FIG 6 : 2 Gearbox fixed parts

Key to Fig 6 : 2 58 Nut 59 Locating pin 60 Screws 61 Reverse stop plate 62 Pivot bolt 63 Fibre washers 64 'Metalistik' bush 65 Cap 66 Cup 67 Cup 68 Spring 69 Snap ring 70 Spring 71 Knob 72 Gearlever 73 Reverse stop bolt 74 Locknut 75 Nylon bushes 76 Distance tube 77 Nylon sphere 78 Taper locking pin 79 1st/2nd selector fork 80 Distance washer 81 Taper locking pin 82 3rd/Top selector fork 83 Taper locking pin 84 Reverse selector 85 Detent plungers 86 Springs 87 Plug 88 Bolt 89 Rubber O-ring 90 Coupling fork 91 Nyloc nut 92 Hollow pin 93 Nyloc nut 94 Gearlever shaft 95 Setscrew 96 Top cover extension housing 97 Gearlever shaft 98 Selector 99 Rubber O-ring 100 Taper locking pin 101 Joint washer 102 Dowel 103 Stud 104 Bolt 105 Top cover housing 106 Joint washer 107 Detent plunger 108 Welch plugs 109 1st/2nd selector shaft 110 Interlock balls 111 Interlock plunger 112 Reverse selector shaft 113 Sleeve 114 3rd/Top selector shaft 115 Dowel 116 Filler/level plug 117 Oil seal 118 Rear ballrace 119 Rear extension 120 Bolt 121 Joint washer 122 Gear casing 123 Speedometer driven gear 124 Rubber O-ring 125 Bearing 126 Oil seal 127 Locating bolt 128 Drain plug 129 Joint washer 130 Oil seal 131 Oil seal housing 132 Pin 133 Bolt 134 Copper washer 135 Bolt 136 Pivot pin 137 Clutch housing 138 Springs

FIG 6:3   Gearbox attachments

and laying them out on a clean sheet of paper in the order of removal.

7 The parts of the synchromesh units are shown in **FIG 6:9.** Wrap each unit in a piece of cloth and press the outer sleeve off while the parts are in the cloth. **If this precaution is not observed the springs and balls will be shot out and lost.**

8 Lift out the countershaft assembly from the casing. Leave the tube in place unless the needle roller bearings are to be changed. If the needle rollers are to be examined, remove the tube, shake out the needles 51 and 55 and prise out the retaining rings 50, 52, 54 and 56. Lift out the reverse idler gear 7 with its bush 3. Undo the nut 4 to remove the parts of the reverse gear actuator.

6:4 Reassembling the gearbox

Thoroughly clean all the parts, washing them at least twice, the second wash being in clean solvent. Carefully examine the parts and renew any that are worn or seem doubtful. Check all shafts and bearing surfaces for fret or chatter marks. Check the gears to make sure that there are no broken, worn or missing teeth. Renew all the oil seals and fit new gaskets so as to ensure against oil leaks after the gearbox has been reassembled and refitted to the car.

1 Refit the balls and springs to the hubs of the synchro-mesh units, holding them in place with grease. Compress the balls back into the hubs using a hose clip tightened around the hub. Insert the hub into the outer sleeve and tap it into place, allowing the hose clip to slide off. until the balls click into the detent grooves in the sleeve. Test each synchromesh unit in a jig as shown in **FIG 6:10.** Apply a gradually increasing pull to the hook, using a spring balance, and note the load required to move the balls out of the detent position. If the load is incorrect, either adjust it by fitting new springs or reset it by fitting shims under the springs. The correct release load for both synchromesh units should be 19 to 21 lb (8.6 to 9.5 kg).

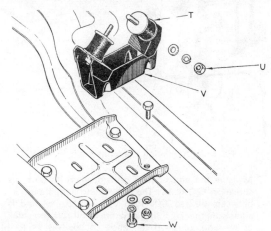

FIG 6:4   Gearbox mounting details

FIG 6:5   Removing the speedometer driven gear

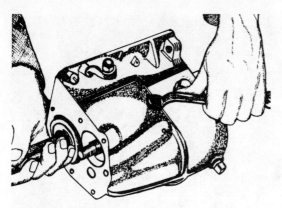

FIG 6:6 Removing the reverse spindle locking bolt

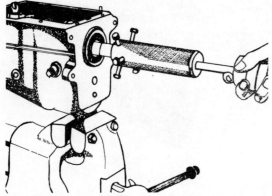

FIG 6:7 Removing the input shaft assembly

2 Measure the end float of each gear on its bush, as shown in **FIG 6:11**. The correct end float should lie between .002 to .006 inch (.05 to .15 mm) and is adjusted either by fitting new bushes if it is too small or by lapping down the ends of the bushes if it is excessive. **Take care not to reduce the length of the bushes by too much, as they partially control the total end float on the mainshaft.**

3 Assemble the thrust washer 23, bush 25, thrust washer 26, bush 27 and circlip washer 29 to the mainshaft, securing the parts in place with part of the old circlip 30. Measure the end float as shown in **FIG 6:12**. If required adjust the end float, so that it lies between the correct limits .004 to .010 inch (.10 to .25 mm), by the selective fitting of the thrust washers.

4 Fit the split collars 17, first speed gear 15, thrust washer 14, bearing 13 (or distance tube when an overdrive is fitted), distance washer 11 and circlip 10 to the mainshaft. Measure the end float as shown in **FIG 6:13** and adjust it to the correct limits of .000 to .002 (.00 to .05 mm) by selectively fitting the right width washer 11.

5 If the needle roller bearings have been removed from the countershaft fit new retaining rings at the dimensions shown in **FIG 6:14**. Replace the needle rollers, holding them in with thick grease and finally retaining them in position using a tube of the dimensions given

earlier. Fit the front thrust washer 57 into place in the casing so that its tag locates in the recess provided. Hold it in place with thick grease and centralize it by partially entering the countershaft. Lower the countershaft gear cluster assembly into position and press in the countershaft so that it ejects the tube and supports the gear cluster. Fit the rear thrust washer 49 correctly into place and pass the countershaft through it. Measure the end float of the gears between them and a thrust washer. Adjust to the correct end float of .007 to .013 inch (.178 to .330 mm) by the selective fitting of the thrust washers. End float may be increased by lapping down the steel faces of the thrust washers but **never the bronze faces.** Once the end float is satisfactory, press back the bearing retaining tube and allow the cluster to slide to the bottom of the casing.

6 Screw the pivot 5 back into the actuator 6 so that one thread protrudes through the boss. Secure the assembly back in place in the casing using the plain washer and nut 4. Refit the reverse idler gear 7 and its bush 3 so that they lie as shown in **FIG 6:15**.

7 Refit the parts to the mainshaft in the reverse order of removal. Refit the circlip 30 using special tool No. S.145 before refitting the remainder of the parts. Replace the mainshaft assembly in the gearbox and support the front end with the abutment plate tool shown in **FIG 6:8**. Set the gearbox on end and support it by clamping the abutment plate in a vice. Slide in the thrust washer 14. Refit the snap ring 12 to the rear

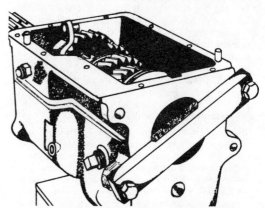

FIG 6:8 Abutment plate tool in position

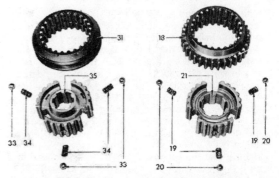

FIG 6:9 Synchromesh unit parts

bearing 13 and drive the bearing back into the casing so that the snap ring is tight against the face of the casing. Refit the distance washer 11 and the circlip 10. Press into place the speedometer drive gear 9. Lay the gearbox back onto the bench and remove the abutment plate.

8 Reassemble the parts of the input shaft assembly, making sure that the oil thrower 40 is kept squarely in position until the bearing 39 has been fully pressed back into position. Fit the baulk ring 36 back onto the mainshaft and drive the input shaft assembly back into position, making sure that the lugs on the baulk ring fit into the slots in the synchromesh hub.

9 Turn the gearbox over, align the countershaft gear cluster and thrust washers. Press out the locating tube by inserting the countershaft 48 from the rear of the gearbox. Keep the tube and countershaft in firm contact throughout this operation to prevent either the thrust washers or needle rollers from becoming misaligned. Make sure that the reverse gear is in the correct position and slide into place the reverse idler spindle 2 followed by the distance tube 8. Hold the spindle in place using the peg bolt 1 and washer.

10 Drive in the bearing 118 and oil seal 117 into place in the rear extension 119. Refit the rear extension, using a new gasket 121 and securing it in place with the bolts 120 (note that one of these bolts supports the exhaust pipe on GT6 models). Replace the driving flange 45 securing it with the washer and nut 46.

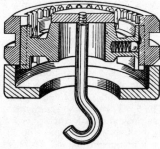

FIG 6:10   Jig for testing axial release loads on synchromesh units

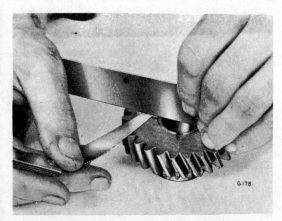

FIG 6:11   Gear end float on bush

FIG 6:12   Total mainshaft end float

FIG 6:13   Determining the thickness of the circlip washer

Refit the speedometer driven gear parts, securing them with the peg bolt (see FIG 6:5).

11 Insert the three springs 138 into their recesses in the front of the gearbox casing. Fit a new oil seal 130 into the housing 131 and refit the clutch cover 137 using a new gasket 138. Use a new copper washer 134 under the bolt 133 if the old washer is damaged or distorted. Refit the parts of the clutch release mechanism.

6:5 Gearchange extension and top cover assembly

Separate the gearchange extension from the top cover assembly by removing the nuts and easing the assemblies apart, taking off the gasket 106.

Gearchange extension:

1 If not already done, unscrew the gearlever knob 71. Unscrew the locknut 93 and withdraw the bolt 95 to separate the gearlever from the rear extension shaft 94. Slacken the locknut 74 and unscrew the reverse stop pin 73. Free the gearlever assembly from the housing by undoing the bayonet-type fitting holding the cap 65 in place. Remove the cups 66 and 67 together

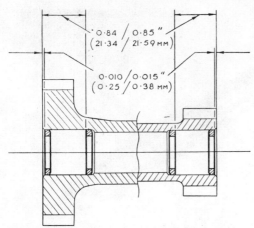

FIG 6:14 Dimensions for fitting countershaft needle roller retaining rings

FIG 6:15 Replacing the reverse idler gear

with the outer spring 68. From the end of the gearlever collect the two nylon stepped washers 75 and the bush 76. Remove the snap ring 69 and slide off the inner spring 70 and nylon sphere 77.

2 A further view of the underside of the extension is shown in **FIG 6:16.** Remove the peg bolt 100 and slide the shaft assembly out of the housing, collecting the selector 98 as it comes free. Unscrew the nut 91 and withdraw the bolt 62 collecting the washers 63 and 'Metalastik' bush 64.

3 The fork 90 can be separated from the front shaft 97 by driving out the hollow steel pin 92. Remove the old O-rings 89 and 99 from the bore in the housing, using a thin blunt screwdriver.

4 The gearchange assembly is reassembled in the reverse order of dismantling. Adjust the reverse stop pin so that the gap between it and the reverse stop plate 61 is as shown in **FIG 6:17,** when the gearlever is in the neutral position of the first/second gate.

The top cover:

1 Tap out the Welch plugs 108 using a $\frac{1}{8}$ inch (3.17mm) pin punch as shown in **FIG 6:18.** Take care to move

the selector shafts out of the way so that they are not damaged by the pin punch. Remove the three taper locking pins 78, 81 and 83 to free the selector forks. Press each selector shaft in turn out of the top cover, sliding off the fork as it comes free. Collect the interlock balls 110. Remove the interlock plunger 111 from the shaft 109 and shake out the three sets of springs 86 and plungers 85 and 107 from the top cover.

2 Thoroughly clean all the parts and examine them for wear. Check that the detents in the shafts are not worn and renew any parts that are worn or damaged.

3 Fit the springs 86 to their plungers and replace them into their recesses in the top cover. Slide the third/top selector shaft 114 into position from the front of the cover, depressing the appropriate plunger until the shaft has passed over it. Press the shaft in until the plunger registers in the middle detent of the shaft. Similarly refit the reverse selector shaft 112 setting this also into the neutral position. As both shafts are sliding into position pick up their respective selector forks on the shafts. Fit the interlock plunger 111 to the first/second selector shaft 109 and partially insert the shaft. This shaft also passes through the third/top selector fork 82 before picking up its own selector fork 79 with the distance washer 80. Before fully sliding the shaft into position replace the two interlock balls 110 as shown in **FIG 6:19.** Secure the selector forks in place on the shafts using the taper locking pins. Make sure that the recesses for the Welch plugs are clean and burr-free. Press new Welch plugs into place using a smear of jointing compound around their edges. Lock the plugs in place by slightly flattening them using a soft-nosed drift.

6:6 The overdrive

The overdrive consists basically of an epicyclic gear train operated by oil pressure from an internal pump. The components of the unit are shown in **FIG 6:20** and the adaptor plate and parts fitted to the gearbox are shown in **FIG 6:21.** Though the components are shown, special tools are required for nearly every operation in dismantling the unit and the work should therefore be entrusted to a competent garage. To check the correct function of the unit a pressure gauge is fitted in place of the operating valve plug 15 and the unit driven by the engine. For this reason the overdrive unit should not be removed from the car but the complete car taken to the garage so that they can carry out full tests.

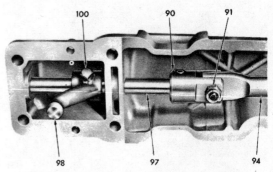

FIG 6:16 Gearchange extension attachments

Under normal conditions the cone clutch 63 is held in firm contact with the cone on the annulus 6, effectively locking the gear train and making the unit act as a solid shaft. When the overdrive is first selected a high operating current (in the order of 20 amps) flows through the solenoid 52 and moves the plunger 50. When the plunger has moved this current is cut to a holding-in current of 2 amps. The solenoid moves the operating valve through the operating lever 49 and cam 48, and the operating valve allows high-pressure oil to act on the pistons 30. The pistons overcome the pressure of the springs and move the cone clutch away from the annulus into firm contact with the brake ring 55. The planet carrier assembly 63 is then free to revolve with the input shaft. The planet wheels 65 rotate about their own axis as well, thus driving the annulus and output shaft at a higher speed.

It may happen that the cone clutch sticks in the overdrive engaged position, this being more likely on new or reconditioned units where the parts are not fully bedded-in. **If this occurs the car must never be pushed or driven backwards as there is a uni-directional clutch fitted between the planet carrier and annulus and parts will be damaged.** Free the cone clutch by raising the car on a ramp or hoist and giving the brake ring several sharp blows with a hide-faced mallet.

The operating valve:

The parts of this, accessible when the gearbox cover has been removed, are shown as 15 to 19 in **FIG 6:20**. With the plug 15 removed, complete with its sealing washer, lift out the spring 16, plunger 17 and ball 18 using a small magnet. Lift out the operating valve 19 using a stiff piece of wire down the central bore, taking great care not to damage the valve seat. Clean the parts in fuel and make sure that the small side orifice connected to the central bore is clean and open. Lay the ball 18 on a clean block of wood, placing the seat of the valve 19 onto the ball. Give the valve a sharp tap but taking care not to close the bore of the valve. Clean out the bore and seat in the casing. Lay the ball into position and give it a firm tap using a copper drift. This will ensure that the

FIG 6:18   Driving out the top cover Welch plugs

FIG 6:19   Replacing the interlock balls

seats are correctly shaped provided that excess force is not used. Reassemble the parts in the reverse order of dismantling.

Solenoid operating lever:

Remove the cover 54 and gasket 53. The solenoid and operating lever will then appear as shown in **FIG 6:22**. Move the operating lever 1 until a $\frac{3}{16}$ inch (4.762 mm) setting pin 2 can be inserted through the lever into the setting hole in the casing. Switch on the overdrive and screw in the adjusting nut 3 until it just contacts the operating lever. De-energize the solenoid, remove the setting pin and again energize the solenoid. Check that the setting holes are again in alignment as well as noting the current consumption. If the current is still at 20 amps (which will cause early failure of the solenoid) the solenoid must be reset. Switch off and fit the setting pin 2. Hold the solenoid plunger firmly against the blanking plug and check that the dimension shown in **FIG 6:23** is correct. If the dimension is incorrect it must be reset. On early models new packing rings of the correct width had to be fitted under the blanking plug but on later models the parts are as shown in the inset in **FIG 6:20** and can be adjusted by screwing the plug 32A in or out.

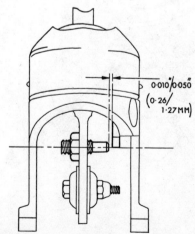

FIG 6:17   Adjustment of the reverse stop pin

0·010″/0·050″
(0·26/
1·27 MM)

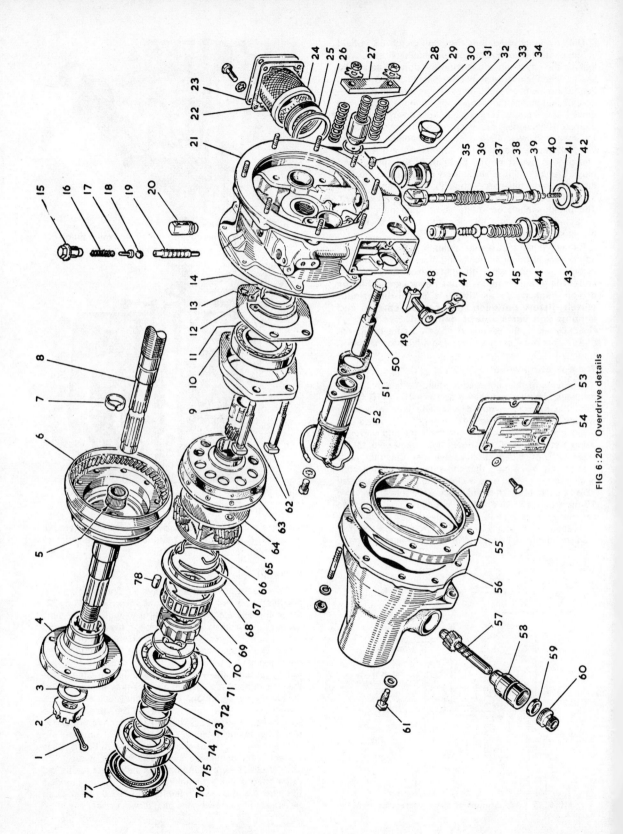

FIG 6:20 Overdrive details

Key to Figs 6:20 and 6:21   1 Splitpin   2 Nut   3 Washer   4 Coupling flange   5 Needle bearing   6 Annulus   7 Spring   8 Mainshaft
9 Sungear   10 Thrust ring   11 Thrust bearing   12 Retaining plate   13 Circlip   14 Plug   15 Plug   16 Spring   17 Plunger   18 Ball
19 Operating valve   20 Lubrication bush   21 Front casing   22 Gasket   23 Coverplate   24 Filter   25 Magnetic rings   26 Rubber/steel washer
27 Bridge piece   28 Bias spring   29 Clutch return spring   30 Piston   31 Piston O-ring   32 Plug   33 Pump locating screw   34 Plug   35 Pump plunger   36 Return spring
37 Pump body   38 Non-return valve body   39 Ball   40 Spring   41 Washer   42 Plug   43 Plug   44 Washer   45 Spring   46 Relief valve plunger
47 Relief valve body   48 Cam   49 Operating lever   50 Solenoid plunger   51 Gasket   52 Solenoid   53 Gasket   54 Coverplate   55 Brake
ring   56 Rear casing   57 Speedometer pinion   58 Speedometer pinion bush   59 Seal   60 Screwed end   61 Locating screw   62 Bolts
63 Cone clutch   64 Planet carrier assembly   65 Planet gear   66 Spring   67 Circlip   68 Oil thrower   69 Cage   70 Inner member   71 Thrust
washer   72 Front bearing   73 Speedometer drive gear   74 Distance piece   75 Spacer   76 Rear bearing   77 Oil seal   78 Roller

FIG 6:21   Gearbox adaptor plate and mainshaft details

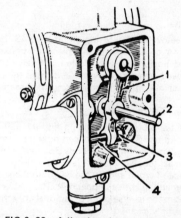

FIG 6:22   Adjusting the operating lever

Key to Fig 6:22   1 Operating pin   2 Setting pin
3 Adjusting nut   4 Solenoid plunger

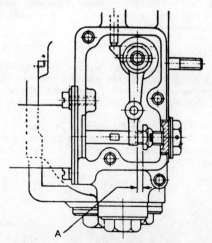

FIG 6:23   Dimensional checks on solenoid

A = .10 to .12 inch (2.54 to 3.05 mm)

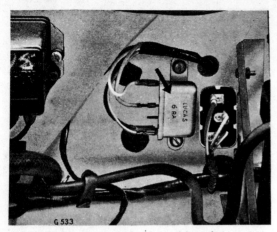

FIG 6:24   Position of overdrive relay

Relief valve:

This is removable after taking off the plug 43. The parts are items 44 to 47. Use a stiff piece of hooked wire through the hole in the side of the relief valve body 47. Once removed, separate the parts and clean them in fuel before reassembling them and refitting the assembly.

Pump non-return valve:

Remove the plug 42 and sealing ring 41. Lift out the spring 40 and ball 39. The parts can now be cleaned but if the seat is doubtful the valve body 38 must be removed using a special tool No. L.213. Place the valve body onto a clean piece of wood and lay the ball onto the seat. Give the ball a smart tap with a copper drift. The parts can then be replaced in the reverse order of removal after they have been thoroughly cleaned.

The oil filter:

This is accessible after the coverplate 23 has been removed. The filter should be cleaned at every oil change or if it is suspected to be choked and preventing the correct operation of the overdrive.

Electrics:

The overdrive requires high currents for its operation and poor connections or bad earthing are very likely causes of the overdrive failing to operate. The wiring circuit is shown in the appropriate Wiring diagram in the Appendix.

In case of failure check the wiring as follows:
1 Switch on the ignition and select overdrive in top gear. Battery voltage should be present on the terminals C.1 and W.2.

2 Short out terminals C.1 and C.2 on the relay (shown arrowed in **FIG 6:24**). If the solenoid now operates then the relay, column switch and gearbox switch are all suspect. Remove the link from between the terminals.
3 Earth terminal W.1. If the solenoid now operates then the gearbox switch is faulty. If the solenoid does not operate the relay is faulty.
4 Earth the yellow/green cable on the switch. If the solenoid now operates then renew the control switch.

6:7 Fault diagnosis

(a) Jumping out of gear

1 Broken spring behind locating plunger
2 Excessively worn detent in selector shaft
3 Worn coupling dogs
4 Fork to selector shaft screw loose

(b) Noisy gearbox

1 Insufficient oil
2 Excessive end float in countershaft gear
3 Worn or damaged bearings
4 Worn or damaged gear teeth

(c) Difficulty in engaging gear

1 Worn clutch
2 Worn synchromesh cones

(d) Oil leaks

1 Damaged gaskets or oil seals
2 Faces damaged on castings

Overdrive:

Only faults which can be dealt with by the owner are given here, and if despite rectification the fault persists the car must be taken to a garage.

(e) Overdrive does not engage

1 Insufficient oil
2 Faulty electric circuit
3 Solenoid valve incorrectly set
4 Pump filter choked
5 Leaking operating valve
6 Leaking pump non-return valve

(f) Overdrive does not release

Do not drive or push the car backwards
1 Sticking cone clutch
2 Blocked restricter passage in operating valve

(g) Clutch slip in overdrive

1 Check for causes of low hydraulic pressure

CHAPTER 7

PROPELLER SHAFT, REAR AXLE AND REAR SUSPENSION

7:1 Description
7:2 Routine maintenance
7:3 Servicing universal joints
7:4 The propeller shaft

7:5 The hub and outer axle shaft assembly
7:6 The differential
7:7 The rear suspension
7:8 Fault diagnosis

7:1 Description

The complete rear suspension fitted to early GT6 cars covered by this manual is shown in **FIG 7:1**. The Vitesse models are very similar except that they use lever and arm type of dampers instead of the telescopic type fitted to the GT6. The details of the rear suspension are shown in **FIG 7:2** and a sectioned view of the hub assembly, complete with brake, is shown in **FIG 7:3**.

The differential unit is fixed to the chassis using rubber bushed mountings. The transverse rear road spring is clamped to the top of the differential case and supports, at its outer ends, the top end of the vertical links 12. The bottom end of the vertical link is attached to the chassis using a wishbone 49. The vertical link also contains the bearings 31 and 34 in which the outer drive shafts rotate. The outer drive shafts, to which the wheel hub 38 is splined, is driven from the differential through the intermediate axle shafts 24. The intermediate shaft is fitted with a universal joint at the inboard end and a Rotoflex rubber coupling at the outboard end. These couplings allow the suspension to move as well as smoothing the drive to the rear wheels.

7:2 Routine maintenance

1 At regular intervals grease the universal joints on the propeller shaft. At the same time check the security of all the coupling nuts and bolts as if these become slack they will be a constant source of noise.
2 At 6000 mile intervals, remove the combined filler and level plug, arrowed in **FIG 7:4**, and check the level of the oil in the differential. Top up if necessary, using the same brand of hypoid oil as is already in the unit. Top up using an oil gun and allow surplus oil to drain out before replacing the plug. Wipe away spillage.

7:3 Servicing universal joints

With the shaft in place try rotating it. If there is any circumferential movement in the universal joint then the joint is worn and should be serviced. Check again with the shaft removed as slight movement in the differential or gearbox can be confused with play in the universal joint. Service kits containing all the necessary parts are supplied for universal joints, so do not attempt to renew individual parts in a universal joint. Service only one joint

FIG 7:1   Rear suspension and axle assembly

at a time and only when this one is completed start on the next. This ensures that there will be no intermixing of the parts or confusion between new and old parts.

A typical universal joint fitted to the propeller shaft is shown in detail in **FIG 7:5**. The universal joints fitted to the inboard ends of the intermediate shafts are very similar except that no grease nipples are fitted to the spider and the seals fit directly onto the bearing cups instead of on the spider.

1 Remove all four circlips 2 using circlip pliers. It may be necessary to clean the bores free from enamel and dirt and also to tap the bearing cups lightly inwards to free stiff circlips.

2 Hold the shaft assembly as shown in **FIG 7:6** and by gentle tapping as shown the bearing cup will start to emerge. Carry on tapping until sufficient of the cup has emerged to allow it to be withdrawn using either the fingers or a pair of grips. Turn the shaft over and remove the opposite bearing in a similar manner.

3 Manoeuvre the trunnions out of the lugs. Lay the exposed trunnions onto two pieces of lead or wood and by tapping as shown in **FIG 7:7** remove the remaining pair of bearings.

4 Thoroughly clean all the parts. Check that the bearing cups are a light drive fit through their bores. In some cases, only after long service and inadequate lubrication, the bores may have worn oval. The flanges 7 can easily be renewed but if the bores in the shaft itself have worn then the only cure is to fit a new shaft assembly.

5 Replace the needle rollers into the bearing cups, using a little grease to hold them in place. The correct number of rollers will exactly fill the bearing cup. Replace the seals. Those fitting onto the spider should be lightly smeared with jointing compound and then driven on using a hollow accurately fitting drift. Lubricate those bearing cups fitted to joints without grease nipples. Those fitted with grease nipples can be lubricated after reassembly.

6 Refit the spider to the flange so that the boss for the grease nipple faces the shaft. Use a mandrel of diameter just smaller than the bearing cup and press the bearings back into position as shown in **FIG 7:8**. **Take great care not to allow any needles to become displaced during this operation otherwise the pressure will snap the needle roller.** If a cup sticks remove it and check the cause without using excessive force in an attempt to fit it. Similarly refit the remaining two bearings and secure all four in place using the circlips. If, after reassembly, the joint is stiff to swivel then lightly tap on the yoke arms to ease the pressure on the bearings.

7:4 The propeller shaft

The type of shaft fitted to all the models covered by this manual is shown in **FIG 7:9**. The universal joints are serviced as described in the preceding section. The sliding joint should not be dismantled under any circumstances and if it is defective a new propeller shaft must be fitted.

Removal:

1 Raise the vehicle and place it on stands or a ramp. Remove the front seats, facia support (GT6 models only), front carpets and gearbox cover (see **Chapter 6, Section 6:2**).

2 Remove the Nyloc nuts and bolts securing the propeller shaft to the gearbox and differential driving flanges. Lower the propeller shaft and draw it out under the rear of the car.

The propeller shaft is replaced in the reverse order of removal. **If the nyloc nuts are slack enough to be run down the threads of the bolts using only finger pressure then they are worn and must be renewed.**

7:5 The hub and axle drive shaft assembly

It should be noted that these assemblies are of completely different design from the equivalent assemblies fitted to the earlier GT6 and Vitesse 2 Litre models, which are not covered by this manual. Several special tools are required to service the assemblies, without which the task will be made far more difficult and in some cases impossible. The owner is advised to read through the instructions and if he feels that he does not possess tools to cope with the task, he should take the car to a suitably equipped garage.

Key to Figs 7:2 and 7:3   1 Rubber bush—spring eye   2 Rear transverse road spring   3 Spring plate   4 Nyloc nut—spring plate to axle housing   5 Rear damper—lever arm type   6 Screw—damper to mounting bracket   7 Damper arm   8 Nyloc nut—damper arm to damper link   9 Ball end taper   10 Link assembly   11 Nyloc nut—rear road spring ends to vertical link   12 Rear vertical link   13 Nyloc nut—damper link to vertical link   14 Tabwasher—vertical link to rear brake   15 Setscrew—vertical link to rear brake   16 Wheel stud   17 Bolt outer drive shaft—rotoflex coupling   18 Outer drive shaft assembly   19 Key—intermediate shaft   20 Bolt—shaft joint to inner axle shaft   21 Nyloc nut—inner axle shaft   22 Flange yoke—coupling   23 Yoke   24 Intermediate drive shaft   25 Driven flange   26 Nyloc nut—driven flange to shaft   27 Nyloc nut—lower wishbone to chassis   28 Bolt—driven flange to rotoflex coupling   29 Inner oil seal   30 Bolt—rear spring ends to vertical link   31 Inner bushing   32 Outer bush (withbone to vertical link)   33 Bolt (withbone to vertical link)   34 Outer bearing   35 Outer oil seal   36 Spacer (outer drive shaft)   37 Shim (outer drive shaft)   38 Rear hub and stud assembly   39 Washer   40 Nyloc nut—rear hub to outer drive shaft 41 Bracket—assembly mounting radius arm to vertical link 42 Distance piece (wishbone to vertical link)   43 Water shield (wishbone to vertical link)   44 Dirt seal (wishbone to vertical link)   45 Nyloc nut (wishbone to vertical link)   46 Washer (wishbone to vertical link)   47 Outer bush (wishbone to vertical link)   48 Rotoflex wishbone assembly   49 Lower wishbone assembly   50 Lower wishbone—inner bush   51 Bolt—wishbone to chassis   52 Bolt—radius arm to vertical link   53 Radius arm   54 Radius arm adjuster   55 Bolt—radius arm to bracket   56 Nyloc nut—radius arm to bracket   57 Bolt—radius arm support bracket   58 Nut—radius arm to bracket   59 Rubber bush—radius arm   60 Brake drum   61 Backplate

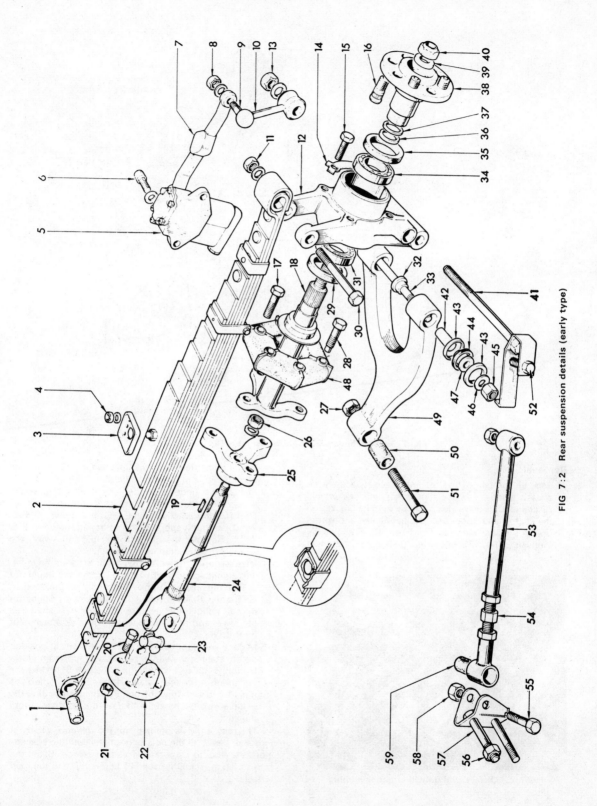

FIG 7:2 Rear suspension details (early type)

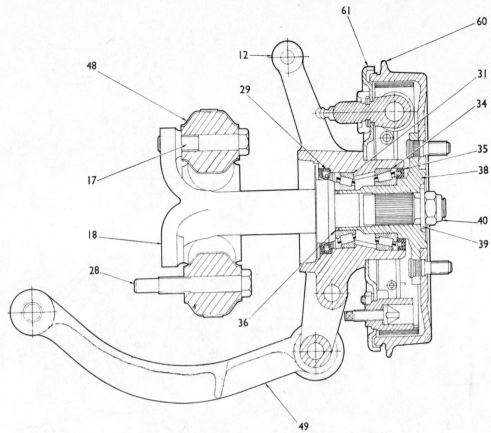

FIG 7:3 Sectioned view of hub assembly (Key as Fig 7:2)

Removal:

1 Jack up the rear of the car and place it securely on chassis stands. Remove the appropriate rear wheel.
2 Disconnect the brake flexible hose from its bracket on the chassis and disconnect the handbrake and spring from the brake unit (see **Chapter 10**). Remove the four sets of nuts 21 and bolts 20 so as to disconnect

FIG 7:4 Differential unit filler and level plug

the intermediate drive shaft flange 22 from the driving flange of the inner axle shaft.

3 Place a jack underneath the vertical link and raise the suspension against the pressure of the road spring. Fit the tool, whose dimensions are shown in **FIG 7:10**, so that it supports the spring as shown in **FIG 7:11**. Remove the nut and bolt 52 and swing the radius arm 53 clear of its bracket 41.

4 **Vitesse only.** Refer to **FIG 7:12**. Slacken the lower link end attachment nut 13 and remove the upper nut 8. Free the link arm 10 from the arm 7 on the damper. **GT6 only.** Refer to **FIG 7:13**. Slacken the upper nut 62 and remove the lower nut 63 with it washer. Pull the lower end of the damper free from its attachment on the axle.

5 Making sure that the retaining bar is firmly in position on the stand, remove the suspension supporting jack. Undo the nut 27 and withdraw the bolt 51 to free the wishbone from its bracket on the chassis. Undo the nut 11 and withdraw the bolt 30 while supporting the vertical link by hand. Withdraw the assembly from the car.

The assembly is refitted in the reverse order of removal. Leave all the nuts finger tight until the suspension is loaded to its normal working position. Bleed the brake system (see **Chapter 10**) before refitting the road wheels.

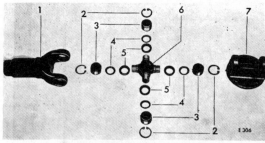

FIG 7:5   Universal joint details

Key to Fig 7:5   1 Sliding yoke   2 Circlips   3 Bearing cups   4 Seals   5 Retainers   6 Spider   7 Flange

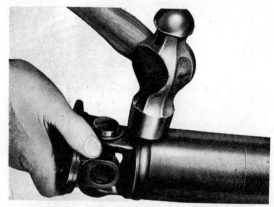

FIG 7:6   Removing bearing cups from shaft

Rotoflex coupling:

1 Remove the hub and axle shaft assembly from the car as described previously. Remove the hub nut 40 and plain washer 39. Take off the brake drum after removing the two countersunk screws. Fit the thread protector No. S.109C to the outer axle shaft 18 and press it out of the hub using tool No. S.109B, collecting the spacer 36 and shims 37.

2 Remove the stone guard and spacer from the outer shaft, preferably using the handpress No. S.4221 and adaptors No. S.4221A-17. Fit the compression clamp No. S.328 around the Rotoflex coupling 48 and free the coupling from both axle shafts by removing the six bolts 17 and 28. Slide off the coupling.

The parts are replaced in the reverse order of removal. No special tools are required. The stone guard and spacer can be drifted into place and the axle shaft drifted into the hub far enough to allow the washer and nut to be replaced and then pulled into position by tightening the nut to a torque of 100 to 110 lb ft (13.825 to 15.208 kg m). Do not forget to replace the shims 37 and spacer 36. New Rotoflex couplings are supplied fitted with a mild steel band which should not be removed until the coupling is bolted into place.

Rear hubs:

1 Remove the hub and axle shaft assembly from the car and press out the axle shaft assembly from the hub as detailed in operation 1 for the Rotoflex coupling.

Remove the wishbone from the vertical link (see under Wishbone in **Section 7:7**).

2 Fit the thrust button S.323/1 and the tool No. S.342, as shown in **FIG 7:14** and by turning the bolt remove the vertical link from the hub.

3 Turn the inner race of the bearing 31 sideways and remove it through the oil seal 29. Use a screwdriver to drive out the oil seal 29 and then drift out the outer race of the bearing 31. Similarly drift out the outer race of the bearing 34 from the vertical link.

4 Fit the thrust button S.323, press the lips of the outer oil seal 35 away from the bearing and fit the adaptors S.323-1 and tool No. S.323 to the bearing as shown in **FIG 7:15**. Make sure that the adaptors are firmly in position under the bearing and tighten down the handle of the tool to withdraw the inner race of the bearing 34. Remove the outer oil seal 35.

Reassembling rear hubs:

Before reassembly clean all the parts and wash the bearings in clean fuel. Examine the surfaces of the rollers and races. Renew both bearings if either show any signs of pitting, wear or scuffing. Rotate the inner race in the outer while pressing them firmly together between the

FIG 7:7   Removing bearing cups from yoke

FIG 7:8   Refitting the bearing cups

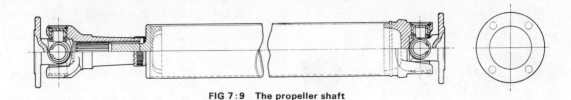

FIG 7:9　The propeller shaft

palms and reject the bearings if they run roughly. It is advisable to fit new oil seals, as the old ones will most likely have been damaged in removal.

1　Fit the gauge S.325-1 over the hub extension and place the plate gauge S.325-3 on the end of the flange. Press down on the plate to make sure that it is squarely in place and use feeler gauges to measure the gap at A shown in **FIG 7:16.**

2　Drive in the outer races of both bearings and replace the inner races, **without lubricant,** into the vertical link. Slide the hub extension S.325-2 through both the bearings and fit the gauge S.325-1 with its slot uppermost. Attach the gauge plate S.325-3 to the body of the gauge. Lightly tighten the thumb screw while rotating the gauge in a clockwise direction to settle the bearings. **Do not overtighten the thumb screw and do not preload the bearings.**

3　Slide feeler gauges, to the thickness measured in operation 1, into the slot in the gauge. Selectively fit a spacer 36 and a maximum of two shims 37 into the slot until they and the feeler gauges tightly pack the slot. The method is shown in **FIG 7:17** and the part numbers and thicknesses of the shims and spacers are given in Technical Data at the end of this manual.

4　Remove the parts of the gauge and bearing inner races from the vertical link. Thoroughly pack the race of the outer bearing 34 with grease and lay it in position in

the vertical link. Drive a new oil seal 35 into the vertical link so that its lips face inwards, preferably using tool No. S.322 and handle 550. Slide the vertical link assembly onto the hub centre and drive it into position using tool No. S.324 located against the inner race of the bearing 34. Remove the tool and liberally pack the inside of the hub with Shell Retinax A or equivalent grease.

5　Pack the inner race of the bearing 31 with grease and lay it into position in the vertical link. Use tool No. S.324 to tap the bearing downwards. **The correct end float is dependent on drawing the bearing into its final position so do not drive it fully home and leave it so that the vertical link can be moved a minimum of $\frac{1}{16}$ inch (1.6 mm).**

6　Drive a new oil seal 29, lips facing inwards, into position on the vertical link. Fit the shims 37 and spacer selected in operation 3 to the outer axle shaft and keep them there with a little grease. Pass the axle shaft through the vertical link and hub assembly, if need be tapping it gently through until a few threads protrude through the hub. Use a slave nut without the plain washer to draw the shaft through until enough threads have come through to safely refit the washer 39 and a new Nyloc nut 40. Tighten the nut 40 to a torque of 110 to 115 lb ft (15.21 to 15.90 kg m) and **rotate the vertical link in order to settle the**

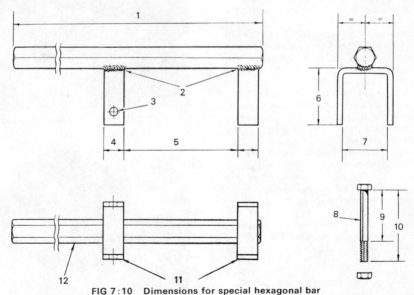

FIG 7:10　Dimensions for special hexagonal bar

Key to Fig 7:10　1　36 inch (91.5 cm)　2　Weld area as shown　3　Drill two holes $\frac{3}{8}$ inch (9.5 mm)　4　1 inch (2.5 cm)
5　$5\frac{3}{4}$ inch (14.6 cm)　6　$2\frac{3}{4}$ inch (7.0 cm)　7　$2\frac{1}{4}$ inch (5.7 cm)　8　$\frac{3}{8}$ inch (9.5 mm) nut and bolt　9　$2\frac{1}{2}$ inch (6.3 cm)
10　$3\frac{1}{2}$ inch (8.9 cm)　11　Make from $\frac{1}{4}$ inch (6.3 mm) mild steel　12　Make from 1 inch (2.5 cm) hexagon bar mild steel

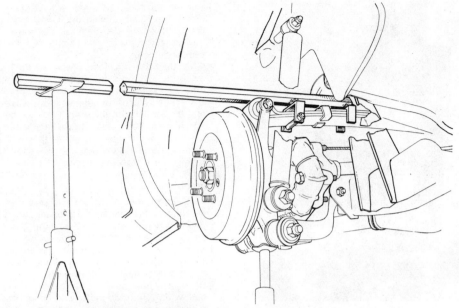

FIG 7:11 Hexagonal bar fitted to support road spring

FIG 7:12 Vitesse damper attachments

FIG 7:13 GT6 damper attachments

bearings while finally tightening the nut. This method will ensure that the end float of the hub is correct between .0005 to .0025 inch (.0127 to .0635 mm).

7 Refit the wishbone assembly to the vertical link (see **Section 7:7**) and replace the assembly to the car in the reverse order of dismantling. Do not forget to bleed the brakes before refitting the road wheels.

7:6 The differential

It is very unwise for the average owner to attempt to dismantle the differential unit. Specialized accurate equipment is essential for ensuring that the pinion and crownwheel gears are meshing correctly. Special equipment is also necessary to set the correct amount of preload on the pinion bearings. Though the rear casing may

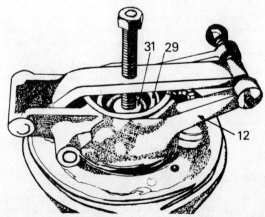

FIG 7:14 Separating the vertical link from the rear hub

FIG 7:15　Removing the outer hub bearing

34
35
38

K128

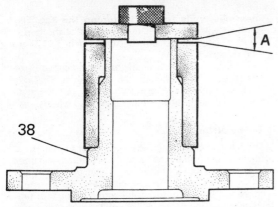

38

A

FIG 7:16　Sectioned view of hub with special tool fitted

be removed, in order to change a leaking gasket, the differential itself cannot be removed from the front casing without the use of a special tool which spreads the casing by just the right amount to allow the parts to be freed.

All the oil seals can be changed, but if the unit presents any other faults the car should either be taken to a suitable garage or consideration given to fitting an exchange unit.

Inner axle shaft assemblies (including oil seals):

1 Drain the oil from the differential unit. Remove both hub and axle shaft assemblies as detailed in **Section 7:5**.
2 Use a $\frac{3}{16}$ inch (6.763 mm) hexagon socket key to remove the four socket-headed screws from each side of the differential casing, as shown in **FIG 7:18**. Withdraw each inner axle shaft assembly, the parts of which are shown in **FIG 7:19**.

3 Remove the circlip 12 and draw the bearing 17 off the shaft 21 preferably using the handpress and adaptor set No. S.4221A-7A. Slide off the housing plate 14 complete with the oil seal 15 and then remove the oil seal from the plate.
4 Wash the parts in fuel and check that the bearing runs smoothly with no signs of roughness or wear. Press a new oil seal 15 into the plate 14 so that the lips of the seal will face the differential on reassembly and refit the assembly to the shaft. Press the bearing back into place and secure it with the circlip. Refit the inner axle shaft assemblies and fill the unit with oil to the correct level. Refit the hub and axle shaft assemblies in the reverse order of removal.

Pinion oil seal:

1 Jack up the rear of the car and place it on stands. Disconnect the rear of the propeller shaft from the pinion driving flange, after draining the differential and removing the exhaust tail pipe.
2 Extract the splitpin and remove the nut securing the driving flange to the pinion. Withdraw the driving flange and lever out the old oil seal.
3 Drive in a new oil seal, using an accurately fitting hollow drift. Replace the driving flange and secure it with the nut and splitpin. Refill the unit with oil. Reconnect the propeller shaft and lower the car back to the ground.

Removal:

1 Jack up the rear of the car and place it securely on chassis stands. Support each suspension using a jack under the vertical link. Disconnect the dampers from the vertical link (see Operation 4 under Removal in **Section 7:5**). Remove the exhaust tail pipe.
2 Disconnect the intermediate shaft couplings from the inner axle shaft flanges. Disconnect the rear end of the propeller shaft from the driving flange on the pinion.
3 Take out the front luggage floor panel on GT6 models or the rear seat assembly on Vitesse models. Remove the access plate for the spring clamping plate from the floor. The attachment will then appear as shown in **FIG 7:20**. Remove all six Nyloc nuts and washers and take out the three rear studs. (GT6 Mk 3 models have four studs and nuts.)
4 The unit mountings are shown in **FIG 7:21**. Undo the nut and withdraw the long bolt of the rear

36
37
K138

FIG 7:17　Selecting spacer and shims

mounting. Have an assistant to support the weight of the unit and remove the nut, washer and rubber pad from each front mounting. Manoeuvre the unit down and forward to clear it from the car.

The unit is replaced in the reverse order of removal. Make sure that all the rubber pads and bushes are in good condition and only fully tighten the nuts when the unit is in position and the bushes are in their normal positions.

7:7 The rear suspension

Details of the rear suspension as used on early cars are shown in **FIG 7:2**, while the arrangement used on later GT6 Mk 3 models is illustrated in **FIG 7:23** in which it will be seen that the transverse leaf spring is now pivoted about its central mounting and the lower wishbone has been discarded giving a swing axle type suspension.

The dampers:

Before removing the dampers, jack up the rear of the car and place it on chassis stands. Remove the road wheels and take the load off the damper by using a jack under the vertical link.

GT6 Dampers:

Refer to **FIG 7:13**. Remove both nuts 62 and 63 with their washers, and pull the damper clear of its mountings.

Before fitting a new damper, mount it vertically in the padded jaws of a vice and pump it through several short strokes so as to allow any air trapped in the mechanism to pass into the upper chamber. Refit the damper, still keeping it vertical.

Test the damper by pumping it through several full strokes. If the resistance is not constant in either direction or it is so high that the damper can hardly be moved, then the unit must be discarded and a new damper fitted. Similarly reject a damper if it has physical damage, such as a bent ram or dented body.

Vitesse dampers:

Refer to **FIG 7:12**. Remove the two screws 6 holding the damper 5 to the chassis, using a $\frac{5}{16}$ inch (7.39 mm) Allen key. Take off the nut 13 and detach the damper complete with the link arm 10. If required, remove the nut 8 and separate the link arm from the lever, either using an extractor or by pulling them firmly apart holding a block of metal against the side of the tapered eye and hitting the opposite side with a hammer.

FIG 7:18 Removing inner axle assembly

FIG 7:19 Inner axle details

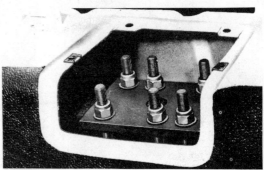

FIG 7:20 Cover removed showing rear road spring attachment

The radius arms:

To remove a radius arm proceed as for the removal of the dampers, adjusting the jack under the vertical link until the two radius arm attachment bolts can easily be withdrawn.

If the rubber bushes are worn or damaged, they should be pressed out and new bushes fitted before refitting the radius arms in the reverse order of removal.

If the radius arm mounting brackets are removed, make sure that the same shims are fitted when re-assembling.

The radius arms also control the rear wheel alignment. On early models adjustment is by means of the adjuster, 54 in **FIG 7:2**, while on the later type suspension it is by means of the shims, 26 in **FIG 7:23**. Removing an equal number of shims from both sides increases the toe-in and vice versa, but this adjustment is preferably carried out by a qualified service station with special equipment for accurate measurement.

The wishbones:

With the rear of the car on stands jack up the suspension underneath the vertical link to relieve the load on the damper. Remove the nuts 27 and 45 then withdraw the bolts 51 and 33 to free the wishbone from the car. Remove the seals and rubber bushes from the wishbone.

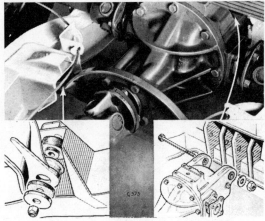

FIG 7:21 Differential unit attachments

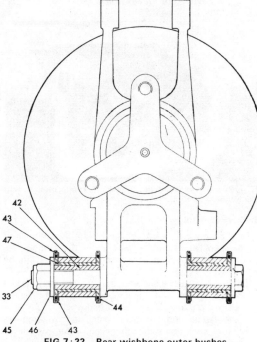

42
43
47
33
44
45   46   43

FIG 7:22 Rear wishbone outer bushes

Refitting the wishbone:

1 Renew any bushes or seals that are worn. Clean off dirt and old grease using newspapers and then washing with clean fuel.
2 Fit the bush 50 back into the inner end of the wishbone 49. A sectioned view of the outer end bushes is shown in **FIG 7:22**. Reassemble the inner halves of the bushes to the wishbone and completely assemble the bushes, pressing in the distance piece 42 on the side which is nearest to the head of the bolt 33.
3 Align the wishbone with the vertical link and pass the bolt 33 fitted with a washer 46 through the assembly so as to keep them aligned. Complete the assembly of the bushes and press in the remaining distance

piece 42. Fit the other washer 46 and secure the bolt in place with the nut 45 finger tight only. As the bushes are assembled they should be packed with sufficient Mobilgrease M.P., or equivalent, to ensure that the space around the bushes is filled with grease.

4 Refit the wishbone assembly to the car and only when the assembly is in position fully tighten the nuts 27 and 45.

The rear road spring:

1 Jack-up the rear of the car and support it securely on chassis stands. Remove the road wheels.
2 Disconnect the two brake hoses from the chassis bracket and pipe. Disconnect the handbrake cable from the lever on the brake backplate and detach the return spring.
3 Jack-up the vertical link to unload the dampers and remove the nuts and bolts to disconnect the inner axle shaft couplings, 20 and 21 in **FIG 7:2**. Remove the dampers.
4 Remove the jack from the vertical link and remove the bolt from the road spring eye.
5 After removing the rear seat assembly on Vitesse or luggage floor on GT6 models, remove the cover over the road spring mounting (see **FIG 7:20**). Remove the six Nyloc nuts (four on GT6 Mk 3) and washers, detach the spring clamp plate and unscrew the rear studs from the axle casing.
6 Withdraw the leaf spring out towards the side of the car.

Refitting:

1 Fit the spring in place noting that it is marked FRONT for correct location.
2 Refit the studs into the axle casing, shorter threaded portion leading. Refit the clamp plate and secure the Nyloc nuts. Apply a suitable sealer and refit the access cover plate.
3 Attach the vertical links to the spring eyes, but do not yet tighten the nuts.
4 Jack-up the vertical links while attaching the dampers (do not tighten at this stage), reconnect the axle shaft couplings.
5 Reconnect the brake cables and hoses, check the brake adjustments and bleed the hydraulic system.
6 Place a jack under the differential casing, remove the chassis stands and, supporting the vertical links at their running heights, load the car and lower the jack until the axle shafts take up their static laden attitude. The securing nuts on the rubber bushed mountings for the vertical link and the dampers can now be secured.

7:8 Fault diagnosis

(a) Noisy axle

1 Insufficient or incorrect lubricant
2 Worn bearings
3 Worn gears

(b) Excessive backlash

1 Worn gears, bearings or bearing housings
2 Worn universal joints
3 Defective Rotoflex couplings
4 Loose coupling bolts

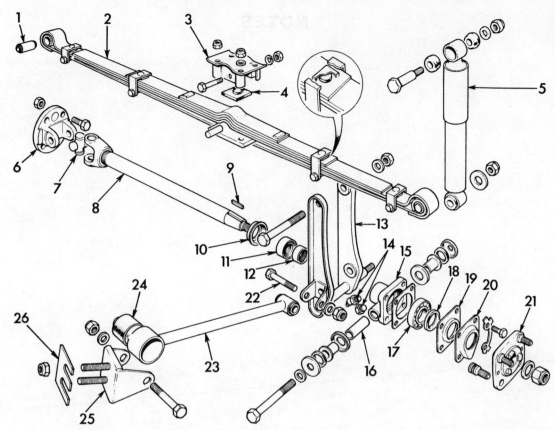

FIG 7:23 Details of the rear suspension fitted to GT6 Mk 3 cars after No. KF20,001

Key to Fig 7:23 1 Bush 2 Road spring 3 Spring clamp plate 4 Pad 5 Damper 6 Flange yoke-coupling 7 Spider 8 Drive shaft 9 Key 10 Flinger 11 Inner oil seal 12 Inner bearing 13 Vertical link 14 Grease nipple or plug 15 Inner hub 16 Distance piece 17 Outer bearing 18 Outer oil seal 19 Oil seal housing 20 Oil catcher 21 Hub and stud assembly 22 Bolt 23 Radius arm 24 Rubber bush 25 Bracket 26 Shim

(c) Oil leakage

1 Defective oil seals
2 Blocked breather on differential case
3 Excessive oil level in the differential unit

(d) Vibration

1 Check 2 and 3 in (b)
2 Propeller shaft out of balance
3 Tyre defects

(e) Rattles

1 Worn rubber bushes on damper
2 Worn bushes in suspension
3 Worn rubber mountings for differential unit
4 Loose clips on road spring

(f) 'Settling'

1 Broken leaf or leaves in road spring
2 Worn suspension bushes

NOTES

CHAPTER 8

FRONT SUSPENSION AND HUBS

8:1 Description
8:2 Routine maintenance
8:3 The front hubs and brake discs
8:4 Ball joints
8:5 The suspension sub-assembly

8:6 Road spring and damper assembly
8:7 The upper wishbone and ball joint
8:8 The vertical link and lower trunnion bearing
8:9 Fault diagnosis

8:1 Description

The assembly follows conventional front suspension design by utilizing unequal length wishbones top and bottom with a vertical link pivoting between the outer ends of the wishbones. The vertical link carries a stub axle about which the wheel and wheel hub rotate on two opposed tapered bearings. The vertical link also supports a bracket on which the disc brake caliper is mounted, the caliper acting on the brake disc which rotates with the wheel hub. A coil spring and damper assembly acts between the subframe attached to the chassis and the lower wishbone assembly, and in this way absorbs and controls the movement of the suspension.

The details of the suspension are shown in **FIG 8:1.** From this it can be seen that the vertical link 18 is free to swivel about a ball joint 15 at its upper end and a trunnion bearing 41 at its lower end. It can also be seen that the wishbones pivot vertically about renewable rubber and nylon bushes. Not shown in the figure is the fact that the suspension assembly is attached to a subframe and that the complete suspension assembly can be removed as a unit from the car.

An anti-roll bar, whose details are shown in **FIG 8:2,** interconnects the lower wishbone assemblies on each suspension and this, by transferring some of the load from the outside wheel in a turn, prevents the body from rolling on corners and also improves the road holding.

8:2 Routine maintenance

1 Remove the plug 27, arrowed in **FIG 8:3,** and replace it with a grease nipple. **Fill a grease gun with Hypoid oil, not engine oil,** and inject the oil into the lower swivel until it exudes from the swivel. Remove the grease nipple and replace the plug. Repeat the operation on the other side suspension. It is recommended that the swivels be oiled every 6000 miles.
2 Adjust and grease the wheel hub bearings every 12,000 miles. Grease may be packed around the outer bearing and the hub adjusted after removing the grease cap, but it is better to take off the hub and pack both bearings with fresh grease. Do not pack the grease cap with grease.

8:3 The front hubs and brake discs

Check for wear in the bearings and vertical link swivels with the front road wheels still fitted and the front of the car jacked up off the ground. Make sure that the wheel

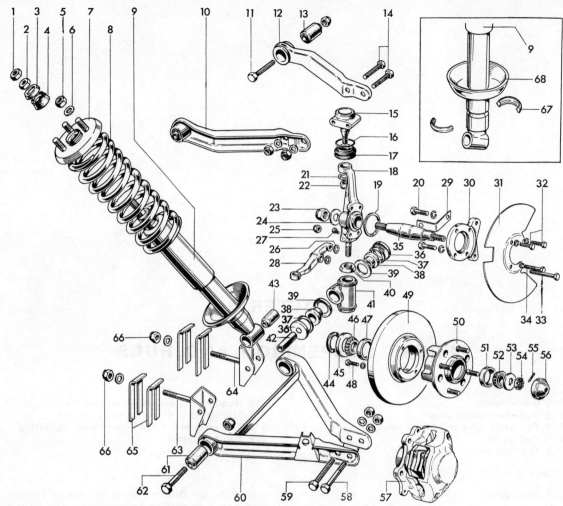

FIG 8:1   Details of lefthand front suspension

Key to Fig 8:1   1 Nut   2 Nut   3 Washer   4 Mounting rubber   5 Nut   6 Washer   7 Upper spring pan   8 Road spring   9 Damper   10 Top wishbone arm   11 Fulcrum bolt   12 Top wishbone arm   13 Fulcrum bush   14 Bolt   15 Ball joint   16 Retainer   17 Rubber seal   18 Vertical link   19 Rubber seal   20 Bolt   21 Washer   22 Nut   23 Nut   24 Washer   25 Nut   26 Spacer   27 Plug   28 Steering arm   29 Bracket   30 Caliper bracket   31 Dust shield   32 Bolt   33 Bolt   34 Stub axle   35 Stub axle   36 Dust seal   37 Rubber ring   38 Nylon bush   39 Dust seal   40 Rubber seal   41 Trunnion   42 Bush   43 Fulcrum bush   44 Felt seal   45 Seal holder   46 Inner race   47 Outer track   48 Bolt   49 Brake disc   50 Hub   51 Outer track   52 Inner race   53 Washer   54 Nut   55 Splitpin   56 Grease cap   57 Brake caliper   58 Trunnion bolt   59 Damper bolt   60 Lower wishbone   61 Fulcrum bush   62 Bolt   63 Front fulcrum bracket   64 Rear fulcrum bracket   65 Shim   66 Nut   67 Collet   68 Lower spring pan

nuts are tight and secure. Grasp the tyre at the six and twelve o'clock positions and try to rock the top of the wheel in and out. If there is play it can easily be felt, though there should be very little play indeed. Repeat the test but this time grasping the tyre at the nine and three o'clock positions. If there was play previously but it has now disappeared, then the vertical link swivels are most likely worn. If the play is still present, then check that it is not caused by steering movement or wear in the tie rod end. If these are satisfactory then the play is most likely caused by worn wheel hub bearings. Spin the road

wheel and check that it rotates freely without any grinding noises or drag from the bearings. Do not confuse noise from the disc brake with that of a defective bearing. Provided that there is only play in the bearings it may be sufficient to readjust them, but if there is any doubt as to their condition the wheel hub should be removed and the bearings checked visually.

Removal:

1 Jack up the car and remove the road wheel. Remove the dust cap 56 by unscrewing a No. 10 UNF bolt

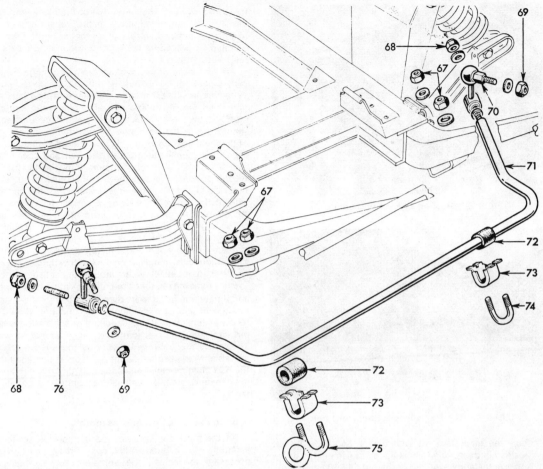

FIG 8:2 Anti-roll bar details

Key to Fig 8:2   67 Nut   68 Nut   69 Nut   70 Link   71 Anti-roll bar   72 Rubber bush   73 Clamp
74 U bolt   75 U bolt (Export models)   76 Stud

through the threaded hole in the end of the cap so as to press it off the hub.

2 Remove the two bolts that secure the brake caliper 57 to the bracket 30 and slide off the caliper, noting the position and quantity of any shims fitted between it and the bracket. Do not disconnect the flexible brake hose and support the caliper with a piece of wire attached to the car so that the hose is not strained. Fit a wedge between the pads to prevent them becoming displaced.

3 Extract the splitpin 55 and remove the nut 54 and D-washer 53. Withdraw the hub assembly from the stub axle taking care to prevent the inner race of the bearing 52 from dropping out as it comes free.

4 Remove the inner race 46 after using a soft-metal drift to tap out the oil seal assembly 44 and 45. If the felt 44 is damaged it should be stripped off the retainer 45 and a new felt glued back with a little jointing compound. This should be done as early as possible to make sure that the jointing compound is dry by the time the parts are reassembled.

5 If required, the outer tracks 47 and 51 can be driven out of the hub using a drift. The brake disc 49 can be separated from the hub 50 after removing the bolts 48.

Reassembly:

Before reassembling the parts, thoroughly clean them in fuel or solvent. Wash the bearings separately so that no dirt from the hub is washed into them. Examine the surfaces of the tracks and rollers and reject the complete bearing if either show signs of pitting, fretting or wear. Rotate the inner race in the track while pressing them firmly together and any roughness in running will be more easily detectable. Ideally both bearings should be renewed if either one shows a fault.

1 Drive the tracks 47 and 51 back into position in the hub, so that they seat fully against the internal flange and so that the largest diameter of the taper faces outwards. If it has been removed then refit the brake disc, making sure that the mating surfaces between the disc and hub are scrupulously clean and free from particles.

FIG 8:3 Steering swivel grease plug

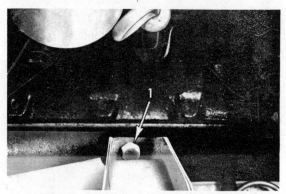

FIG 8:4 Sub-frame inner attachment bolt

2 Pack the inner race 46 with grease and fit it into position in the track 47. Soak the oil seal in engine oil, squeeze the surplus oil out of the felt 44 and carefully drive the assembly back into the hub 50 so as to hold the inner race 46 in position.

3 Liberally pack the inside of the hub 50 with grease and then slide the assembly into position on the stub axle. Pack the inner race 52 with grease and press it back into position in the track 51. Secure the parts in place with the D-washer 53 and nut 54. If a Dial Test Indicator is available the end float on the hub should be set between .003 to .005 inch (.08 to .13 mm). Spin the hub and tighten the nut 54 until drag can just be felt on the bearings. Slacken back the nut one or two flats from this position, make sure that the bearings now spin freely, and secure the nut with a new splitpin 55.

4 Replace the grease cap 56, brake caliper 57 and road wheel in the reverse order of removal. Before refitting the brake caliper wipe the brake disc with a cloth moistened in fuel or solvent so as to ensure that all grease marks or dirty finger prints are removed.

8:4 Ball joints

Ball joints are fitted where two parts are required to swivel about one another while pressure or motion is transmitted from one to the other. The ball joint consists of a tapered pin fitted with a ball head. The ball head is free to revolve in a socket on one of the members, while the taper is firmly fixed into a mating taper on the other member. A nut and washer fit on the end of the tapered part and by tightening the nut the two mating tapers are pulled into firm contact.

After a period of use the two tapers bed together and can appear to be extremely difficult to part. Special extractors which exert strong pressure on the tapers to part them are obtainable but a suitable sized extractor may not be readily available. Under no circumstances should the tapers be parted by hammering on the end of the taper as even with a slave nut fitted the threads are liable to become damaged or the ball and socket distorted. Instead, pull the members firmly apart, using a wedge or some other method. Lay a block of metal on one side of the tapered eye and sharply hit the opposite side of the tapered eye using a copper-faced hammer. An ordinary hammer may be used but it is more likely to damage the parts. A few smart blows should be sufficient to free the tapers. To prevent the parts from suddenly flying apart and causing damage it is a wise precaution to leave the nut on the last few threads.

A ball joint usually wears around the socket and ball. Excess wear means that the ball joint must be scrapped and a new one fitted in its place. The ball joint is usually fitted with a dust excluding gaiter and this should be renewed separately if it is damaged or split, as otherwise dirt can enter the ball joint and cause premature wear. The tapers are unlikely to wear as there is no relative movement between them, but if a taper is damaged then the part must be renewed as the ball joint relies to a very great extent on the extremely accurate mating of the tapers.

8:5 The suspension sub-assembly

All the parts can be removed or replaced while the assembly is still fitted to the car. It may, however, be necessary to remove the complete sub-assembly so proceed as follows:

1 Apply the handbrake, jack up the front of the car and place it securely onto chassis stands. Remove the road wheels, having slackened but not removed the nuts before jacking up the car.

2 Remove the engine bay valance. Disconnect the brake flexible pipe from its bracket on the chassis, preventing the hose from rotating and removing the union and locknut from the hose. Plug the metal pipe to prevent the loss of fluid.

3 Disconnect the anti-roll bar from the lower wishbone assembly. Remove the two nuts 66 securing the lower fulcrum brackets 63 and 64 to the chassis, carefully noting the quantity and position of any shims 65 fitted under the brackets.

4 Remove the inner sub-frame bolt, and packing piece if fitted, arrowed in **FIG 8:4.** Support the engine with a jack and block of wood under the sump and remove the nuts and bolts securing the engine mounting rubber to the sub-frame. If the driver's side suspension is being removed, then disconnect the steering column lower clamp from the steering rack pinion, slacken the impact clamp and withdraw the steering column from the rack (see **Chapter 9**).

5 Remove the nut and washer and then disconnect the tie rod from the steering arm·28. For lefthand side

suspensions support the bonnet and disconnect the bonnet stay from the sub-frame.

6 Remove the four bolts 1, washers and tapping plates from the outside of the sub-frame, shown in **FIG 8:5** and withdraw the suspension sub-assembly from the car.

Refit the sub-assembly in the reverse order of removal. The brake system should be filled and bled before the road wheels are replaced (see **Chapter 10**). It is advisable to have the steering and suspension geometry checked and adjusted on specialized equipment by a suitable garage.

8:6 Road spring and damper assembly

Removal:

1 Securely jack up the front of the car and place it on chassis stands. Slacken the trunnion bearing bolt 58 a few turns and then remove the damper lower mounting bolt 59 with its nut and washer.

2 Remove the three nuts 5 that secure the upper spring pan 7 to the sub-frame. Lower the assembly through the suspension to remove it from the car.

The assembly is replaced in the reverse order of removal, but only fully tightening the nuts on the bolts 58 and 59 when the suspension is loaded to its normal working position.

Dismantling:

1 Use the handpress S.4221A and adaptor to compress as many of the coils of the spring 8 as can be safely picked up. Compress the spring sufficiently to remove the pressure on the upper spring pan 7. The method is shown in **FIG 8:6**.

2 Remove the locknut 1 and carefully, in case there is still spring pressure, unsrew the nut 2. Remove the washer 3 and rubber mounting 4. Carefully release the pressure on the spring and remove the handpress.

3 Withdraw the damper 9 from the spring and remove the other rubber mounting and washer from the damper. On Woodhead-Monroe units tap up the lower spring pan 68 and remove the collets 69. If the fulcrum bush 43 is worn or damaged press it out of the damper eye.

The parts are reassembled in the reverse order of dismantling, after having checked both the damper and the spring as well as renewing damaged or defective mounting rubbers or bush.

The road spring:

When the spring has been removed, first examine it for cracks or obvious damage. Measure the free length of the spring and compare the figure with the dimension given in Technical Data. If the spring is short it should be renewed as it will have weakened in service.

The damper:

A defective damper cannot be rectified and it must be rejected and a new damper fitted in its place. First examine the damper for physical defects such as a bent ram, dented body or fluid leaks. Provided the damper is satisfactory in appearance then mount it vertically in the padded jaws of a vice. A new damper, or one that has been kept in storage for some time should have the air

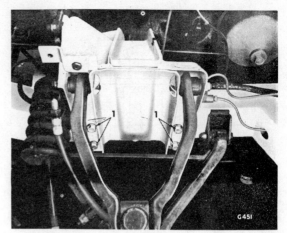

FIG 8:5 Sub-frame attachments

FIG 8:6 Removing the road spring from the damper

bled to the top sealed chamber by gently pumping the damper using several short strokes. After bleeding test the damper by pumping it through several full strokes. A damper is defective if any of the following are present; resistance so high that the damper can hardly be moved by hand, none or slight resistance in either direction, or pockets of no resistance when reversing direction. A satisfactory damper will have appreciable and constant resistance in either direction, an old damper having slightly less resistance than a new one.

8:7 The upper wishbones and ball joint

Test for wear using the method described in the first paragraph of **Section 8:3**. Excessive wear is difficult to detect once the parts have been dismantled.

Before removing these parts the car should be jacked up, with the handbrake on and the front end placed on chassis stands. Partly raise and support the suspension using a small jack under the vertical link, after removing the appropriate road wheel.

The ball joint 15 can be removed by removing the nut 22 and washer 21 then separating it from the vertical link 18 by a method described in **Section 8:4**. Take out the nuts and bolts 14 to free it from the upper wishbones.

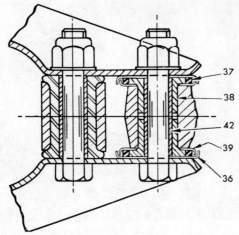

FIG 8 : 7 Lower wishbone outer attachments

When the ball joint is separated from the vertical link, support the brake assembly and use a piece of wire or string to hold it in position.

After removing the ball joint the wishbones 10 and 12 can be removed from the sub-frame by taking off the nuts and withdrawing the bolts 11. Label the wishbones to ensure that they are replaced in their correct positions.

If the fulcrum bushes 13 are worn or damaged then press the old bushes out and press in new bushes using a pilot tool and a little soft soap as lubricant. The new bushes should be pressed in so that they protrude equally on either side of the wishbone.

The parts are replaced in the reverse order of removal, but only tightening the nuts fully when the suspension is in its normal working position.

8 : 8 The vertical link and lower trunnion bearing

1 Remove the hub assembly (see **Section 8 : 3**). Slacken the nut on the damper bottom attachment bolt 59 a few turns and remove the trunnion securing nut and bolt 58 to free the trunnion from the wishbones.
2 Disconnect the upper ball joint 15 from the vertical link 18, and the tie rod end from the steering arm 28 (see **Section 8 : 4**). Lift out the vertical link assembly from the car.
3 Remove the bolts 33 and 34 securing the steering arm 28 and spacers 26 to the vertical link. Remove the bolts 32 that secure the dustshield 31, caliper mounting bracket 30 and seal 19 to the vertical link.
4 Unscrew the trunnion 41 from the vertical link and remove the seals, washers and bushes. If required, the stub axle 35 may be pressed out from the vertical link after removing the nut 23 and washer 24.

Reassemble the parts in the reverse order of dismantling. The trunnion 41 is screwed fully into place on the vertical link and it is then unscrewed to the first working position, ensuring that it has a range of at least 60 deg. on either side of the straight ahead position without binding. A sectioned view of the lower wishbone outer attachments are shown in **FIG 8 : 7.**

If the lower trunnion is worn it must be renewed and a new vertical link also fitted. It should be noted that the assemblies are handed and the righthand trunnion can readily be identified by the reduced diameter on the base. The righthand assembly is machined with a righthand thread while the lefthand assembly is machined with a lefthand thread.

Lower wishbones:

These may be removed after disconnecting the trunnion and lower damper attachment. Either take off the nuts 66 and remove the wishbones complete with their brackets 63 and 64 or else withdraw the bolts 62. The bushes 61 are a press fit in the wishbones.

Suspension geometry:

The suspension geometry is controlled by the number and position of the shims 65 under the brackets 63 and 64. Accurate specialized equipment is essential for measuring the angles in the suspension and the average owner should not attempt to adjust the geometry under any circumstances.

8 : 9 Fault diagnosis

(a) Wheel wobble

1 Worn hub bearings
2 Weak or broken front springs
3 Uneven tyre wear
4 Worn suspension bushes
5 Loose wheel nuts
6 Unbalanced wheels

(b) Bottoming of suspension

1 Check 2 in (a)
2 Dampers not working

(c) Rattles

1 Check 2 and 4 in (a)
2 Worn damper mountings
3 Worn anti-roll bar bushes

(d) Excessive rolling

1 Check 2 in (a) and 2 in (b)
2 Broken anti-roll bar

CHAPTER 9

THE STEERING SYSTEM

9:1 Description
9:2 Routine maintenance

PART I   THE STEERING UNIT
9:3 Removal and replacement
9:4 Dismantling
9:5 Reassembly

9:6   Front wheel alignment (Track)

PART II   THE STEERING COLUMN
9:7   Removal and replacement
9:8   Servicing
9:9   Steering column assembly GT6 Mk 3
9:10 Fault diagnosis

9:1 Description

A rack and pinion steering unit is fitted to all models covered by this manual. The pinion on the unit is attached by a coupling directly to the lower end of the steering column. As the pinion rotates with the steering wheel, a gear on the end of the pinion engages in the teeth of the rack, moving it from side to side. A tie rod is attached to each end of the rack by the inner ball joints, and the outer end of each tie rod is attached to the steering arm on the suspension, again using a ball joint. As the rack moves from side to side the front wheels are turned about the steering swivel by the levers, and the vertical motion of the suspension is allowed for by the ball joints at either end of the two tie rods. It will be seen that all the connections are direct and no idler parts are required, thus giving a very precise and accurate method of steering.

The steering lock is limited by the maximum movement of the rack in the unit and the front wheel alignment is controlled by the effective length of the tie rods. For these reasons it is vital that the steering unit is reassembled to the correct dimensions.

The steering column is designed to telescope in the event of a serious accident. This design also allows a limited adjustment in the height of the steering wheel

and it is achieved by connecting the upper and lower inner columns using an impact clamp. The switches and horn push are mounted at the top of the outer column in such a way that the cables are led out through a hole in the side of the column and no stator tube is required.

On 1971 cars a lock for the steering column, incorporating the ignition/starter control, is fitted beneath the facia panel.

9:2 Routine maintenance

At 12,000 mile intervals remove the grease plug from the top of the steering unit, arrowed in **FIG 9:1,** and replace it with a grease nipple. Apply a grease gun and give the unit five strokes only. **Do not overlubricate otherwise the bellows will be damaged.**

The bellows on the steering unit and the outer tie rod ends should be regularly examined for damage and renewed if required. The bellows contain the lubricating grease and prevent the entry of dirt and water, so if they are damaged the wear rate will be excessive.

PART I   THE STEERING UNIT

The details of the steering unit are shown in **FIG 9:2,** and its mountings in **FIG 9:3.** The dimensions to which the unit must be reassembled are shown in **FIG 9:4.**

FIG 9:1 Steering unit grease plug and coupling attachments

9:3 Removal and replacement:

1 Remove the grease plug 28 to free the earth cable 45 that is secured underneath it. Loosely replace the grease plug to prevent the ingress of dirt. Remove the nut 8 and bolt 9 securing the lower coupling 7 to the pinion shaft 15, also shown in **FIG 9:1**.

2 Remove the nuts 19 and washers 18, then disconnect the tie rod ends 44 from the steering arms on the suspension (see **Chapter 8, Section 8:4**). Remove the lefthand engine bay valance.

3 From underneath the car remove the nuts and washers 24 as well as the plates 23. Pull out the U-bolts 20 from above and remove the rubber bushes 21, which are split for easy removal.

4 Support the weight of the engine on a sling and hoist. Remove the front engine mounting bolts from the lefthand side, arrowed A in **FIG 9:5**. Raise the left-hand side of the engine approximately 1½ inches (4 cm) taking great care not to damage the radiator hoses.

5 Move the steering unit forwards to disengage the coupling from the pinion shaft and manoeuvre the unit out of the car from the driver's side. If the unit is going to be out of the car for any length of time, lower the engine and reconnect the engine mounting.

Replacement:

Before replacing the unit check that it conforms to the dimensions shown in **FIG 9:4**.

1 Raise the lefthand side of the engine as described earlier. Set the steering wheel in the straight-ahead position. Count the exact number of revolutions required to turn the pinion from one full lock to the other. Rotate the pinion back half this number of turns so that the unit is also in the straight-ahead position. Without allowing the pinion to turn, manoeuvre the unit back into the car and reconnect the pinion shaft to the lower coupling.

2 Fit the rubber bushes 21 to the rack tube and then place the U-bolts 20 into position. Replace the plates 23, flanges inwards, and loosely secure them with the nuts and washers 24. Lower the engine back into place and correctly secure the front mounting with the nuts and bolts (see **FIG 9:5**).

3 An assistant will be required for this operation. Press the U-bolts outwards until the gap between the retainers on the U-bolts and the flange plates on the

rack tube, shown at A in **FIG 9:3,** is ⅛ inch (3.17 mm) on both sides. Hold both U-bolts in position while the assistant slides both plates 23 inwards until the flange on the plate abuts fully along the flange of the chassis member shown at B. With the parts in place, fully tighten the nuts 24.

4 Reconnect the outer tie rod ends to the steering levers. Secure the coupling to the pinion with the Nyloc nut and bolt. Reconnect the earthing strap under the grease plug 28.

5 Before road testing the car first jack up the front end and check that the steering moves freely from lock to lock, then with the car back on the ground check the front wheel alignment (see **Section 9:6**).

9:4 Dismantling

With the unit removed from the car, proceed as follows:

1 Release all three clips 42 and the wire 40 so that the bellows 41 can be slid outwards to expose the inner ball joints. Slacken the locknuts 33 and unscrew both tie rod assemblies from the rack 32. Remove the springs 36 and locknuts 33 from the ends of the rack.

2 Unscrew the cap nut 27 and withdraw the shims 29, spring 30 and plunger 31. Extract the circlip 10 and withdraw the pinion assembly, taking care not to lose the dowel 5. Slide off the retaining ring 11, shims 12, bush 13 and thrust washer 14 from the pinion 15. Use a small blunt screwdriver to remove the O-ring from inside the retaining ring 11.

3 Slide out the rack 32 from the rack tube 25. Shake out the thrust washer 16 and bush 17 from the housing.

4 Free the lockwasher 35 and unscrew the sleeve nut 34 from the cup nut 39. Withdraw the shims 26 and cup 37 from inside the cup nut. Slacken the locknuts 43 and unscrew the tie rod ends 44 from the tie rods 38. Unscrew the locknuts 43, after which the bellows 41 and cup nuts 39 can be slid off the tie rods.

9:5 Reassembly

Before reassembling the parts they should be thoroughly cleaned. Any solvent may be used on the metal parts, but the only safe solvent for the bellows is methylated spirits. Most other solvents will attack the rubber to a greater or lesser degree. Renew any worn or damaged parts.

The parts are reassembled in the reverse order of dismantling, but to ensure the correct and precise operation of the unit it is essential that the correct clearances and dimensions are adhered to.

Pinion end float:

1 Fit the bush 17 and thrust washer back into position and introduce the rack 32 through the housing 25. Make sure that the rack is positioned as shown in the cross-section in **FIG 9:6**.

2 Fit the parts back onto the pinion 15, omitting the shims 12 and O-ring. Slide the pinion assembly into position and secure it with the circlip 10.

3 Mount a DTI (Dial Test Indicator) on the rack tube so that its stylus rests vertically on the end of the pinion. (A DTI is not essential as the adjustment can be reached by trial and error). Press the pinion firmly

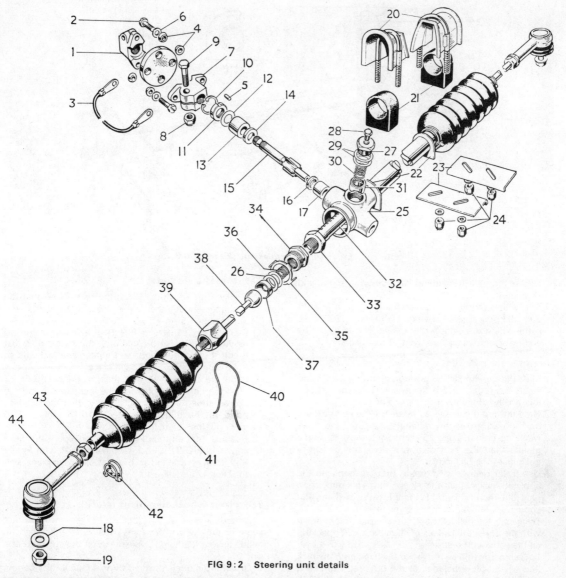

FIG 9 : 2   Steering unit details

Key to Figs 9 : 2 and 9 : 3   1 Steering coupling (upper)   2 Bolt   3 Earth cable (soldered in position)   4 Rubber bushes
5 Dowel   6 Washer   7 Steering coupling (lower)   8 Nyloc nut   9 Pinch bolt   10 Circlip   11 Retaining
ring   12 Shims   13 Bush   14 Thrust washer   15 Pinion shaft   16 Thrust washer   17 Bush
18 Washer   19 Nyloc nut   20 U bolts   21 Rubber bushes   22 Abutment plates   23 Locating plates
24 Nyloc nuts   25 Rack assembly   26 Shims   27 Cap   28 Grease plug   29 Shims   30 Spring
31 Plunger   32 Rack   33 Locknut   34 Sleeve nut   35 Lock tab   36 Spring   37 Cup   38 Tie-rod
39 Cup nut   40 Locking wire   41 Rubber gaiter   42 Clip   43 Locknut   44 Tie-rod end   45 Earth cable

down into the housing and zero the DTI. Pull the pinion out against the circlip and note the reading on the DTI. Remove the DTI, circlip 10 and retaining ring 11. Fit a new O-ring in the retaining ring.

4 Make up a shim pack 12 that is just thinner than the dimension measured, and fit it over the pinion. Replace the retaining ring 11 and secure the parts in place with the dowel 5 and circlip 10. Correctly adjusted the pinion should rotate freely with minimum end float.

Pinion pressure pad:

1 Refit the plunger 31 and cap nut 27 only. Tighten the cap nut until all end float is eliminated.

2 Use feeler gauges to measure the gap between the underside of the cap nut and the face of the housing, and then remove the cap nut and plunger.

3 Make up a shim pack 29 which is .004 inch (.1 mm) thicker than the dimension just measured. Pack the unit with grease and reassemble the parts in the

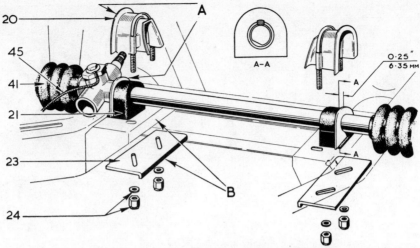

FIG 9:3   Steering unit mountings (Key as Fig 9:2)

reverse order of dismantling, including the spring and shim pack.

4 Check that the pinion rotates freely when a load of 2 lb (.9 kg) is applied at a radius of 8 inch (20.3 cm). If the pinion does not rotate correctly then adjust by adding or removing shims from under the cap nut.

Tie rod inner ball joints

1 Slide the cup nut 39 into position on the tie rod 38 and insert into it the cup 37. Screw the sleeve nut 34 and lockwasher 35 tightly into the cup nut.

2 Hold the cup nut in a vice and by pulling and pushing on the tie rod roughly estimate the total end float. Make up a shim pack 26 whose thickness is a little greater than the estimated end float and fit it into position in the ball joint.

3 Use feeler gauges to measure the gap between the cup nut, lockwasher and sleeve nut. This dimension plus .002 inch (.05 mm) is the thickness of shims that should be removed from the shim pack 26.

4 Dismantle the ball joint and then reassemble it again with the correct thickness of shim pack, after packing all the parts with grease.

5 Loosely screw the tie rod assembly back onto the rack and use a spring balance at the outer end to check that the tie rod articulates freely at a load of $1\frac{1}{2}$ lb (.681 kg). If necessary, adjust the load by varying the quantity of shims 26. When the load is satisfactory unscrew the assembly from the rack, and lock the cup nut and sleeve nut with the lockwasher.

Refitting the tie rods:

1 Replace the locknuts 33 on the rack 32 so that the distance between their inner faces corresponds to the dimensions 3+4+5+3 (total of 24.40 inch— 619.76 mm) shown in **FIG 9:4**. Screw the tie rod assemblies back into place until the sleeve nuts just touch the locknuts and then tighten the locknuts so the assemblies are secured in place.

2 Slide the bellows 41 and their securing clips back onto the tie rods. Screw on the locknuts 43 and the tie rod ends 44, adjusting them so that they correspond to the dimensions 1+2 (10.14 inch—25.75 cm), and lock them in position.

3 Recheck that all the dimensions correspond to those shown in **FIG 9:4**. Pack each bellows 41 with $\frac{1}{2}$ oz of Retinax A grease and secure the bellows in place with the clips 42 and wire 40.

9:6 Front wheel alignment (track)

An indication that the front wheels are not in correct alignment is when the tyres wear unevenly and the treads have a feathered appearance on the edges of one side.

On all the models covered by this manual the correct alignment is $\frac{1}{16}$ to $\frac{1}{8}$ inch (1.6 to 3.0 mm) toe-in with the car in an unladen condition, and 0 to $\frac{1}{16}$ inch (0 to 1.6 mm) when the car is fully laden with all the seats occupied or 150 lb (68 kg) weights placed in each seat. Adjustment is by slackening the locknuts 43 and clips

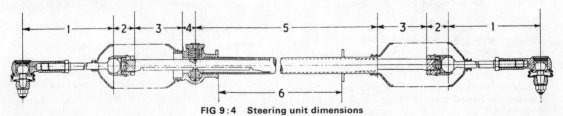

FIG 9:4   Steering unit dimensions

Key to Fig 9:4   1 8.72 (22.15 cm)   2 1.42 (3.61 cm)   3 3.33 (8.45 cm)   4 .88 (2.23 cm)   5 16.88 (42.87 cm)   6 12.65 (32.13 cm)

42 on the tie rods and rotating the tie rods so that they screw either in or out of the tie rod ends thus effectively altering the length of the assemblies. Unless the adjustment required is very small, both tie rods should be adjusted by equal amounts to ensure that the steering wheel will still be in the straight-ahead position when the front wheels are so.

The wheel alignment is best checked using a proper gauge but if care is taken then the measurements can be taken without special equipment. With the car on level ground and the wheels in the straight-ahead position, roll it forwards for a few yards to settle the suspension and bearings.

Measure, as accurately as possible, the distance between the inside wheel rims on the front of the front wheels and at wheel centre height. Mark the point of contact of the tyre with the ground with a piece of chalk and roll the car forwards so that the wheels turn exactly half a revolution. **Never push the car backwards or the measurements will be inaccurate.** Again measure the distance between the rims at wheel centre height but at the rear of the front wheels. The difference between the two dimensions gives the wheel alignment, the correct condition being when the first measurement is smaller than the second by the specified toe-in dimension.

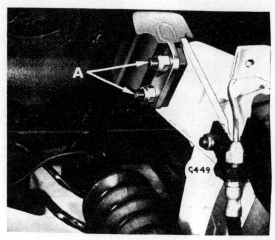

FIG 9:5 Engine mounting bolts

PART II THE STEERING COLUMN

Details of the steering column assembly fitted to early cars are shown in **FIG 9:6** and its attachments in **FIG 9:7**, details of the assembly used on GT6 Mk 3 cars are given in **FIG 9:8** and its servicing described in **Section 9:9**.

9:7 Removal and replacement

1 Remove the nut and bolt that secure the coupling to the lower steering column 1. Disconnect the electrical cables from the steering head at the snap connectors under the facia, labelling the cables if the colours have faded.

2 Undo the nuts and bolts securing the lower outer column support clamp 30 and the bottom half of the upper clamp 40, while supporting the column.

3 When both clamps are removed then withdraw the assembly up and out of the car.

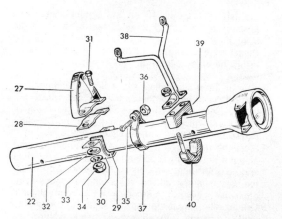

Steering column attachments (Vitesse)

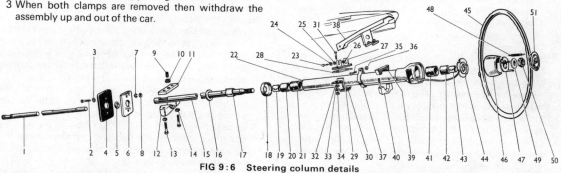

FIG 9:6 Steering column details

Key to Figs 9:6 and 9:7 1 Inner steering column (lower) 2 Bolt 3 Washer 4 Rubber seal 5 Washer 6 Retaining plate 7 Spring washer 8 Nut 9 Impact clamp adjusting screw 10 Lock nut 11 Impact clamp (upper) 12 Impact clamp (lower) 13 Impact clamp bolts 14 Spring washers 15 Upper inner steering column 16 Nylon washer 17 Direction indicator cancelling ring 18 End cap 19 Nylon bush 20 Steel sleeve 21 Rubber bush 22 Outer steering column 23 Bolt 24 Spring washer 25 Plain washer 26 Nut 27 Bracket 28 Felt pad 29 Felt pad 30 Outer column support clamp (lower) 31 Bolt 32 Plain washer 33 Spring washer 34 Nut 35 Bolt 36 Nut 37 Cable trough clip 38 Support bracket 39 Outer column upper support clamp (top half) 40 Outer column upper support clamp (lower half) 41 Rubber bush 42 Steel sleeve 43 Nylon bush 44 Horn contact ring 45 Steering wheel 46 Steering wheel boss 47 Spring clip 48 Contact brush 49 Washer 50 Steering wheel nut 51 Horn push assembly

FIG 9:7 Steering column attachments

Replacement:

1 Slacken the locknut 10 on the impact clamp and unscrew the adjusting screw 9 two complete turns using an Allen key.
2 Replace the assembly and secure it loosely in place using the clamps 30 and 40. Do not forget to refit the felt 29.
3 Turn the front wheels into the straight-ahead position and set the steering wheel so that the two spokes are level and the third spoke is vertically downwards. Refit the lower steering column 1 into the coupling and secure it in place with the Nyloc nut and bolt.
4 Slide the steering wheel up or down to the desired height and clamp the column by tightening the nuts and bolts securing the clamps 30 and 40. Do not set the column at the bottom of its range of movement, otherwise it cannot telescope if an accident occurs.
5 Use an Allen key to tighten the adjusting screw 9 as hard as possible without actually bending the Allen key and then lock it in place by tightening the locknut 10. Reconnect the electrical cables.
6 It is advisable to jack up the front of the car and check that the steering travels freely from lock to lock.

9:8 Servicing

Remove the steering column from the car as described in the previous section. If the coupling requires dismantling, then remove the nut and bolt securing it to the steering unit pinion and manoeuvre it out of the car.

1 Undo the nut 36, withdraw the bolt 35 and remove the cable trough 37. Prise out the horn push 51 and withdraw the contact brush 48. Remove the electrical switches from the steering column after taking off their covers.
2 Remove the bolts 13 and spring washers 14 to free the two halves of the impact clamp 11 and 12 from the steering column. Withdraw the lower column 1 downwards and the upper column 15 and steering wheel 45 upwards after sliding off the nylon washer 16.
3 Hold the upper column 15 in the padded jaws of a vice and remove the nut 50, washer 49 and clip 47.

Use a suitable extractor to separate the steering wheel from the column.

4 Take off the end cap 18 and depress the two protrusions on the rubber bush 21 so that the lower bush assembly can be driven out of the column using a long rod. Separate the nylon bush 19 and steel sleeve 20 from the rubber bush 21. Similarly remove the upper bush assembly and then dismantle it.

Examine all the parts for wear or damage, especially the nylon and rubber bushes. Ensure that both the inner steering columns are straight and true. Renew any parts that require it.

Reassemble the parts in the reverse order of dismantling. When refitting the steering wheel to the upper inner column align the spokes with the lugs on the indicator cancelling ring 17 and peen the nut 50 to prevent it from working loose in service.

9:9 Steering column assembly GT6 Mk 3

The steering column assembly is shown exploded into component form in **FIG 9:8** which will assist in servicing if this should be necessary. The procedure for removing the column from the car is as follows:

1 Disconnect the battery and remove the driver's parcel shelf.
2 Remove the pinch-bolt from the clamp securing the mast to the flexible coupling.
3 Remove the nuts from the two bolts securing the forward column mounting bracket and withdraw the forward support housing and felt liner.
4 Disconnect the connections for the horn, direction indicators and lights. Disconnect the plug from the steering column lock.
5 Remove the two screws securing the rear mounting bracket and withdraw the two halves of the clamp and the upper screwed plate.
6 Withdraw the steering column together with the tie bar.

Dismantling and reassembly should not present any difficulty if a careful note is made of the location of the various parts as they are removed. Note that the two bolts securing the safety clamp are not tightened until after the assembly has been installed in the car. Refit as follows:

1 Turn the road wheels to the straight-ahead position and then with the steering wheel central, engage the lower end of the mast in the splines of the flexible coupling. Fit and tighten the pinch-bolt.
2 Slide cardboard tube towards the rear and fit the felt over the mast housing so that the ends of the felt are below the mast housing.
3 Engage the forward ends of the tie bar in the forward mounting bolts. Fit the felt housing and engage the forward mounting bolts. Fit the plain and spring washers and retaining nuts.
4 See that the spring clip is fitted on the mast housing in line with the rear clamp bracket. Fit the upper and lower clamp halves to the mast housing, fit the screwed plate in the bracket above the clamp halves, install and secure the retaining bolts.
5 Secure the nuts and bolts on the forward bracket.
6 Restore the electric connections, refit the parcel tray and connect the battery.

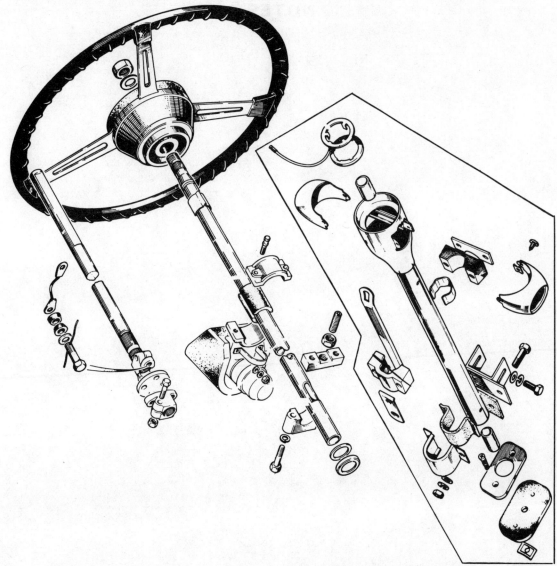

FIG 9:8   Components of the steering column assembly fitted to GT6 Mk 3

9:10 Fault diagnosis

(a) Wheel wobble

1 Unbalanced wheels and tyres
2 Slack steering connections
3 Incorrect steering geometry

(b) Wander

1 Check 2 and 3 in (a) . .
2 Damaged suspension or chassis
3 Uneven tyre pressures
4 Weak dampers or springs

(c) Heavy steering

1 Check 3 in (a)
2 Very low tyre pressures
3 Neglected lubrication
4 Wheels out of alignment
5 Steering unit incorrectly adjusted
6 Steering column bushes tight
7 Seized tie rod ends

(d) Lost motion

1 Loose steering wheel
2 Worn splines or loose bolts securing coupling
3 Worn steering coupling
4 Worn ball joints

NOTES

CHAPTER 10

THE BRAKING SYSTEM

10:1 Description
10:2 Routine maintenance
10:3 Servicing precautions

PART 1   THE FRONT DISC BRAKES
10:4 Renewing the friction pads
10:5 Servicing the brake caliper
10:6 The brake disc

PART II   THE REAR DRUM BRAKES
10:7 Relining the rear brakes
10:8 Servicing the rear brake

PART III   THE HANDBRAKE
10:9   Cable adjustment
10:10 Renewing the cables

PART IV   THE HYDRAULIC SYSTEM
10:11 Removing a flexible hose
10:12 The tandem master cylinder
10:13 The Pressure Differential Warning Actuator
        (PDWA)
10:14 Bleeding the brakes

PART V   THE BRAKE SERVO UNIT
10:15 Operation
10:16 Maintenance
10:17 Servo unit testing and faults
10:18 Fault diagnosis

10:1 Description

All models covered by this manual are fitted with disc brakes to the front wheels and drum brakes to the rear wheels. All four brakes are operated hydraulically when the foot pedal is depressed but only the rear drum brakes operate when the handbrake is used. The rear brakes are connected mechanically to the handbrake lever so that the handbrake is totally independent of the hydraulic system.

A master cylinder is used to generate the hydraulic pressure and this pressure is fed to the wheel brakes through a system of metal pipelines and flexible hoses. On standard models the master cylinder is a single-chamber unit of exactly the same design and construction as the master cylinder fitted to the clutch hydraulic system, the only difference being that the cylinder for the brakes has a larger reservoir than the one for the clutch system.

A safety device which may be fitted to later GT6 cars is the dual-circuit master cylinder. This has two chambers interconnected by a sliding piston and each chamber serves only half the brakes. The master cylinder is so designed that if one half of the system fails the other half will still operate at its full efficiency. A PDWA (Pressure Differential Warning Actuator) is fitted between the two halves of the system so that if there is a pressure differential between the two a warning light will be lit.

Wear in the front friction pads is taken up automatically but one adjuster is fitted to each rear brake. Adjusting the rear brakes automatically adjusts the handbrake as well.

Later models of the GT6 Mk 3 are fitted with rear wheel brakes which are self-adjusting, using a screwed ratchet wheel operated by the handbrake linkage.

10:2 Routine maintenance

1 At regular intervals check the level of the fluid in the master cylinder reservoir. If required, top up to the level marked on the side of the reservoir. Wipe the top clean before removing the cap so as to prevent dirt from falling into the reservoir. As the front friction pads wear the fluid will fall steadily, but a sudden drop must be investigated as it can be caused by a leak in the system.

FIG 10:1 Handbrake compensator sector and secondary cable guides

FIG 10:2 Friction pad renewal

2 At regular intervals adjust the rear brakes. Securely jack up the rear of the car, leaving the handbrake off. Turn the adjusters in clockwise until the brakes lock. Unscrew each adjuster, a single notch at a time, until the road wheel rotates freely without the brake dragging or binding. Do not confuse resistance from the rear axle with drag from the brakes. Lower the car and remove the jacks.

3 At 6000 mile intervals apply grease liberally around the handbrake secondary cable guides and compensator, arrowed in **FIG 10:1**.

Preventative maintenance:

Regularly examine the friction pads, rear brake linings, flexible hoses and metal pipelines. Corroded pipelines must be changed as they will have weak spots which may fail under stress.

Ideally the system should be stripped down every three years and old fluid and seals discarded. Dirt or gummy deposits in the system can be flushed out by draining the system and pumping a quart of methylated spirits (denatured alchohol) through the system, half a pint out through each bleed nipple.

10:3 Servicing precautions

Absolute cleanliness is essential in all operations involving the hydraulic system. Use only the recommended cleaning fluids and lay the parts on clean sheets of paper so that they cannot pick up dirt or contaminant.

Use only the recommended brake fluid, Castrol Girling Crimson Clutch and Brake Fluid to specifica-SAE.70 R3, or other makes which meet this specification. Other brake fluids will attack the material of the seals causing them to fail. Keep the fluid in sealed clean containers so that it cannot absorb moisture from the air or become contaminated with dirt. Fluid that has been bled or drained from the system should be discarded unless it is perfectly clean. Such fluid must not be returned directly to the master cylinder reservoir as it contains minute air bubbles. Allow the fluid to stand for 24 hours in a sealed container so that the air bubbles can dissipate.

After dismantling a part examine all the components for wear. Bores of cylinders must be smooth and highly polished. If the bore shows pitting, scoring or wear the whole assembly must be renewed. The only fluids that should be used for cleaning the parts are methylated spirits (denatured alcohol), brake fluid or Girling hydraulic cleaning fluid. The metal parts may be washed in trichlorethylene or similar solvents but all traces of solvent must have evaporated before the unit is reassembled and the solvent must not come into contact with any of the rubber parts.

When internal parts are refitted they should all be dipped into clean hydraulic fluid and refitted wet. Seals must be replaced using only the fingers and worked around so that they are fully and squarely onto their recesses. It is advisable to discard all old seals and fit new ones in their place as a matter of principle. Many of the components use a cup seal on a piston and often this cup seal will have to be entered into the bore with the lips leading. Take great care during this operation not to roll back or damage the lips of the seal. Use hydraulic fluid as lubricant and very carefully ease the seal into the bore.

The importance of cleanliness cannot be over-stressed.

PART I THE FRONT DISC BRAKES

10:4 Renewing the friction pads

The pads must not be allowed to wear thinner than $\frac{1}{8}$ inch (3.17 mm). **FIG 10:2** shows the method of renewing the pads.

1 Securely jack up the front of the car and remove the road wheels.

2 Take out the spring clip retainers 8 and withdraw the pad retainers 9. Remove the damping shims 12 and withdraw the brake pads 4. Do not attempt to reline the brake pads.

3 Use an airline and a brush to remove all the dust and dirt from inside the caliper. Open the bleed screw and press both pistons back into their bores. Use a tube or container to catch the fluid ejected from the bleed nipple. Close the bleed nipple.

4 Refit the parts in the reverse order of removal, noting that the arrows on the damping shims must point in the direction of forward rotation.

5 Pump the brake pedal several times to adjust the front brakes. Check the fluid level in the reservoir and replace the road wheels. Avoid heavy or prolonged braking until the new pads have become bedded-in.

10:5 Servicing the brake caliper

The brake caliper is shown sectioned in **FIG 10:3**. Remove the caliper from the suspension as described in **Chapter 7, Section 7:5,** after disconnecting the flexible hose as instructed in **Section 10:11.**

1 Remove the friction pads and damping shims as described in the previous section. Brush out dirt and dust, then withdraw the pistons 5.

2 Take off the dust excluder 7 and extract the piston seal 6 taking great care not to damage or score the bore. Discard the seal 6 as new seals must be fitted on reassembly. Clean and examine the parts as instructed in **Section 10:3.** Do not part the two halves of the caliper and if the seal 1 has failed the caliper must be renewed.

3 Fit a new seal 6 into the bores and secure the lips of the dust excluders 7 into their recesses in the cylinders. Press the pistons 5, closed ends leading, back into the bores, taking great care to ensure that the pistons are squarely entered into the bore. If the pistons are allowed to tilt initially then they will jam and damage the surface of the bore. Fit the dust excluders 7 into their recesses in the pistons.

4 Refit the caliper to the suspension in the reverse order of removal. When the flexible hose has been reconnected fill and bleed the hydraulic system as instructed in **Section 10:14,** before replacing the road wheels.

10:6 The brake disc

Before this can be removed from the wheel hub the hub must be removed from the suspension as instructed in **Chapter 8, Section 8:3.**

A scored brake disc will cause poor braking and excessive pad wear. If the damage is only shallow it can be machined off provided that no more than .020 inch (.0508 mm) is removed from each face and the limiting dimensions shown in **FIG 10:4** are observed. A very high standard of finish is required, so the machining must be left to firms specializing in this sort of work.

If the scoring is too deep to be machined off then the disc must be renewed. When the disc and hub have been refitted to the car, with the correct end float, mount a DTI (Dial Test Indicator) on the caliper. Set the DTI so that the stylus rests vertically on the outer face of the brake disc at a distance of .5 inch (12.7 mm) from the outer edge of the disc. Press the hub assembly inwards to take up the end float and rotate it so that the runout on the brake disc is measured. The runout must not exceed .006 inch (.152 mm) and if this figure is exceeded check the mating surfaces of the disc and hub for dirt. Reassemble the disc to the hub, aligning different securing holes. If the runout is still excessive the disc will either have to be machined or scrapped.

PART III THE REAR DRUM BRAKES

The details of the lefthand side rear brake assembly are shown in **FIG 10:5.**

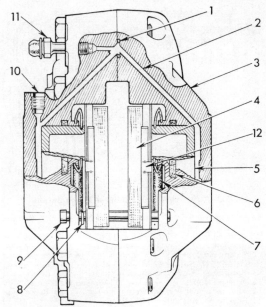

FIG 10:3 Sectioned front brake caliper

Key to Fig 10:3
1 O-ring seal
2 Fluid transfer passage
3 Caliper body
4 Brake pad
5 Piston
6 Piston seal
7 Dust excluder
8 Spring clip retainer
9 Pad retainer
10 Hose connection
11 Bleed nipple
12 Damping shim

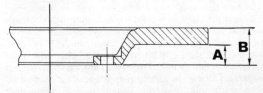

FIG 10:4 Brake disc limiting dimensions

Key to Fig 10:4   **A** .612 inch (15.54 mm)
B 1.072 inch (27.23 mm)

10:7 Relining the rear brakes

Replacement shoes and linings must be fitted if the old linings are worn below $\frac{1}{16}$ inch (1.6 mm) thickness or if they are contaminated with oil or grease.

1 Jack up the rear of the car, leaving the handbrake off, and remove the rear road wheels. Slacken the brake adjusters right off.

2 Take out the two countersunk screws 20 and withdraw the brake drum 21. Hold the steady pins 8 at the rear of the backplate 9 and grip each steady pin cup 14 in turn with a pair of pliers. Press the cup in against the spring pressure and turn it through 90 degrees so as to free it from the T-shape on the steady pin. Remove the cups 14 and 12, springs 13 and withdraw the steady pins 8 from the rear of the backplate.

3 Remove the splitpin 2 from the handbrake lever 1. Lever or pull both shoes 19 and 25 out of their abutment slots to relieve the spring tension. Free the

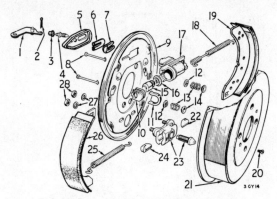

FIG 10:5   Lefthand side rear brake details

Key to Fig 10:5   1 Handbrake lever   2 Splitpin
3 Dust cap   4 Bleed nipple   5 Dust excluder
6 Retaining clip   7 Retaining clip   8 Steady pins
9 Backplate   10 Dust excluder   11 Clip
12 Steady pin cups   13 Springs   14 Steady pin cups
15 Piston   16 Seal   17 Wheel cylinder   18 Return spring
19 Brake shoe   20 Countersunk screw   21 Brake drum
22 Adjuster tappet   23 Adjuster wedge and body
24 Adjuster tappet   25 Return spring   26 Brake shoe
27 Shakeproof washers   28 Nuts

springs 18 and 25 from one shoe and remove the shoes and springs from the brake.

Remove dirt and dust from inside the brake using an airline and stiff brush. Grease or oil can be removed with the careful use of a brush and fuel. If there has been a leakage of grease or oil into the brake then the source must be traced and cured before refitting new shoes.

Smear the slots with a little white, zinc-based grease and refit the brake shoes in the reverse order of removal. Assemble the springs and shoes loosely in the brake then pull the front shoe into its position first, after which the rear shoe should be pulled or levered into position. Do not forget to replace the steady pins 8 and their associated parts and a new splitpin 2. Tap the shoes along their slots until they are concentric with the brake drum. When the drum has been refitted adjust the rear brakes and pump the brake pedal hard so as to centralize the shoes.

Self-adjusting drum brakes:

This type of brake is fitted to the rear wheels of late GT6 Mk 3 models and the essential details are shown in **FIG 10:6**. To dismantle these units for brake shoe renewal proceed as follows:

1 Jack-up the rear of the car and remove the road wheel. Release the handbrake and remove the brake drum.

2 Move the ratchet lever 3 clear of the ratchet wheel and screw the wheel inwards to release the brake adjustment.

3 Release the two steady springs 4 as described earlier to free the shoes and withdraw the steady pins.

4 Pull the leading shoe 5 out of engagement with the anchor plate and then release it from the wheel cylinder.

5 Release the trailing shoe 7 from the anchor plate, detach the shoe return springs 8 and withdraw the two shoes. Note carefully the location of the return springs for later reassembly.

Reassembly:

This is carried out as follows:

1 Arrange the two shoes for fitting and engage the upper spring ends in the webs, the spring being on the inboard side.

2 Offer up the shoes and engage the two appropriate ends in the anchor plate.

3 Similarly fit the lower spring ends to the webs and engage one shoe in the handbrake operating lever ensuring that the lever pad is correctly located in the shoe web and the other shoe in the ratchet spindle as shown.

4 Fit the shoe steady pins, springs and caps, centralise the shoes and fit the brake drum and road wheel.

5 Lower the car to the ground and bring the brake shoes into adjustment by operating and releasing the handbrake several times.

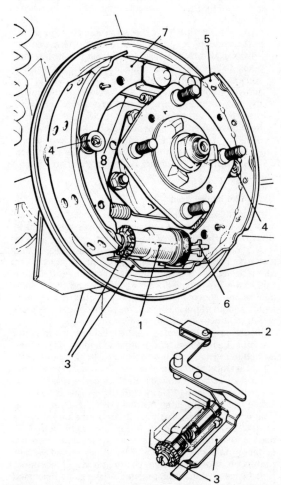

FIG 10:6   The drum brake and self-adjusting mechanism fitted to later GT6 Mk 3 models

Key to Fig 10:6   1 Wheel cylinder   2 Handbrake cable fork end   3 Ratchet wheel and lever   4 Steady springs
5 Leading shoe   6 Backplate lever   7 Trailing shoe   8 Shoe return springs

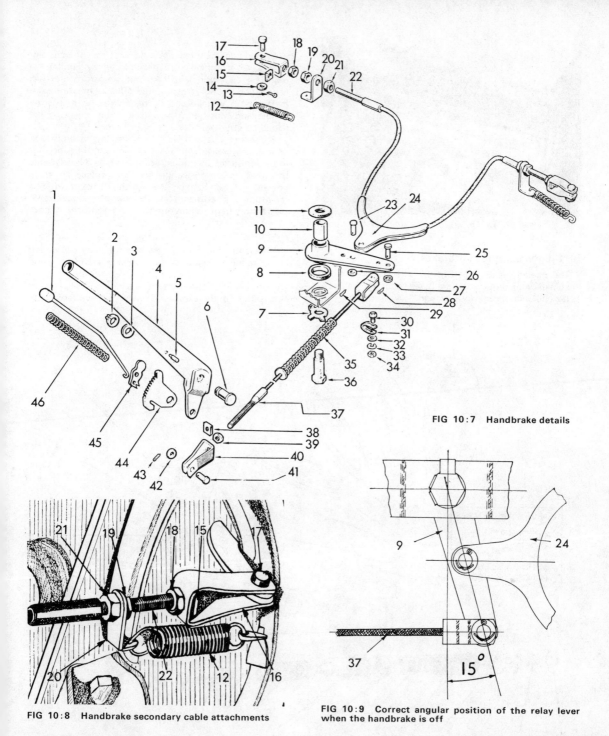

FIG 10:7 Handbrake details

FIG 10:8 Handbrake secondary cable attachments

FIG 10:9 Correct angular position of the relay lever when the handbrake is off

Key to Figs 10:7, 10:8 and 10:9 1 Pawl release rod   2 Circlip   3 Plain washer   4 Handbrake lever   5 Pawl pivot pin
6 Pivot pin   7 Lockplate   8 Rubber seal   9 Relay lever   10 Bush   11 Felt seal   12 Pull-off spring   13 Splitpin
14 Plain washer   15 Square nut   16 Clevis   17 Clevis pin   18 Locknut   19 Adjusting nut   20 Adjustable spring anchor
21 Locknut   22 Secondary cable   23 Clevis pin   24 Compensator sector   25 Clevis pin   26 Plain washer
27 Plain washer   28 Splitpin   29 Splitpin   30 Clamp bolt   31 Clamp   32 Plain washer   33 Spring washer   34 Nut
35 Spring   36 Pivot bolt   37 Primary cable   38 Square nut   39 Locknut   40 Clevis   41 Clevis pin   42 Plain washer
43 Splitpin   44 Ratchet   45 Pawl   46 Pawl spring

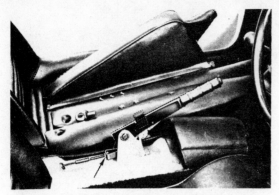

FIG 10:10   Primary cable adjuster

10:8 Servicing the rear brakes

The operations described in this chapter, apart from the brake drum, require that the brake shoes are removed as described in the previous section.

Brake drum :

Check that the working surface of the drum is not scored. Light damage can be removed by turning the drum on an arbor in a lathe but deeper scoring will necessitate fitting a new drum. Check the drum for cracks, both visually and by hanging it on a wooden handle and tapping with a small metal object. A flat sounding note indicates a crack.

Brush out dirt and dust from inside the drum and remove any grease with a suitable solvent. If the drum is to be left off the car for any length of time it is advisable to lightly oil or grease the working surface so as to prevent rust from forming. **Before the drum is refitted it must of course be thoroughly degreased, preferably using a solvent such as trichlorethylene.**

Adjuster :

Unless the unit is to be renewed the body can be left bolted to the backplate. Withdraw the two tappets 22 and 24 and screw the wedge out through the body. If the wedge is difficult to turn then use a wire brush to remove corrosion from the exposed threads. Remove the grease

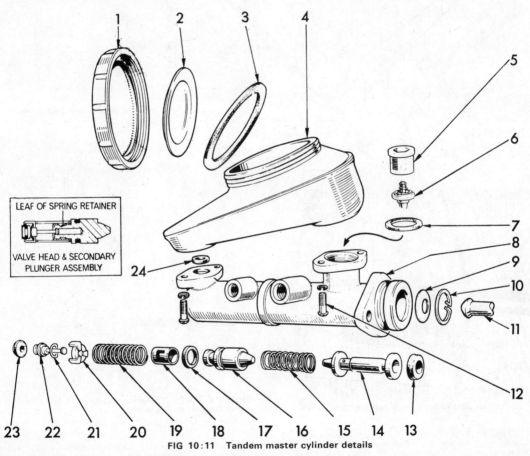

FIG 10:11   Tandem master cylinder details

Key to Fig 10:11   1 Cap   2 Baffle plate   3 Seal   4 Reservoir   5 Tipping valve securing nut   6 Tipping valve   7 Seal reservoir to body   8 Body   9 Abutment washer   10 Circlip   11 Pushrod   12 Screw, reservoir to body   13 Seal   14 Primary plunger   15 Intermediate spring   16 Secondary plunger   17 Seal   18 Spring retainer   19 Secondary spring   20 Valve spacer   21 Spring washer   22 Valve   23 Seal   24 Seal, reservoir to body

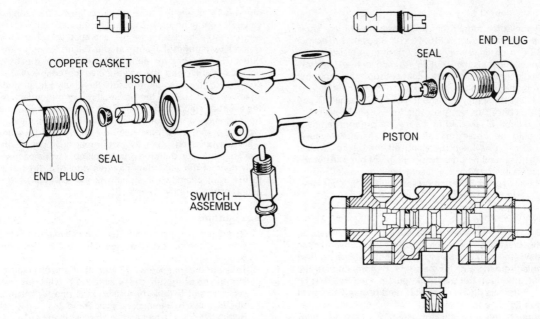

FIG 10:12 Pressure Differential Warning Actuator (PDWA) details

with a piece of rag, washing carefully with clean fuel. Reassemble the adjuster in the reverse order of dismantling, using zinc-based grease as a lubricant.

The wheel cylinder:

1 Remove the flexible hose as instructed in **Section 10:11**. Disconnect the handbrake cable from the lever 1 on the brake and take off the rubber dust excluder 5.
2 Use a screwdriver to drive off the retaining plate and spring 6 and 7 from the neck of the wheel cylinder body 17. Withdraw the assembly from the backplate, at the same time manoeuvring off the handbrake lever 1.
3 Take off the spring clip 11 and rubber dust excluder 10 from the wheel cylinder. Withdraw the piston 15 and seal 16 from the cylinder and then separate the seal from the piston.

The parts are reassembled and refitted in the reverse order of dismantling and removal, while following the instructions given in **Section 10:3**. Bleed the brakes as instructed in **Section 10:14**.

PART III   THE HANDBRAKE

The details of the handbrake are shown in **FIG 10:7** and the secondary cable attachments to the wheel brake are shown in **FIG 10:8**.

10:9 Cable adjustment

Normally adjusting the rear brakes will also adjust the handbrake but after a long period of service the cables stretch slightly and will require adjustment. However before adjusting the cables check the whole system to ensure that there is no other cause. Excessively worn rear brake linings or worn clevis pins and forks can cause excessive movement on the handbrake lever, so replace these if any are defective. Only when the cause has been narrowed down to stretched cables should the cables themselves be adjusted.

1 Securely jack up the rear of the car and leave the handbrake off.
2 From underneath the car, check that the relay lever 9 is correctly set at the angle shown in **FIG 10:9**. If the angle is incorrect then remove the tunnel trim to expose the primary cable adjuster, as shown in **FIG 10:10**. Slacken the locknut 39 and by turning the cable screw it in or out of the clevis fork 40 until the relay lever is set at the correct angle. Tighten the locknut 39 and replace the tunnel trim.
3 Extract the splitpins 13 and remove the washers 14 and clevis pins 17 so as to free the clevis forks 16 from the levers on the brakes. Turn the brake adjusters as far clockwise as they will go and until the brake shoes are in contact with the brake drums. Slacken the locknuts 18 and screw the forks 16 equally along the cable so as to remove the slack. The cable is at the correct length when the clevis pins 17 can just be refitted without having to pull hard or strain the cable. Use new splitpins 13 to secure the clevis pins in place.
4 Unscrew both brake adjusters, a notch at a time, until the wheels rotate freely and the brakes do not bind or drag. Position the spring anchors 20 so that the springs 12 are just in tension when the handbrake is off. Lower the car back to the ground and remove the jacks.

10:10 Renewing the cables

The handbrake will have to be adjusted as described in the previous section if either of the cables are renewed.

Primary cable:

1 Remove the tunnel trim to expose the primary cable adjuster, as shown in **FIG 10:10**. Slacken the locknut 39 and unscrew the cable 37 from the clevis fork 40, collecting the square nut 38 as it comes free. Unscrew the locknut 39 from the cable and pull the cable out from the hole in the floor, so that it is all under the car.

2 Extract the splitpin 28 and remove the washer 27 and clevis pin 25 to free the cable from the relay lever.

The cable is replaced in the reverse order of removal. It should be noted that the whole handbrake lever assembly can be freed by taking off the circlip 2, plain washer 3 and then withdrawing the pivot pin 6. After the primary cable has been adjusted position the clamp 31 so that the spring 35 is compressed by 1 inch (25.4 mm) with the handbrake off.

Secondary cable:

1 Disconnect the secondary cable 22 from the levers on the brakes. Slacken the locknuts and unscrew the clevis forks 16 and spring anchors 20, including their nuts, from the ends of the cable. Pull the ends of the cable through the two cable guides (see **FIG 10:1**).

2 Free the ears on the lockplate 7 and unscrew the pivot bolt 36. Free the relay lever from the chassis and disconnect the compensator sector 24 from the relay lever by withdrawing the clevis pin 23. The cable 22 can be slid out of the compensator sector and removed from the car.

Replace the cable in the reverse order of removal. Grease the bush 10 when replacing it and note that the rubber seal 8 is underneath. With the cable still slack, liberally pack the compensator sector and cable guides with grease. Slide the cable backwards and forwards through them to distribute the grease.

PART IV   THE HYDRAULIC SYSTEM

The master cylinder fitted to standard (European) models only differs from the master cylinder fitted to the clutch system by having a larger reservoir. Servicing instructions apply equally in each case so for all details of the brake master cylinder refer to **Chapter 5, Section 5:3**.

10:11 Removing a flexible hose

Never twist the flexible portion of a hose as this will cause damage and early failure.

Unscrew the metal pipeline nut while holding the adjacent hexagon of the hose with a spanner. Take care not to twist the metal pipe while undoing the nut or it will fracture. Still holding the flexible hose take off the locknut holding it to its bracket. The hose can then be freed from the bracket and the other end unscrewed from the brake, allowing the flexible portion to rotate freely.

Replace the hose in the reverse order of removal, securing it to the brake first and then to its bracket on the car.

10:12 The tandem master cylinder

The details of this are shown in **FIG 10:11**.

Operation:

The pushrod 11 is attached to the brake lever. When the pedal is depressed the pushrod presses the primary plunger 14 down the bore of the cylinder. The tipping valve 6, connecting the chamber to the reservoir, closes and pressure builds up in the chamber to act on the secondary plunger 15 and on the brakes through the outlet. The secondary plunger moves down the bore immediately, closing the valve 22 which connects that chamber to the reservoir. Pressure then builds up in both chambers and acts on the brakes through the outlets. In the event of failure in the half of the system served by the front chamber, the secondary plunger 16 will stop moving when the spring 19 becomes coil bound and pressure will then build up normally in the rear chamber. If the rear chamber fails then the primary plunger will mechanically contact the secondary plunger forming a direct link to the front chamber. The plungers are returned by the action of the springs 15 and 19.

Dismantling:

1 Remove the master cylinder by the same method as the standard master cylinder (see **Chapter 5, Section 5:3**).

2 Take out the four screws 12 and lift off the reservoir 4. Lightly press in on the pushrod 11, unscrew the securing nut 5 (using an Allen key) and lift out the tipping valve 6. Remove the seals 7 and 24.

3 Remove the dust cover and again press in the pushrod. Use a pair of long-nosed pliers to remove the circlip 10. The pushrod 11 and the abutment washer 9 can be withdrawn. Carefully shake or blow out the internal parts.

4 Separate the spring 15 and primary plunger 14 from the secondary plunger assembly. Part the coils of the spring 19 and use a small blunt screwdriver to lift the leaf on the retainer 18 over the shoulder on the secondary plunger 16 so that the plunger can be separated from the retainer. Slide the stem of the valve 22 into the larger offset hole in the end of the retainer 18 and remove the retainer. Remove the remaining parts from the valve. Remove the seals 13, 17 and 23.

Reassemble the master cylinder in the reverse order of dismantling, observing the precautions given in **Section 10:3** and noting the additional following points:

1 The spring washer 21 is fitted to the valve 22 so that the concave side of the washer is away from the valve.

2 When reassembling the secondary plunger and valve assembly compress the spring 19 by mounting the assembly between the protected jaws of a vice and press the retainer onto the plunger using a small screwdriver. Part the coils and use a long-nosed pair of pliers to gently squeeze the leaf down squarely behind the shoulder on the plunger.

3 The primary plunger 14 must be pressed down the bore of the cylinder when refitting the tipping valve 6. Tighten the securing nut 5 to a load of 35 to 40 lb ft.

10:13 The Pressure Differential Warning Actuator (PDWA)

This is only fitted in conjunction with a tandem master cylinder, and its details are shown in **FIG 10:12**.

Removal:

1 Make sure that the ignition is switched off and then remove the electrical connections from the unit.

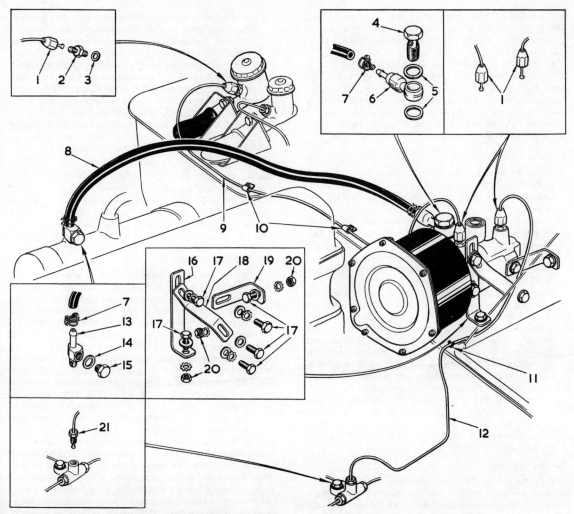

FIG 10:13   Details of the Girling Powerstop vacuum servo unit installation

Key to Fig 10:13   1 Union (female)   2 Adaptor   3 Copper washer   4 Banjo bolt   5 Copper washers   6 Non-return valve   7 Clips   8 Vacuum hose   9 Brake pipe   10 Clips   11 Clip   12 Brake pipe   13 Adaptor   14 Copper washer   15 Plug   16 Bracket   17 Bolts   18, 19 Brackets   20 Nuts   21 Union (male)

2 Disconnect all four pipes from the unit, plugging the pipes so as to prevent the loss of fluid or the ingress of dirt.

3 Remove the bolt securing the unit to the car and then remove the unit from the car.

Reverse the order of removal to replace the unit. After refitting the unit both halves of the brake system must be bled.

Dismantling:

Remove both end plugs and the switch assembly. Carefully push out the valves taking great care not to damage the bore. Discard the old copper gaskets and take off and discard the rubber seals.

Test the switch assembly by reconnecting it into the circuit and with the ignition switched on press the plunger of the switch against an earthed metal part on the car, when upon the warning light should glow.

Reassembly:

1 Fit new seals to the pistons, observing the precautions given in **Section 10:3**. Insert the longer piston, slotted end outwards, until the radiused groove is opposite the hole for the switch plunger. **Do not press in the piston so far that the seal passes the hole for the plunger or the seal will be damaged.** Screw in the switch tightening it to a torque of 2 to 2.5 lb ft.

2 Refit the short piston, again slotted end outwards. Use new copper washers and screw in the end plugs to a torque of 16 to 20 lb ft.

10:14 Bleeding the brakes

Hydraulic fluid is virtually incompressible but air, being a mixture of gases, can be compressed. If air has entered the system it must be bled out otherwise the brake pedal will operate with a spongy feel and preciseness and efficiency will be lost. Air will enter when the system is dismantled or if the level in the reservoir has fallen so low that it is drawn in.

Because of the PDWA the brake system fitted with a tandem master cylinder cannot be bled in exactly the same manner as the standard system. However, **on all types of system hydraulic fluid will be continuously used up, so before starting bleeding fill the reservoir as full as possible and keep it topped up throughout the operation.**

Standard system :

1 Bleed the brakes in the order of decreasing pipe runs, starting with the rear brake furthest from the master cylinder and ending on the front brake nearest the master cylinder.
2 Attach a length of $\frac{1}{4}$ inch (6 mm) bore plastic or rubber tubing to the bleed nipple on the brake to be bled. Dip the free end of the tube into a little clean hydraulic fluid in a glass container. On the rear brakes the adjusters should be screwed in so that the shoes are hard against the brake drums.
3 Open the bleed nipple by half a turn. Have a second operator to work the brake pedal in a sequence as follows: push the pedal right down through a full stroke and then pump it rapidly for two or three short strokes, allow the pedal to return fully unaided and then repeat the sequence. Carry on this method until air ceases to be ejected with the fluid through the bleed tube. Tighten the bleed nipple either on a down stroke or when the pedal is fully depressed.
4 When all the brakes have been bled readjust the rear brakes. If difficulty is experienced in removing the air then tighten the bleed screw at the end of each full stroke and open it again at the beginning of the next downstroke.

Tandem system :

Only the half of the system that has been dismantled requires bleeding as the two halves are hydraulically independent. Again first bleed the brake furthest from the master cylinder and when bleeding the rear brakes lock the shoes to the drums using the adjusters. Readjust the rear brakes after bleeding is complete.

1 Connect a bleed tube to the nipple and open it as described for the standard system. Allow the fluid to run through on its own until it comes out reasonably air free. Repeat this on all the remaining nipples to be bled. Replace the bleed tube on the first nipple and again open it.
2 The second operator must depress the pedal with light pressure allowing it to return unassisted. **Do not use heavy pressure, press the pedal through the end of its stroke or 'try' the pedal before bleeding is fully completed.**
3 If excessive pressure is used then the pistons in the PDWA will move over and have to be centralized. This is done as follows:

Centralizing the PDWA :

1 Finish bleeding the half of the system. When completed transfer the bleed tube to a bleed nipple on a brake at the opposite end of the car to the brakes just bled.

2 Switch on the ignition but **do not start the engine.** With the PDWA pistons off centre the brake warning light will glow and the oil pressure warning light will remain off.
3 Exert a steadily increasing pressure on the brake pedal until a click is felt in the pedal and the brake light dims while the oil pressure light starts glowing. The pistons have now centralized and any further pressure will move them off centre in the opposite direction.
4 Switch off the ignition and tighten the bleed nipple.

PART V   THE BRAKE SERVO UNIT

Later cars are fitted with a Girling Powerstop vacuum servo unit as standard, it can also be obtained as a kit of parts for adding to cars not already equipped. This kit is Part Number 514600 and the details of the complete installation are shown in **FIG 10:13**. The internal components of the vacuum servo unit are shown in **FIG 10:14**.

10:15 Operation

Normally the valve assembly 7 is positioned by the control piston 13 so that it closes off the connection to atmospheric pressure (via the filter assembly) and the chambers on both sides of the vacuum piston 40 are interconnected to the vacuum from the inlet manifold. The operating piston 26 has a tapered passage through it and fluid pressure from the master cylinder passes directly through this hole to the brakes. This allows the brakes to operate even if the servo has failed. At this stage the fluid pressure on either side of the control piston is equal but, as it acts on different area at either end face, the control piston will move so that the valve closes the interconnection between the vacuum chambers and opens the rear chamber to atmosphere. The pressure difference moves the piston 40 forwards and the seal 42 closes the hole through the operating piston 26. The operating piston is pressed forward and the fluid in front of it is further pressurized by this action thus increasing the pressure to the brakes. This brake pressure fluid is acting on the smaller face of the control piston and as it is higher than the pressure from the master cylinder a point is reached where the pressure difference cancels out the effect of the differential areas on the control piston. The control piston then closes both valves and the pressure is held until the input pressure from the master cylinder is varied. When the input pressure is released the control piston is returned to its original position by the spring 16 and the two chambers are again interconnected to vacuum so that the piston 40 is returned by the spring 41. The seal 42 is retracted from the operating piston 26 and the hydraulic pressure throughout the system returns to atmospheric pressure.

Basically then the servo uses different air pressures on either side of a piston to augment the hydraulic pressure from the master cylinder and feedback is provided in the hydraulic circuit to vary the output in relation to the input The system is fail-safe in that a direct hydraulic linkage to the brakes is provided in the event of vacuum failure.

10:16 Maintenance

1 The air filter 4 should be renewed at regular intervals, depending on the climatic conditions in which the car is used.

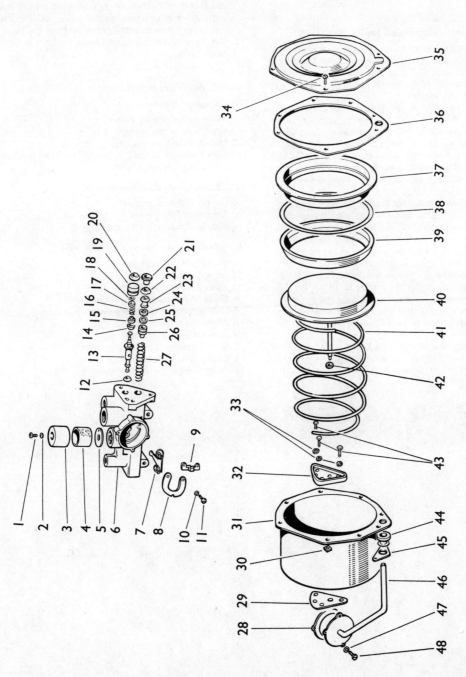

FIG 10:14   Brake servo unit details

Key to Fig 10:14   1 Screw   2 Washer   3 Filter cover   4 Filter element   5 Rubber pad   6 Servo body   7 Valve assembly   8 Spring   9 Retainer   10 Washer
11 Screw   12 Secondary seal   13 Control piston   14 Primary seal   15 Abutment plate   16 Spring   17 Retainer   18 Circlip   19 Plug   20 Taper seal   21 Bush
22 Gland seal   23 Spacer   24 Circlip   25 Washer   26 Output piston   27 Spring   28 Joint washer   29 Joint washer   30 Nut   31 Vacuum cylinder
32 Clamping plate   33 Washers   34 Screw   35 Screw   36 Joint washer   37 Seal retainer   38 Backing ring   39 Seal   40 Vacuum piston   41 Spring
42 Seal   43 Screws   44 Grommet   45 Retainer   46 Vacuum pipe   47 Washer   48 Screw

2 An exchange unit should be fitted every 36,000 miles (or 3 years). If need be the unit can be dismantled and all the seals renewed instead of exchanging the unit. A service kit provided for this contains all the necessary parts.

10:17 Servo unit testing and faults

Apply the handbrake firmly and securely jack up the front wheels. This is really only necessary for the final test but all the tests can be carried out with the front wheels off the ground. Make sure that the gearlever is in neutral, and start the engine.

1 Pump the brake pedal slowly. It should be possible to hear the hiss of the air inlet, and feel the unit working by laying a hand on the vacuum cylinder. If the unit does not operate check that vacuum is reaching it. Also check the non-return valve between the hose to the inlet manifold and the banjo connection on the unit. If both of these are satisfactory then there is an internal fault.

2 Leave the engine running for at least half a minute and then switch it off. After two minutes with the engine off apply the brakes and check that the servo operates as detailed in test 1. If the unit does not operate then repeat the test and clamp the vacuum hose just before switching off the engine. If the test is now satisfactory then the non-return valve in the hose is defective. Check for leaks through the air valve by removing the filter assembly and placing a finger over the air inlet. If the suction is slight then the air valve assembly is satisfactory and there is an air leak elsewhere in the system.

3 Restart the engine and apply the brake hard for 15 to 20 seconds. If the brake pedal creeps then there are scores or leaks in the components of the brake system.

The whole system must be systematically checked until the defective component is found.

4 Apply the brakes and release them. The front wheels should be free to spin within half a second of releasing the brake. If the brakes stick on then repeat the test with the vacuum hose to the servo disconnected. If the brakes now operate correctly then the fault is in the servo and a misaligned vacuum piston is the most likely fault.

10:18 Fault diagnosis

(a) Spongy pedal

1 Air in the hydraulic system
2 Fluid leak in the system
3 Defective master cylinder
4 Gap between the underside of the friction linings and shoes on rear brakes

(b) Excessive pedal movement

1 Check 1, 2 and 3 in (a)
2 Excessive lining wear
3 Very low fluid level in reservoir

(c) Brakes grab or pull to one side

1 Wet or oily friction linings
2 Seized wheel cylinder
3 Seized handbrake cable
4 Cracked or distorted front brake disc
5 High spots on rear brake drum
6 Worn out friction linings
7 Uneven tyre pressures
8 Mixed linings of different grades
9 Broken shoe return springs
10 Defective suspension or steering

CHAPTER 11

THE ELECTRICAL SYSTEM

11 : 1 Description
11 : 2 The battery
11 : 3 Servicing motors
11 : 4 The generator
11 : 5 The generator control box
11 : 6 The starter motor
11 : 7 The alternator
11 : 8 The windscreen wipers

11 : 9 The horns
11 : 10 The fuses
11 : 11 The headlamps
11 : 12 The direction indicators
11 : 13 Fuel and temperature gauges
11 : 14 Seat belt warning system
11 : 15 Fault diagnosis

11 : 1 Description

All the models covered by this manual are fitted with a negative earthed electrical system. **It is particularly important to observe the correct polarity of the circuit when items containing diodes or transistors are fitted. These items, such as alternators, radios etc. may be irreparably damaged if a reversed voltage is applied to them.** For this reason such circuits should be disconnected if the battery is being boost-charged or if any arc-welding operations are to be carried out on the car.

A 12-volt lead/acid battery stores electrical power for starting the engine and running accessories and lights when the engine is not running. On the Vitesse models power is supplied by a generator but on GT6 models an alternator replaces the generator. In all cases the generator or alternator is driven by a belt from the engine pulley. The generator output is controlled by a separate control box while the alternator has its control unit integral with the alternator. In all cases a warning light is fitted to the dash to indicate that the battery is not being charged.

A 12-volt test bulb or any reasonable voltmeter are quite suitable for carrying out continuity checks and to a limited degree high resistance in the circuit can be detected. However, high-grade moving coil instruments are essential whenever tests or adjustments are made on components, as cheap and unreliable instruments are incapable of measuring to the accuracy required.

Wiring Diagrams are shown in Technical Data at the end of this manual so that the wiring can be traced and faults cured. Detailed instructions for servicing the electrical equipment are given in this chapter but it is foolish to attempt to repair any item that is seriously defective, either electrically or mechanically. It is better to renew such items on an exchange basis than to carry out expensive and possibly unsatisfactory repairs.

11 : 2 The battery

The battery is one of the most vital parts of the electrical system and is also the part most likely to suffer if maintenance is neglected. If the following instructions are regularly carried out the full life of the battery will be assured and starting troubles will be minimized:

1 Always keep the top of the battery clean and dry. Dirt or moisture will provide a leakage path to the adjacent metal parts. If the battery surround has become corroded, then the battery should be taken out of the car, and all acidity neutralized using either dilute

FIG 11 : 1 Heavy discharge check

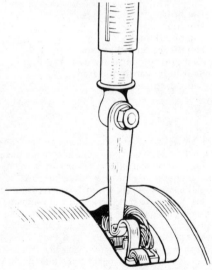

FIG 11 : 2 Checking brush spring tension

ammonia or baking powder in warm water. Wash the area with plenty of clean water and when the parts are dry, paint them with anti-sulphuric paint.

2 Keep the battery terminal posts and their connectors clean and tight. Galvanic corrosion products should be washed off with dilute ammonia (or baking powder solution) and the terminal posts and connectors lightly smeared with petroleum jelly before they are reconnected. The petroleum jelly will prevent the formation of more corrosion. Special tools are available for cleaning the terminal posts but light

coatings of oxide can be scraped off with a sharp knife. Make sure that the connectors are secure but do not overtighten the securing screws.

3 Check that the level of the electrolyte is above the separators, or up to the bottom of the filling tubes on Auto-Fil batteries. If the level is low, top up using only pure distilled water. On Auto-Fil batteries this is accomplished by removing the cover and filling the trough until all the tubes are filled. Replacing the cover automatically displaces the balls and breaks the air lock, allowing the electrolyte to fall to the correct level.

4 If the battery is removed from the car for storage or the car is not in use for long periods, the battery should be given a freshening up charge at monthly intervals. If this is not carried out the plates will sulphate and the battery become ruined. Normally vent plugs are removed from the battery when charging but on Auto-Fil batteries the cover should be left in place, holding back the balls and allowing a free passage for the gases given off.

Electrolyte :

Never add concentrated acid to the battery. Electrolyte of the correct specific gravity should only be added to the battery to replace any that has been lost by spillage or leakage, and distilled water only is required to replace evaporation losses. It is best to obtain ready mixed electrolyte, but if it is to be made up from concentrated sulphuric acid and distilled water take great care in handling the acid as it is extremely dangerous. Use a suitable container as a great deal of heat is given off in the mixing, and **add the acid to the water. Never add water to concentrated acid.**

The condition and specific gravity of the electrolyte will give a great deal of information on the battery. Use an hydrometer to measure the specific gravity, drawing up sufficient electrolyte to ensure that the float is suspended freely. The indications of the readings are as follows:

For climates below 32°C (90°F)	Specific gravity
Cell fully charged	1.270 to 1.290
Cell half-charged	1.190 to 1.210
Cell discharged	1.110 to 1.130

Replace spillage with electrolyte of specific gravity 1.270.

For climates above 32°C (90°F)	Specific gravity
Cell fully charged	1.210 to 1.230
Cell half-charged	1.130 to 1.150
Cell discharged	1.050 to 1.070

Replace spillage with electrolyte of specific gravity 1.210.

These figures are given for a standard electrolyte temperature of 16°C (60°F) and for accurate results the reading should be converted to standard by adding .002 for every 3°C (5°F) rise and subtracting for every increment fall in temperature.

All the cells should give approximately the same readings and if one is out then that cell is suspect. If the electrolyte appears dirty or full of small specks then this is another indication of a faulty cell.

The individual cells can be tested using a heavy discharge tester across the inter-cell connections, as shown in **FIG 11 : 1**. Do not hold the tester in place for more than 6 seconds as the current flow is in the order of 150 to 200 amps per cell. All six cells should give the same readings and, depending on the type of instrument, each cell should maintain 1.2 to 1.7 volts for five seconds. A rapid voltage drop indicates a defective cell. Do not carry out this test on a battery that is known to be low in charge.

11:3 Servicing motors

A generator can be considered as a motor that is driven and produces current so the instructions in this section are equally applicable to generators.

The design of motors will vary in detail but the following will apply in general to all motors, and to the generator.

Brushgear:

Dismantle sufficiently to examine the brushgear. Renew the brushes if they are worn to less than their minimum length (given in Technical Data). If the brushgear is pivoted check that it moves freely on its pivots. Brushes fitted in brushboxes should slide freely; check by pulling gently on the flexible connectors. If the brushes stick, then remove them and polish their sides on a smooth file, cleaning the brushboxes with a petrol-moistened piece of cloth. Replace brushes so that they are in their original positions and the bedding is not disturbed.

All brushes are fitted with some type of spring to keep them in firm contact with the armature. Use a spring balance, modified if necessary, to measure the spring tension or pressure. A spring balance suitable for starter motors is shown in **FIG 11:2**. Renew the springs if they are weaker than the limits given (see Technical Data).

Commutators:

Normally these should only require wiping over with a petrol-moistened cloth and cleaning out carbon dust from between the segments. The commutator should have a darkened but smooth and polished surface. Minor scores and pitting can be polished off using a strip of fine glass-paper (never use emerycloth as this will leave particles embedded in the copper). Deeper damage can be taken off in a lathe, using the highest speed possible and a very sharp tool. The best finish is obtained by taking a light final cut using a diamond tipped tool but a good finish can be obtained by polishing with very fine glasspaper. The insulation between the segments on starter motors must not be undercut. On generators, the insulation is already sufficiently undercut and the slots only need cleaning out.

Armatures:

Special equipment is required to test the coils of the armature winding. If isolated commutator segments are burned then it is likely that some of the coils are damaged. If any of the laminations on the armature are scored the cause is either a bent armature shaft (scoring on one side only), loose polepieces, or badly worn bearings (the latter two will cause scoring all round). **Never try to straighten a bent armature shaft and never machine an armature.** If it is suspected that the armature is faulty, either have it tested at a garage or fit one of known performance as a check.

Bearings:

On larger motors either porous bronze bushes or ball-bearings will be fitted. Smaller motors with have either bushes or spherical self-aligning bearings.

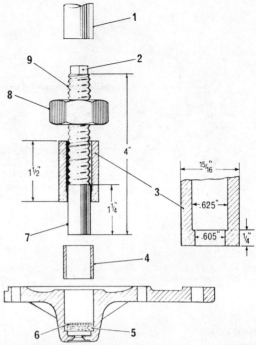

FIG 11:3 Refitting porous bronze bushes. The dimensions given are for the generator bush

Key to Fig 11:3   1 Press   2 Squared end   3 Sleeve
4 Porous bronze bearing bush   5 Felt ring
6 Felt ring retainer   7 Fitting pin (.5924 inch diameter)
8 Extracting nut   9 Thread ($\frac{5}{8}$ inch BSF truncated 614 inch)

Spherical bearings are usually held in place by a riveted spring clip and if they are worn the assembly must be replaced complete. They should be checked for freedom of movement in the clip and lightly lubricated all over with a little engine oil.

Porous bronze bushes can be removed by screwing a suitably sized tap squarely in for a few threads and withdrawing the old bush on the tap. Before fitting, a new bush must be soaked in engine oil for at least 24 hours. The period can be reduced by heating the oil to 100°C (over a bath of boiling water) and soaking at this temperature for 2 hours, removing the bush from the oil when it is cool. **FIG 11:3** shows the method of refitting the bush to the generator end bracket. A similar method must be used for the starter motor bushes, but use a highly polished fitting pin .7490 ± .0005 inch for the drive end bracket bush and .4985 ± .0005 inch for the commutator end bracket bush. Take care to replace any felt or metal washers fitted under the bush.

Ballbearings are usually held in place by a retainer secured with rivets. Drill off the heads of the rivets and use a suitable pin punch to drive out the rivet stems. The parts can then be removed or pressed out. Pack the new bearing with Shell Alvania RA grease or equivalent before refitting the parts in the reverse order of removal. It should be noted that on the generator the bearing and its associated parts are held in place by a circlip.

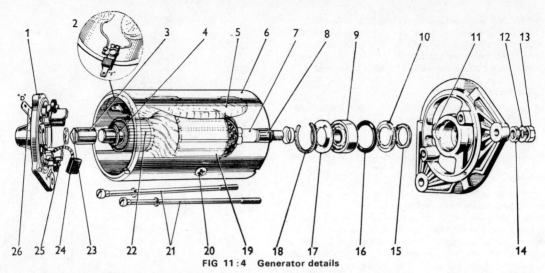

FIG 11:4   Generator details

Key to Fig 11:4   1 Commutator end bracket   2 Field connector and field winding earth lead   3 Porous bronze bearing bush
4 Fibre thrust washer   5 Field winding   6 Yoke   7 Shaft   8 Key   9 Ballrace   10 Pressure ring and felt ring retaining plate
11 Drive end bracket   12 Washer   13 Shaft nut   14 Pulley spacer   15 Felt ring   16 Pressure ring   17 Bearing retaining plate
18 Circlip   19 Armature   20 Pole shoe screw   21 Through-bolts   22 Commutator   23 Felt ring retainer   24 Brush
25 Felt ring   26 Output connector

Field coils:

On the generator and starter motor these are held in place by the polepieces. The screws which hold the pole-pieces require a special wheel screwdriver to remove or replace them, so the task is best left to a garage. Some smaller motors may be fitted with permanent magnets instead of field coils.

If the resistance of the field coils is given (see Technical Data) then this should be checked either using an ohmeter or connecting an ammeter and 12-volt supply in series with the coil. Use Ohms law $(V = I \times R)$ to determine the current. A high resistance and a low or nil current indicates an open circuit or break in the wire. A low resistance and high current indicates a short circuit. If the resistance is not given, then the coils should be checked for continuity using a test bulb (12-volt will do but a 110 AC volt check is better). The coil should also be tested for a short circuit by connecting the test bulb and supply between the terminal and the yoke.

11:4 The generator

The generator details are shown in **FIG 11:4**. Refer also to **Section 11:3** for details on checking and servicing the parts.

Routine maintenance:

1 At 6000 mile intervals check that the fan belt is at the correct tension, as described in **Chapter 4, Section 4:4**. Renew the fan belt if it is fraying or showing signs of wear.

2 At 12,000 mile intervals inject a few drops of oil through the hole in the commutator end bracket. Do not overlubricate otherwise oil will find its way onto the commutator and brushgear.

3 At 24,000 mile intervals remove the generator and inspect the brushgear and commutator.

Generator tests:

1 Check that the driving belt is at the correct tension and not slipping.

2 Disconnect the electrical cables from the D and F terminals on the generator and bridge the terminals with a short length of wire. Connect an accurate 0–20 voltmeter between the interconnected terminals and a good earth on the car.

3 Start the engine and gradually increase the speed, noting the readings on the voltmeter. The reading should rise steadily and rapidly with the engine speed. An engine speed of 730 rev/min should be sufficient to reach 20 volts. **Do not race the engine and do not exceed an output of 20 volts.** If the reading fluctuates violently then there is a defect in the generator. No reading indicates faulty brushgear. If the maximum reading only reaches 1-volt then it is likely that the field coils are faulty and a reading of only 4 to 5 volts indicates defective armature coils.

4 If the generator performs satisfactorily, then stop the engine and reconnect the cables to the generator, leaving the jumper wire in place. Disconnect the same cables from the D and F terminals on the control box and the earth cable from the E terminal. Repeat the test between the individual D and F cables and the earth cable. In both cases the readings should be exactly the same as for the generator alone. If the readings differ then there is either a fault in the cables or in the earthing of the control box.

5 Remove the jumper wire from between the generator terminals and reconnect all the cables to their correct terminals.

Dismantling the generator:

1 Remove the generator by slackening all three mounting bolts and easing the fan belt off the generator pulley. Free the generator from the car by removing the three

mounting bolts after disconnecting the cables from the D and F terminals.

2 Remove the two through-bolts 21 and ease off the commutator end bracket 1. The yoke 6 can be slid off the armature.

3 Further dismantling is only necessary if the bearing 9 needs renewal or another armature 19 needs to be fitted. Remove the nut 13, washer 12, generator pulley and spacer 14. Carefully remove the key 8 from the shaft 7 and press the armature shaft out of the bearing. The bearing 9 and its parts can be removed from the drive end bracket 11 after taking out the circlip 18.

The generator is reassembled in the reverse order of dismantling. When refitting the commutator end bracket slide the brushes up into their brushboxes and hold them there by resting the brush springs on the side of the brushes. When the end bracket is refitted use a thin screwdriver through the bracket slots to lift the springs back into position on the brushes. Both end brackets are cast with little pips and these fit into slots on the end of the yoke to ensure alignment of the parts.

Generator data :

Brush minimum length	$\frac{9}{32}$ inch
Brush material	H.100 grade carbon
Brush spring tension	17 to 32 ozs
Minimum diameter of commutator	1.430 inch
Field coil resistance	5.9 ± .3 ohm (2 amps at 12 volts)
Porous bronze bush removal replacement	Use $\frac{5}{8}$ inch tap .5924 inch highly-polished mandrel

11 : 5 The generator control box

It is essential that only high-grade instruments are used to test or adjust the Lucas RB.340 control box. Before carrying out any adjustments on the control box check through the following points to ensure that the fault does not lie outside the control box.

1 Test the generator and its cables, as well as the control box earth point as described in **Section 11 : 4**.

2 Check the battery to ensure that it is capable of holding a charge and check the battery connections to ensure that high resistance there is not preventing the battery from charging or supplying sufficient current.

3 If the main symptom is that the battery is flat, check that the car has not been used only for low-mileage journeys not long enough to allow the generator to recharge the battery after frequent starts.

Cleaning contacts :

Dirty contacts can cause erratic operation of the unit. All regulator contacts—Use a fine carborundum stone or silicone carbide paper.

Cut-out contacts—Use only fine glasspaper, **never emery, silicone carbide or carborundum.**

After the points have been cleaned remove loose dirt and filings with a clean piece of cloth moistened in methylated spirits.

A view of the control box with the cover removed is shown in **FIG 11 : 5**. On some units the cover will be held in place by a special type of rivet expanded by a removable plug.

VR   CR   CO
FIG 11 : 5   Control box with cover removed

Key to Fig 11 : 5   **VR** Voltage regulator
CR Current regulator   **CO** Cut-out

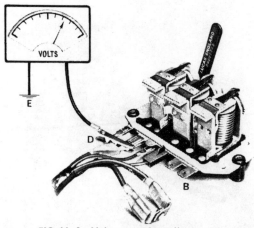

FIG 11 : 6   Voltage setting adjustment

Voltage setting :

The cover need only be removed if the setting has to be adjusted. Adjustments are made by turning the cam with a special tool. Checks and adjustments should be completed as rapidly as possible to avoid heating of the coils from giving spurious readings.

1 Refer to **FIG 11 : 6**. Disconnect both leads from the B terminals and connect the leads together to allow battery voltage to reach the ignition. Either partially withdraw the lead to the D terminal or disconnect the warning light lead from the WL terminal which is in electrical contact with the D terminal. Connect a voltmeter between the terminal and earth as shown.

2 Start the engine and run it at 2200 rev/min. The voltmeter reading should be steady between the following limits:

Ambient temperature	Voltage setting
10°C (50°F)	14.9 to 15.5
20°C (68°F)	14.7 to 15.3
30°C (86°F)	14.5 to 15.1
40°C (104°F)	14.3 to 14.9

If the voltage fluctuates then clean the contact points. If the voltage still fluctuates, there is an internal fault in the unit.

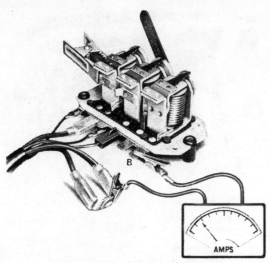

FIG 11:7   Current setting adjustment

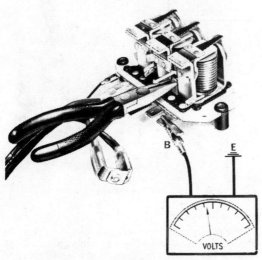

FIG 11:8   Drop off voltage adjustment

3 The unit may be adjusted provided that the voltage is steady though outside the limits. Turning the adjustment cam clockwise will decrease the reading and turning it anticlockwise will increase the voltage reading. When the adjustment is satisfactory, replace the cover and correctly connect the cables.

Current setting:

Again the adjustments must be completed as rapidly as possible. **FIG 11:7** shows the circuit for testing, the adjusting tool in place and a bulldog clip shorting the voltage regulator contacts to prevent it from operating.
1 Switch on all the lights so that the generator will develop its maximum output. Start the engine and run it at 3300 rev/min. **Do not switch on the lights while the engine is running, only before starting, otherwise the bulbs will blow.**

2 The ammeter should give a steady reading between 24 and 26 amps. If the reading fluctuates, then clean the cut-out points and repeat the test. Provided that the reading is steady but outside the limits, it can be raised by turning the adjusting cam anticlockwise to increase the current or clockwise to decrease the current. Replace the cover and restore the circuit to normal after completing the checks and adjustments.

Cut-in voltage:

Connect a voltmeter between the partially exposed D terminal (or the WL terminal) and a good earth point.
1 Start the engine and switch on all the lights. Gradually increase the engine speed while noting the voltmeter reading. The reading should rise steadily until the points close and then it will drop back slightly.
2 Note the maximum reading that the voltmeter reaches just before the points open. This should lie between 12.7 and 13.3 volts. Turn the adjusting cam on the cut-out in an anticlockwise or clockwise direction to increase or decrease the voltage reading.
3 Repeat the test, using small adjustments every time, until the reading is within the correct limits. Replace the cover and restore the circuit to normal.

Drop off voltage:

The circuit and point of adjustment are shown in **FIG 11:8**.
1 Start the engine and run it up to approximately 2200 rev/min. Slowly decrease the engine speed noting the voltmeter readings.
2 When the cut-out operates the voltage will drop to zero. Note the minimum reading on the voltmeter before this occurs; this should lie between 9.5 and 11.0 volts.
3 If the drop-off voltage is incorrect then remove the control box cover. Bend the cut-out fixed contact slightly to reduce the gap if the reading is low and outwards to slightly increase the gap if the reading is high. Repeat the test and adjustments until the reading is correct. Replace the cover and correctly reconnect the circuit.

11:6 The starter motor

The starter motor details are shown in **FIG 11:9**.

Starter motor does not operate:

1 Check the condition of the battery and pay especial attention to the terminal, posts and connectors, as high resistance at the connections is a common cause of the battery failing to provide sufficient current to operate the starter motor.
2 Switch on the lights and again attempt to operate the starter motor. If the lights dim then current is being taken by the motor, and it is possible that it is jammed in mesh. Either use a spanner on the squared end of the shaft to rotate the motor and free it, or engage a gear and rock the car backwards and forwards to unjam the starter motor. If these methods fail to free the starter motor then it must be removed for further checks. Worn pinion or flywheel ring gear teeth can cause the motor to jam.

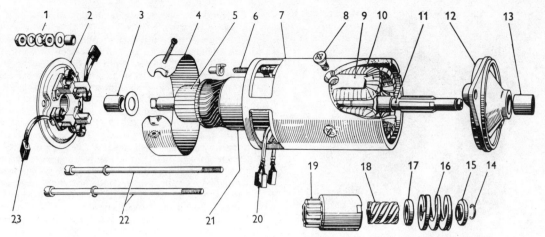

FIG 11:9 Starter motor details

Key to Fig 11:9   1 Terminal post nuts and washers   2 Commutator end bracket   3 Commutator end bracket bearing bush   4 Coverband   5 Commutator   6 Terminal post   7 Yoke   8 Pole shoe screw   9 Pole shoe   10 Field windings   11 Shaft   12 Drive end bracket   13 Drive end bracket bearing bush   14 Jump ring   15 Shaft collar   16 Main spring   17 Buffer washer   18 Screwed sleeve   19 Pinion and barrel   20 Field winding brush   21 Armature   22 Through-bolts   23 Earth brush

3 If the lights do not dim then there is probably a fault in the wiring. Manually press the rubber covered button on the starter solenoid, shown in **FIG 11:10**. If the starter motor now operates then it is likely that the starter switch or its wiring is defective, though the possibility of a coil failing in the starter solenoid should not be discounted. If the motor still does not operate, the short across the solenoid terminals using either a pair of old pliers or thick piece of rod. If the starter now operates then the starter solenoid is defective and must be renewed. When the solenoid operates it will do so with a click. Very low battery voltage will cause the solenoid to engage and then free rapidly, giving a series of clicks.

4 If the circuit is satisfactory and power is reaching as far as the motor but the motor does not operate, then it must be removed for further examination.

Dismantling the starter motor:

1 The brushgear and commutator can be examined after removing the cover band 4.
2 Remove the field winding brushes 20 from their brushboxes. Remove the terminal nuts, washers and insulating bush 1.
3 Unscrew the two through-bolts 22 and remove the commutator end cover 2. The yoke 7 can now be slid off the armature.
4 For further dismantling the starter drive must be removed.

Reassemble the motor in the reverse order of dismantling. Slide the brushes 23 up into their brushboxes and hold them there by resting the springs on the sides of the brushes until the commutator end bracket 2 is refitted. Do not overtighten the locknuts 1 otherwise the terminal post may be damaged.

Starter drive:

Compress the spring 16, preferably using handpress No. S.4221A and adaptor set No. S.4221A-14, and remove the jump ring 14. The parts can then be slid off the shaft.

Wash the parts in clean fuel and then lubricate them lightly with clean engine oil. Replace them in the reverse order of removal. Renew both the screwed sleeve 18 and the pinion and barrel 19 as an assembly if either are worn.

Test the starter motor after reassembly. For full tests a torque measuring rig and high current ammeter are required (the data is given in Technical Data). Clamp the starter motor in a vice so that the bared end of a heavy duty cable is clamped against the yoke. Connect the other end of the cable to the negative terminal on a 12-volt battery. Similarly connect another heavy duty cable between the positive terminal of the battery and the terminal on the motor. The motor should run at high speed and turn freely taking a maximum current of 60 amps.

Starter motor data:

Brush minimum length	$\frac{5}{16}$ inch
Brush spring tension	30 to 34 oz
Minimum diameter of commutator	$1\frac{9}{32}$ inch

Commutator end porous bronze bush

Removal	Use $\frac{9}{16}$ inch tap
Replacement	.4985 $\pm$ .0005 inch mandrel

Drive end porous bronze bush

Removal	Use $1\frac{3}{16}$ inch tap
Replacement	.7490 $\pm$ .0005 inch mandrel

11:7 The alternator

The alternator details are shown in **FIG 11:11. Never disconnect or reconnect any part of the charging circuit when the engine is running, otherwise the components may be damaged.**

FIG 11:10 Starter solenoid

Before checking the alternator for defects check the following points:
1 The drive belt must be at the correct tension and not slipping on the pulleys.
2 Check the condition of the battery and the battery terminals.
3 Run the engine at 2870 rev/min (alternator running at 6000 rev/min), switch on the headlamps and check that the voltage drop between the alternator + blade and battery positive terminal does not exceed .5-volt. Similarly check that the voltage drop between the alternator — blade and the battery negative terminal does not exceed .25-volt.

Alternator checks:

This method tests only the alternator, leaving the control unit inoperative. If the equipment is not available to carry out this check then a diode check should be carried out as described later. If the alternator is found to

be defective on test this diode check should be carried out before any other checks.
1 Disconnect the multi-socket connectors and remove the moulded cover 1. Connect up a test circuit as shown in **FIG 11:12, taking great care to observe the correct polarity of the circuit.** Leave the variable resistor 3 disconnected until just before starting the engine otherwise it will drain the battery.
2 Start the engine and gradually increase its speed. At 720 engine rev/min (1500 alternator rev/min) the light 4 should go out.
3 Hold the engine speed steady at 2870 rev/min (6000 alternator rev/min) and adjust the variable resistance 3 until the voltmeter reads 14 volts. Leave the alternator to attain its normal operating temperature and check that the voltmeter still reads 14 volts. The ammeter should then be reading 28 amps.
4 If the ammeter reading does not reach 28 amps then there is a fault in the alternator. Provided that the alternator is satisfactory stop the engine, replace the cover 1 and carry out a control unit check.

Control unit check:

This test should also be performed with the alternator as near as possible to its normal operating temperature.
1 With the multi-socket connector removed, connect up a test circuit as shown in **FIG 11:13, taking great care to observe the correct polarity of the circuit.**
2 Start the engine and gradually increase the speed. The light 3 should go out at an engine speed of 720 rev/min (1500 alternator rev/min).
3 Increase the speed and then hold it steady at 2870 engine rev/min (6000 alternator rev/min). The voltmeter should be steady at 14.0 to 14.4 volts. If the reading is not steady within the limits but the alternator is satisfactory then the control unit is defective and must be renewed.

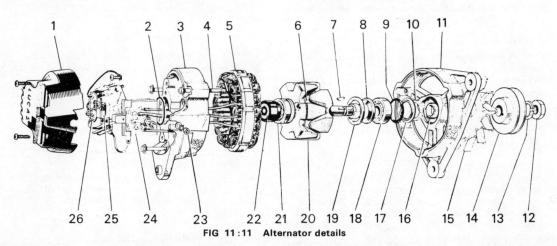

FIG 11:11 Alternator details

Key to Fig 11:11   1 Moulded cover   2 Rubber O-ring   3 Slip ring end bracket   4 Through-bolts   5 Stator windings
6 Field winding   7 Key   8 Bearing retaining plate   9 Pressure ring   10 Felt ring   11 Drive end bracket   12 Nut
13 Spring washer   14 Pulley   15 Fan   16 Spacer   17 Pressure ring and felt ring retaining plate   18 Drive end bearing
19 Circlip   20 Rotor   21 Slip ring end bearing   22 Slip ring moulding   23 Nut   24 Rectifier pack   25 Brushbox assembly
26 Control unit

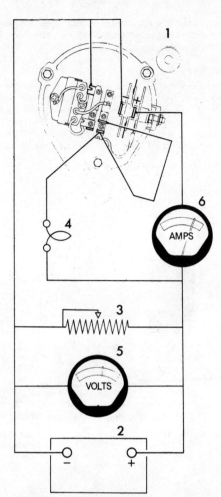

FIG 11:12 Alternator functional check, with control unit inoperative

Key to Fig 11:12   1 Alternator   2 12-volt battery
3 0–15 ohm (35 amp) variable resistor   4 12-volt (2.2 watt)
light   5 0–20-volt voltmeter   6 0–40-amp ammeter

Diode check :

1 Remove the moulded cover and disconnect the 'Lucar' connector from the rectifier pack 24.
2 Carefully note the position of the three stator wires on the diodes. Unsolder the wires from the diodes, **carefully gripping the pin with a pair of pliers so that they act as a heat sink.**
3 Test each diode in turn by connecting a bulb and 12-volt battery as shown in **FIG 11:14.** Test with the voltage in one direction and then reverse the polarity. The bulb should light in one direction only. If it does not light at all or lights in both directions then the diode is faulty and the complete rectifier pack must be renewed.
4 Refit the rectifier pack and solder back the stator wires using a pair of pliers as a heat sink and carrying out the soldering as rapidly as possible.

Dismantling the alternator :

1 Remove the alternator from the car, take off the cover 1 and remove the rectifier pack as described in Diode Check. Remove the brush box and control unit assembly from the rectifier pack by unscrewing the three screws. The control unit may be removed, if required, after noting the position of the three wire eyelets, removing the three screws securing the eyelets and the screw securing the control unit.
2 Place an extractor tool, as shown in **FIG 11:15,** so that it engages with the outer race of the bearing 21. Surplus solder may have to be filed away from the connections on the slip ring moulding 22 so as to allow the tool to pass over the moulding. Have an assistant to hold the slip ring end bracket 3 and carefully drive the bearing out of the bracket by tapping the end of the extractor tool. Leave the rubber O-ring 2 in place unless it is damaged. Remove the stator windings 5 from the drive end bracket 3.
3 Wrap the pulley 14 with a length of old fan belt and grip it carefully in a vice. Unscrew the nut 12, remove

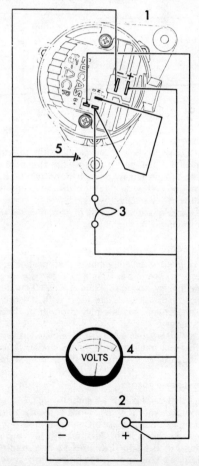

FIG 11:13 Control unit functional check

Key to Fig 11:13   1 Alternator   2 12-volt battery
3 12-volt (2.2 watt) light   4 0–20-volt voltmeter
5 Earth connection to alternator body

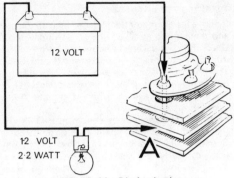

FIG 11:14 Diode check

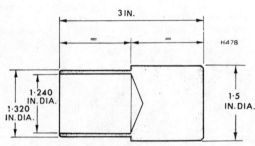

FIG 11:15 Dimensions for extractor tool

the washer 13 and pulley 14. Extract the key 7 from the shaft.

4 Use a press to remove the rotor 20 from the drive end bracket 11. **Do not hammer on the end of the shaft otherwise the threads will become damaged.** The renewal of the bearings will be dealt with separately.

Reassemble the alternator in the reverse order of dismantling.

Brush gear:

Check that the brushes protrude at least .2 inch from the brush box when free. Use a modified spring balance to check that the spring pressure is 7 to 10 ounces when the faces of the brushes are flush with the brush box. Renew the brush box assembly if either of these limits are not reached.

Clean the brushes with petrol-moistened cloth and check that they move freely in the brush box. If necessary polish the sides of the brush lightly, using a smooth file.

Slip rings and rotor:

Check that the slip rings are smooth and clean, cleaning them with a petrol-moistened cloth. If the slip rings show any burn marks, polish these off using very fine glasspaper. **Never use emerycloth, as this will leave particles imbedded in the slip ring, and do not machine the slip rings as this may affect the high speed performance of the alternator.**

The resistance of the field coil winding may be measured between the slip rings and this should be 4.33 ± 5 per cent ohm at 20°C. A 110-volt AC test lamp may be used

between each slip ring and the rotor to ensure that the insulation has not broken down. Renew the rotor if it is defective.

The stator:

After removing the stator the windings may be checked. Connect a 12-volt battery and 36 watt test bulb in series with any pair of stator wires. The bulb should light. Repeat the test by disconnecting any one wire and replacing it with the third wire, and again the bulb should light. A 110 volt AC test bulb may be used to test the

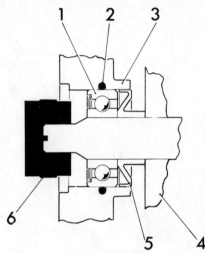

FIG 11:16 Slip ring end bearing details

Key to Fig 11:16   1 Bearing   2 Rubber O-ring
3 Slip ring end bracket   4 Rotor   5 Grease retainer
6 Slip ring moulding

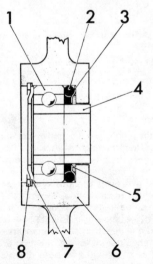

FIG 11:17 Drive end bearing details

Key to Fig 11:17   1 Bearing   2 Pressure ring
3 Pressure ring and felt ring retaining plate   4 Spacer
5 Felt ring   6 Drive end bracket   7 Bearing retaining plate
8 Circlip

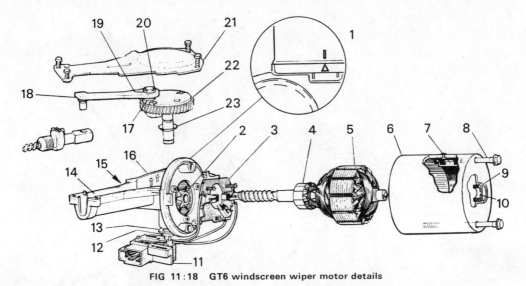

FIG 11:18   GT6 windscreen wiper motor details

Key to Fig 11:18   1 Aligning marks   2 Self-aligning bearing   3 Brush assembly   4 Commutator   5 Armature   6 Cover
7 Permanent magnet   8 Through-bolt   9 Cover bearing   10 Felt washer   11 Limit switch unit   12 Final gear shaft spring clip
13 Washer   14 Cross-head guide channel   15 Thrust screw (non-adjustable) or Thrust screw and locknut (adjustable)
16 Gearbox   17 Washer   18 Connecting rod   19 Washer   20 Crankpin spring clip   21 Gearbox cover   22 Final gear
23 Dished washer

insulation between the wires and the stator core. Renew the stator if it is defective.

The bearings:

Dismantle the alternator as far as is required.

Refer to **FIG 11:16**. Unsolder the two field winding connections to the slip ring moulding 6 and remove the moulding from the shaft. Use a suitable extractor to remove the bearing 1 from the slip ring end bracket 3. Pack the new bearing with Shell Alvania RA grease or equivalent and use a suitable tube to drive the inner race of the bearing into position on the rotor shaft. Replace the slip ring moulding 6 on the shaft, ensuring that the slot in the shaft engages in the projection in the moulding. The moulding may be fitted either way round. Resolder the connections, using Fry's HT 3 solder.

Refer to **FIG 11:17**. Use a large screwdriver to remove the circlip 8 and take out the bearing retaining plate 7. Push out the bearing 1 and its associated parts. Pack the new bearing 1 with Shell Alvania RA grease and reassemble it in the reverse order of dismantling.

11:8 The windscreen wipers

The details of the two speed motor fitted to the GT6 models are shown in **FIG 11:18** and the details of the single speed motor fitted to Vitesse models are shown in **FIG 11:19**.

On the GT6 models there is no adjustment for the park position other than positioning the wiper arms on different blades of the wiper wheelbox spindles, though the relationship of the cam to the crankpin is shown in **FIG 11:20**.

The single speed motor fitted to Vitesse models contains an adjustable parking switch. Slacken the screws securing the gearbox cover and rotate the domed cover to the desired position. On righthand drive models

the identifying pip on the dome should be directly towards the cable rack and on lefthand drive models the pip should be furthest away from the cable rack.

Testing the wiper motor:

If the motor fails to operate then use a voltmeter or test bulb to check that supply is reaching the motor. If supply is not reaching the motor then check the fuse and the wiring. If this is satisfactory remove the gearbox cover and take out the connecting rod linking the final drive gear to the cable rack. Remove the wiper arms and use a spring balance to check that the cable rack moves with a force of less than 6 lb (2.7 kg). If this force is exceeded check that the wheelboxes are aligned and that the tubing is neither pinched or distorted.

Connect an ammeter in series with the motor and switch it on. After running for 60 seconds the motors are correct if they are within the following limits:

Two speed motor (Lucas 14W):

Normal speed 46 to 52 rev/min taking a current of 1.5 amp.

High speed 60 to 70 rev/min taking a current of 2.0 amp.

Single speed motor (Lucas DR3A):

Running speed 45 to 50 rev/min at a current of 2.7 to 3.4 amp.

Motor data:

Two speed motor:
Minimum brush length:

Normal brushes	$\frac{3}{16}$ inch
High speed brush	.28 inch (when narrow portion is worn off).
Brush spring pressure	5 to 7 oz (with brush bottom aligned with brushbox slot end).

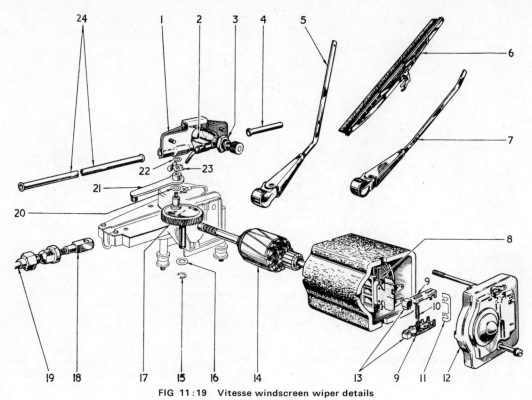

FIG 11:19 Vitesse windscreen wiper details

Key to Fig 11:19   1 Wheel box   2 Jet and bush assembly   3 Nut   4 Righthand side rigid tubing   5 Wiper arm
6 Blade   7 Wiper arm   8 Field coil assembly   9 Brushgear   10 Tension spring and retainers   11 Brushgear retainer
12 End cover   13 Brushes   14 Armature   15 Circlip   16 Washer   17 Final drive wheel   18 Cable rack
19 Lefthand side rigid tubing   20 Spacer   21 Connecting rod   22 Circlip   23 Parking switch contact   24 Centre section
rigid tubing

Single speed motor:

Brush tension	125 to 140 grammes
Field winding resistance	8.0 to 9.5 ohms
Stall current	13 to 15 amps

Armature end float:

On two speed motors the armature end float should be
.002 to .008 inch. On original motors the adjusting screw
is of set length and the end float can only be adjusted by
fitting shims under the head of the screw or by turning off
the underside of the head in a lathe. If a replacement
armature is fitted then a new adjusting screw is supplied
complete with locknut so that the correct end float can
easily be set.

Single speed motor armatures should have an end
float of .008 to .012 inch. The adjusting screw in this case
is always fitted with a locknut.

Wheelboxes:

The wheelboxes on the Vitesse models are shown in
FIG 11:21. The wheelboxes for GT6 models are similarly
attached but to gain access to them facia parts and the
heater demister ducts must also be removed.

1 Remove the wiper arms. Disconnect the cable rack from
   the motor and withdraw the cable rack.

2 From outside the car remove the locknuts and rubber
   bushes securing the wheelboxes and partially press in
   the wheelboxes.

3 Working inside the car, remove sufficient parts to gain
   access to the wheelboxes. Disconnect the windscreen washer tubing. Undo the screws holding the
   cable rack tubing in place and remove the wheelboxes
   from the car.

Replace the wheelboxes in the reverse order of removal ensuring that they align with the cable rack tubing
so that the cable rack will have a smooth run.

11:9 The horns

All the models are fitted with a similar horn system. The
model of horns fitted to the GT6 require a higher operating
current than those fitted to the Vitesse models so a 6RA
horn relay is fitted to the GT6 models.

If the horns are out of adjustment they will not change
pitch but instead will sound rough and consume
excessive current, which will lead to early failure. Before
adjusting the horns check that their mounting bolts are
secure and that the horns are not fouling against any
adjacent structure.

Remove the fuse and bridge the terminals with a piece
of wire. Test one horn at a time. Connect an ammeter in

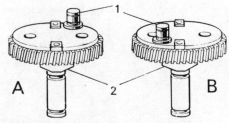

FIG 11:20 Relationship of crankpin to cam for correct parking position on GT6 models

Key to Fig 11:20   **A** Park position (cable rack retracted)
B Park position (cable rack extended)   **1** Crankpin
2 Cam

series with the horn and turn the adjusting screw until the operating current is 7.0 to 7.5 amps on GT6 models and 3.5 to 4.0 amps on Vitesse models. **Do not slacken or disturb the centre slotted core or its locknut.**

If an ammeter is not available then unscrew the adjusting screw anticlockwise until the horn just fails to sound. Screw the adjusting screw back clockwise for quarter of a turn and this will be a reasonably accurate setting.

A defective horn cannot be dismantled and must be renewed.

11:10 The fuses

GT6:

The fuse box is illustrated in **FIG 11:22**. The cover is transparent and need not be removed to examine the fuses. Three operational fuses are fitted and there is space for two spare fuses. All the fuses are 35 amp rated and colour coded white.

The top fuse protects all the circuits controlled by the ignition switch, apart from the ignition circuit itself. The centre fuse protects the side lights and number plate illuminating lamp. The bottom fuse protects the following circuits; horn, headlamp flasher, roof lamp and hazard warning (if fitted).

Vitesse:

A fuse box containing two operational and two spare fuses is fitted to the bulkhead. The fuse fed by the white cable protects the circuits controlled by the ignition switch. Both fuses in the fuse box are 35 amp rated and colour coded white. A separate line fuse, shown in **FIG 11:23**, is fitted to protect the side light and number plate illumination circuits. If the fuse is not visible pull gently on the brown/red and red wires to draw the fuse out. The actual fuse is held in the unit by a bayonet type fitting and is 25 amp rated and colour coded pink.

11:11 The headlamps

Four headlamps are fitted to Vitesse models but only two to GT6 models. All the headlights are fitted with sealed units where the filaments are sealed into the reflector and lens to form one complete unit. If a fault develops in the unit, such as a blown filament or cracked lens (which will cause the filaments to burn out) then the unit must be replaced. On both models the headlamps are held in place by small screws. Remove the trim and these screws, **taking care not to turn the adjusting screws**, and turn the headlamp assembly anticlockwise

to free it from the adjusting screws. The sealed unit can then be disconnected from the adaptor and removed from its case.

Beam adjustment is set by turning the adjusting screws, but this should only be done using specialized equipment to ensure that the beams are set not only for best illumination but also to comply with current lighting regulations.

11:12 The direction indicators

The GT6 is fitted with a Lucas 8FL 3.6A flasher unit below the facia panel on the righthand side of the bulkhead. The Vitesse is fitted with a Lucas FL5 flasher unit located behind the facia on the lefthand side dash panel.

The units are similar in that they are sealed and are operated by the alternate cooling and heating of a bimetallic strip, and that mishandling will damage them both. Once defective, a unit cannot be repaired but must be renewed.

If the direction indicators cease to function then remove the flasher unit and check that battery voltage is reaching the B terminal. If voltage is not reaching the terminal, check the fuse and trace back along the wiring until the fault is found.

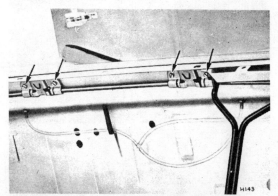

FIG 11:21 Vitesse wiper wheelbox attachments

FIG 11:22 GT6 fuse box

FIG 11:23 Vitesse line fuse

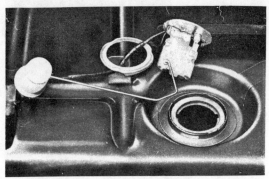

FIG 11:24 GT6 tank unit

FIG 11:25 Vitesse tank unit fitted

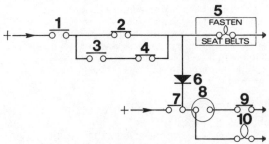

FIG 11:26 Schematic wiring diagram for the seat belt warning and key warning systems

Key to Fig 11:26 1 Gearbox switch 2 Driver's belt switch 3 Passenger's seat switch 4 Passenger's belt switch 5 Warning light 6 Diode 7 Driver's door switch 8 Buzzer 9 Key switch 10 Key light

If voltage is reaching the terminal, then connect the B and L terminals of the socket together with a jumper wire and operate the direction indicator switch in both directions with the ignition switched on. If the appropriate lamps now light then the flasher unit is faulty and must be replaced. If the lamps do not light then the fault lies either in the switch, wiring or bulbs. If one lamp does not light check both the bulb and the earthing of the lamp.

11:13 Fuel and temperature gauges

The supply for both these systems is provided by a voltage stabilizer. This is mounted on the back of the speedometer. If the unit is removed it must be refitted so that the B and E terminals are uppermost and the unit is not tilted more than 20 deg.

The voltage stabilizer uses the heating and cooling of a bi-metallic strip to open and close the output contacts giving, over a period of time, the exact equivalent of a steady 10 volts for the same period of time. If an ordinary voltmeter is used to measure the output the voltage will slowly fluctuate between battery voltage and some lower figure. For this reason special test equipment is required to check the systems, which will take about a minute to reach their operating figures.

The transmitters vary their resistance in proportion to the quantity to be measured (either fuel level or coolant temperature) and as the supply voltage is equivalent to a constant over a period of time, the current, over a period of time, that flows through the circuit will also be proportional to the quantity to be measured. This current flows through the instrument and heats a small coil. This coil is wrapped around a bi-metallic strip and the bending of the bi-metallic strip moves the instrument pointer.

All the components of the system are sealed and must be renewed if defective.

GT6 tank unit:

The unit is shown in FIG 11:24 and is removed by tapping the locking ring anticlockwise. No sealing compound is required when replacing the unit. Access is by folding forward the luggage floor carpet, removing the spare wheel cover and then removing the fuel tank cover panel.

Vitesse tank unit:

The installation is shown in FIG 11:25. Before removing the unit check that the fuel tank contains less than 3 gallons of petrol to ensure that the level is below the fuel tank unit. Drain out excess fuel if the tank contains more than 3 gallons.

The unit is held in place by six screws and is sealed with a cork washer and jointing compound on the mating faces. When refitting the unit a new cork washer must be used and all traces of old jointing compound removed.

When removing a tank unit take great care not to bend or damage the float arm.

Faulty readings:

Never connect battery voltage directly across the instruments. Before checking the instruments and transmitters check through the wiring and fuse. Defective insulation will cause high readings while broken wires will cause nil readings. Loose or faulty connectors will cause the readings to fluctuate. If the readings are still incorrect then the faulty component will have to be isolated by a process of elimination, unless a suitable tester is available. If there is no output but a voltmeter shows that power is reaching the voltage stabilizer unit then the unit is defective and must be replaced. A defective voltage stabilizer will affect both instruments.

11:14 Seat belt warning system

The electrical circuit for this device, fitted to USA cars only, is shown in **FIG 11:26**, its operation is as follows:

The light 5 on the instrument panel will light up and the buzzer 8 sound if the ignition is switched on and a gear selected without the driver's seat belt being fastened and actuating the switch 2.

If the front passenger seat is occupied the seat belt must be fastened to actuate switch 4, otherwise the light and the buzzer will operate since the passenger's weight will actuate switch 3.

Also shown in the diagram are the connections for the key warning system which causes the buzzer to sound if the driver's door is opened while the ignition key is still in the ignition lock.

11:15 Fault diagnosis

(a) Battery discharged

1 Terminals loose or dirty
2 Insufficient charging current
3 Shortcircuit in parts of system not protected by fuses
4 Battery defective internally

(b) Battery will not hold charge

1 Low electrolyte level
2 Battery plates sulphated or plate separators ineffective
3 Electrolyte leakage from cracked casing or top sealing compound

(c) Generator output low or nil

1 Driving belt broken or slipping
2 Control box out of adjustment or defective
3 Generator mechanically defective
4 Insulation standing proud between commutator segments
5 Commutator worn, dirty or burned
6 Brushes sticking or excessively worn
7 Weak or broken brush springs
8 Armature or field coils defective

(d) Alternator output low or nil

1 Driving belt broken or slipping
2 Defective control unit
3 No battery supply to field coils
4 Brushes excessively worn or slip rings dirty
5 Weak or broken brush springs
6 Multi-socket connectors not properly connected
7 Diodes failed in rectifier pack
8 Stator or field coils defective

(e) Starter motor lacks power or will not operate

1 Battery discharged, loose or dirty battery connections
2 Starter pinion jammed in mesh
3 Defective starter switch
4 Defective starter solenoid
5 Brushes excessively worn or sticking, leads detached or shorting
6 Weak or broken brush springs
7 Commutator dirty or worn
8 Defective armature or field coil windings
9 Starter motor mechanically defective
10 Engine abnormally stiff

(f) Starter motor runs but does not turn engine

1 Pinion sticking on screwed sleeve
2 Broken teeth on pinion or flywheel gear

(g) Starter motor rough or noisy

1 Bent armature shaft
2 Loose polepieces
3 Excessively worn bearing bushes
4 Mounting bolts loose
5 Starter pinion spring broken
6 Damaged pinion or flywheel gear teeth

(h) Lamps inoperative or erratic

1 Defective wiring or loose connections
2 Bulbs burned out
3 Poor earth points
4 Battery discharged or dirty connections on battery
5 Battery defective and incapable of holding a charge
6 Lighting switches defective
7 Fuse blown (check for cause)

(j) Wiper motor sluggish and takes high current

1 Defective cable rack or wheelboxes
2 Insufficient armature end float
3 Dirty or worn commutator
4 Defective field coil or armature windings
5 Brushes worn or brush springs weak

(k) Wiper motor operates but does not drive arms

1 Defective cable rack or wheelboxes
2 Gearbox components badly worn

(l) Oil pressure and brake warning lights glow dimly

(Only applicable on tandem brake installations)
1 Low or nil oil pressure

NOTES

CHAPTER 12

THE BODYWORK

12:1 Bodywork repairs
12:2 Windscreen glass

PART I   THE GT6

12:3 The doors
12:4 The bonnet
12:5 Facia components
12:6 The heater

PART II   THE VITESSE

12:7   The doors
12:8   The bonnet
12:9   The sliding roof
12:10 Facia components
12:11 The heater
12:12 Modifications

12:1 Bodywork repairs

Both the GT6 and Vitesse models use a chassis on which the components are mounted, so the bodywork does not provide the mountings for suspension and transmission. The bodywork is also divided up into panels which can be renewed. As a result it will often be found cheaper to renew a damaged panel than to have that panel dressed out by a skilled panel beater.

Minor dents and scratches are best filled and then sprayed, using a self-spraying can of matching paint. It should be remembered that paint changes colour with age, so it is better to spray a complete panel, or at least to spray a larger area than the damage and to feather in the edges of the patch by thinning the application of paint.

Clean off any wax polish in the area and mask surrounding areas with newspaper and masking tape. Lightly scuff the damaged area. Use a primer filler or paste stopper according to the amount of filling required and, when it is dry, rub down using 400 grade 'Wet and Dry' paper and water. Spend plenty of time and patience in obtaining the best finish possible, using more coats of filler if required, as small blemishes in the matt surface will stand out glaringly in the polished final surface. Spray on paint, using at least two thin coats rather than one thick

one which may run, and lightly rubbing down paint between coats. Lightly polish and remove spray dust from the final coat with cutting compound. Leave the paint for at least several days before applying wax polish.

12:2 Windscreen glass

The rear quarter lights and backlights on Vitesse models, as well as the backlights on GT6 models, are fitted in the same manner as the windscreen glass, so the following instructions apply provided that differences in mouldings are noted and instructions for windscreen wiper arms are ignored.

Removal:

1 Use a screwdriver, whose sharp edges have been ground off, to work around between the weatherstrip and body to break the seal. **Take care to keep the tool firmly under the rubber and avoid damaging the paintwork.**
2 Remove the windscreen wiper arms. From inside the car apply heavy hand pressure (or foot pressure) to the lower corners of the glass to push it out. Have an assistant outside the car to take the glass as it comes free and give assistance as required.

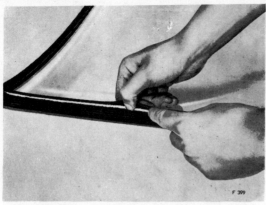

FIG 12:1   Inserting cord into weatherstrip

FIG 12:2   Fitting windscreen

3 If necessary, remove the mouldings from the weatherstrip and take the weatherstrip off the glass. Clean off old sealant with petrol or white spirits. Examine the weatherstrip for deterioration, cuts or splits, and renew it if defective.

If the glass has broken, care should be taken to remove all the particles. **Demister ducts and hoses should be removed and cleaned out in case any glass has fallen down them.** If particles are left in these may be blown out into the passenger's or driver's face when the demisting system is operated. It is also advisable to obtain a new weatherstrip with the replacement glass as the old one will most likely be damaged, either by broken glass or in the attempt to remove all the particles stuck to it. The aperture flange should be carefully examined and any dents in it dressed out with a block and hammer. Any protrusions should be filed to the level of the flange, otherwise they may set up local stress points and cause the new glass to break. Clean old sealant off the flange with petrol or white spirits.

Replacement:

1 Refit the rubber weatherstrip around the glass, with its join at the bottom, and inject sealant between the glass and weatherstrip. Refit the mouldings into the weatherstrip, wiping away surplus sealant with a cloth moistened in white spirits or petrol.

Key to Figs 12:3 and 12:4

1 Clip
2 Door glass
3 Clip
4 Outer weatherstrip
5 Glazing strip
6 Glass channel
7 Vent rubber channel
8 Channel stop
9 Pivot socket
10 Vent frame
11 Locking plate
12 Washer
13 Bracket
14 Screw
15 Weatherstrip
16 Vent inner frame
17 Pivot pin bracket
18 Washer
19 Bolt
20 Vent glass
21 Bolt
22 Washer
23 Hinge pin
24 Hinge
25 Bolt
26 Bolt
27 Check strap
28 Sealing rubber
29 Clip
30 Sealing rubber
31 Push button
32 Spring washer
33 Bracket
34 Bolt
35 Washer
36 Bolt
37 Washer
38 Bracket
39 Washer
40 Washer
41 Bolt
42 Nut
43 Nut
44 Vent bracket
45 Spring
46 Glazing strip
47 Collar
48 Washer
49 Spring
50 Nut
51 Pin
52 Locking handle
53 Tabwasher
54 Rubber washer
55 Spring
56 Escutcheon
57 Pin
58 Handle
59 Handle
60 Screw
61 Escutcheon
62 Spring
63 Pin
64 Handle
65 Sealing rubber
66 Sealing rubber
67 Trim pad
68 Clip
69 Clip
70 Finisher strip
71 Trim pad
72 Bolt
73 Washer
74 Regulator mechanism
75 Washer
76 Washer
77 Bolt
78 Glass stop bracket
79 Washer
80 Bolt
81 Remote control
82 Screw
83 Washer
84 Glass stop
85 Bracket
86 Bolt
87 Washer
88 Bolt
89 Washer
90 Glass run channel
91 Grommet
92 Rubber channel
93 Washer
94 Spring washer
95 Spring clip
96 Washer
97 Spring washer
98 Lock
99 Screw
100 Screw
101 Screw
102 Door panel
103 Striker
104 Washer
105 Spring clip
106 Private lock
107 Washer
108 Handle
109 Washer
110 Bolt
111 Bolt
112 Washer
113 Washer
114 Spring
115 Plunger

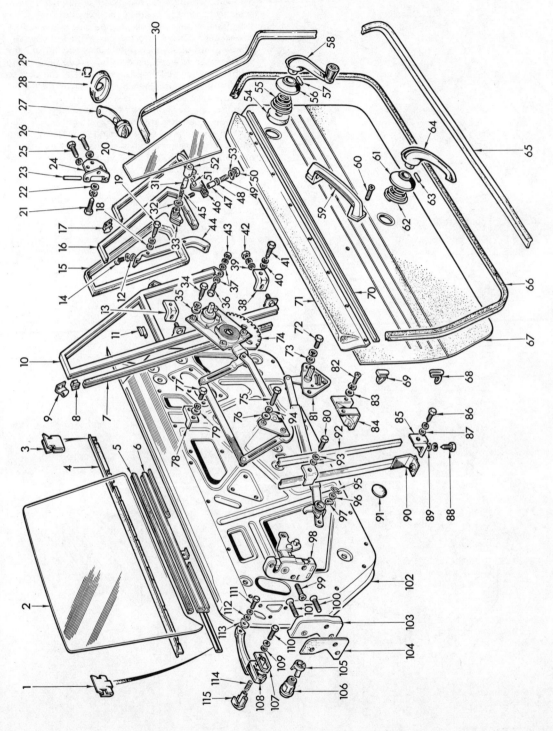

FIG 12:3   GT6 door details

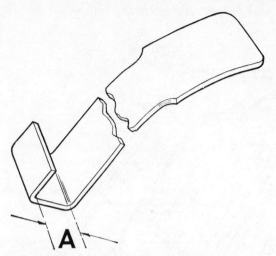

FIG 12:4 Tool for refitting weatherstrip clips

2 Lay a long length of thick cord all round the groove in the weatherstrip, as shown in **FIG 12:1**, and leave the ends protruding freely. Wipe the aperture flange with soapy solution as a lubricant. Have an assistant place the glass into position outside the car, with the ends of the cord passed into the car. With the assistant pressing the glass firmly into place and driving the weatherstrip in as required using gentle blows of a rubber hammer, pull firmly on the ends of the cord so that the lip of the weatherstrip is lifted over the flange, as shown in **FIG 12:2**.

3 Inject sealant between the weatherstrip and the body. Press the weatherstrip firmly in to effect the seal, and wipe away surplus sealant using a piece of cloth moistened in petrol or white spirits. **Do not use so much solvent that it creeps into the joint and destroys the bond.**

PART I   THE GT6

12:3 The doors

Typical door details are shown in **FIG 12:3**. The door itself may be removed by drilling out the rivet in the door check strap and, with the bonnet open, removing the

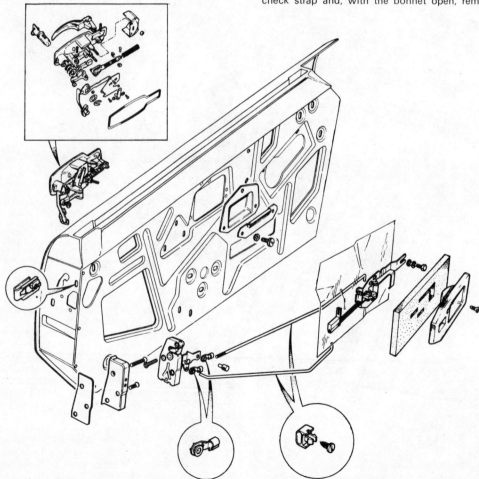

FIG 12:5   Showing later type door lock mechanism as fitted to GT6 Mk 3 models

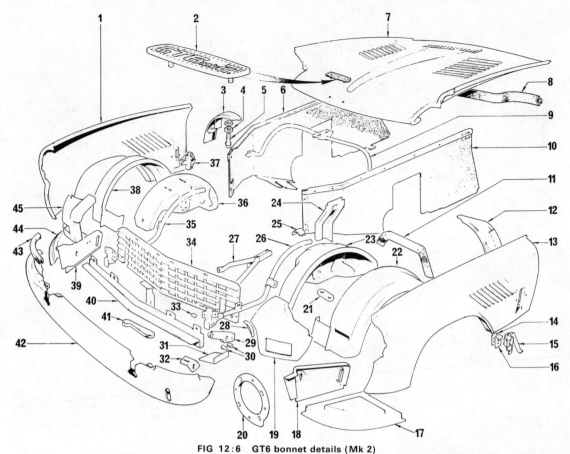

FIG 12:6   GT6 bonnet details (Mk 2)

Key to Fig 12:6   1 Righthand front side wing   2 Bonnet top name plate   3 Front wing side reinforcement   4 Nut jam   5 Bonnet location peg   6 Righthand engine bay valance   7 Bonnet top assembly   8 Bonnet sealing rubber   9 Rear tube assembly   10 Lefthand engine bay valance   11 Wheelarch to dash rear seal   12 Front wing side reinforcement   13 Lefthand front side wing   14 Tapping plate   15 Bonnet catch assembly   16 Dash side catch plate   17 Nose to wheelarch filler panel   18 Closing panel assembly   19 Nose panel   20 Headlamp mounting bracket   21 Backing plate anchor brackets   22 Wheelarch outer panel   23 Wheelarch inner panel   24 Wheelarch to wing support   25 Bonnet hinge tube anchor bracket   26 Bonnet hinge tube   27 Support stay   28 Nose panel reinforcement   29 Bonnet hinge bracket assembly   30 Distance piece   31 Valance bracket   32 Front valance support   33 Bonnet hinge tube spacer   34 Front grille assembly   35 Bonnet hinge tube   36 Wheelarch inner panel   37 Bonnet catch assembly   38 Wheelarch outer panel   39 Closing panel assembly   40 Grille mounting   41 Front valance support bracket   42 Front valance   43 Bonnet seal   44 Nose filler panel   45 Nose panel

six bolts that secure the hinges to the body. Limited adjustment to the position of the door is obtainable by slackening the bolts securing the hinges to the door and body and moving the door to the required position.

To gain access into the door, remove the trim panel. Press the escutcheons 56 and 61 firmly towards the panel and use a thin rod to press out the securing pins 57 and 63. The interior handles, escutcheons and springs can then be removed. Take out the two screws 60 and remove the grab handle. The trim panel can then be gently prised off the door.

Door glass:

Remove the trim panel. Remove the glass stop 84 and wind down the window until the runners disengage from the glass channel 6. If required, the window regulator

mechanism can now be removed by pulling up the glass and taking out the six screws 34 and 75.

Prise off the weatherstrips and lift the glass out of the door.

Once the door glass has been removed the quarter light vent can be removed. Remove the three nuts 42 and 43. Take out the rubber grommet from the front closing face of the door and remove the screw 14. The quarter light vent assembly can now be lifted out of the door.

Refit the parts in the reverse order of removal. Make sure that both the runners of the window regulator are engaged in the glass channel. When refitting the weather-strips make up a tool as shown in **FIG 12:4** to pull the clips back into place. On the inner clips the dimension A should be $\frac{3}{16}$ inch (4.75 mm) and for the outer clips it should be $\frac{1}{4}$ inch (6.35 mm).

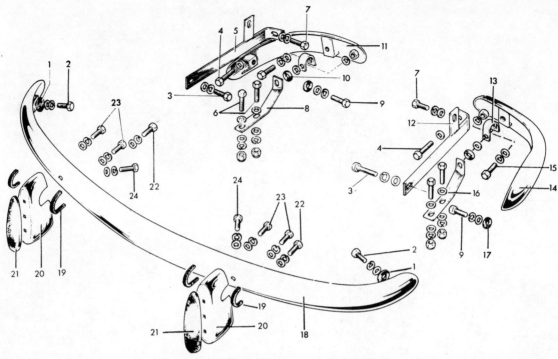

FIG 12:7   GT6 bumper details (Mk 2)

Key to Fig 12:7   1 Rubber washer   2 Front bumper to body bolt   3 Support bracket bolt   4 Spring bar bolt
5 Upper spring bar   6 Support bar bolt   7 Spring bar bolt   8 Rear bumper support   9 Body side bolt   10 Rubber washers
11 Righthand rear bumper   12 Upper spring bar   13 Rear bumper support extensions   14 Lefthand rear bumper
15 Support extension bolt   16 Rear bumper support   17 Rubber washer   18 Front bumper   19 PVC moulding
20 Overrider assembly   21 Overrider rubber buffer   22 Lower overrider attachments bolt   23 Front bumper to body bolt
24 Overrider to front bumper bolt

Door lock:

Remove the trim panel. Remove the spring clip 95 and washers 96 and 97 which secure the remote control link to the door lock. The remote control unit 81 can now be removed by taking out the three securing screws 72 and withdrawing the unit through the aperture in the inner panel. The lock assembly 98 can be removed, with the remote control unit in place, after taking out the three screws 99.

The parts are refitted in the reverse order of removal. When refitting the lock 98 make sure that it engages with the private lock 106.

The private lock 106 can be removed after compressing the legs of the spring clip 105. When refitting the private lock, make sure that it engages with the anti-burst lock 98.

Changes to the door lock mechanism and fittings for the GT6 Mk 3 are shown in **FIG 12:5**.

Adjustment:

The adjustment of the door position has already been dealt with. Slacken the two screws 100 and the third screw 101 that secure the striker plate 103. Move the striker plate to the desired position and check it by gently closing the door. Always make sure that the striker plate is parallel to the swing of the door and never slam the door when the striker plate is out of adjustment. Fully tighten the securing screws when, after trial and error, the adjustment is correct.

12:4 The bonnet

The bonnet details are shown in **FIG 12:6**.

Removal:

1 Disconnect the battery. Disconnect the lighting and horn cables from the snap connectors situated at the top centre of the front grille. Label the cables if the colours have faded to ensure that they will be correctly reconnected.

2 Refer to **FIG 12:7**. Remove the bolts 2, 22 and 23 and then take off the front bumper assembly.

3 Disconnect the bonnet stay from the wheel arch and lay the bonnet down to the closed position. Refer to **FIG 12:8** and remove the two sets of nuts and bolts 2 from the hinge. With the help of an assistant lift the bonnet assembly from the car.

Refit the bonnet in the reverse order of removal. Adjustments are provided to ensure that the bonnet can be made to fit accurately to the body.

Horizontal adjustment:

This is achieved by slackening the two bolts, 2 in **FIG 12:8** or **12:9** and moving the bonnet as necessary to obtain a parallel gap of $\frac{3}{16}$ inch (5 mm) between the bonnet scuttle and doors. On later cars it may be necessary to remove the underriders and the stop plates to give the correct location for the buffers.

Vertical adjustment:

Slacken the bolts, 1 in **FIG 12:8** or 6 in **FIG 12:9**, and raise or lower the bonnet as required. It will also be necessary to adjust the height of the rubber buffers and the fasteners for the bonnet catches to ensure rattle-free closing and security. Do not forget to secure all the attachment bolts when the correct locations have been found.

12:5 Facia components

The facia details are shown in **FIG 12:10**.

Parcel shelf:

The parcel shelf attachments are shown in **FIG 12:11**. 1 and 2 are screws, 3 are the screws securing the fresh air vent to the shelf, and 4 are nuts and bolts. The parcel shelf can be removed after undoing all the attachments. On the driver's side the speedometer trip cable must also be detached.

Instrument panel:

The instrument panel can be pulled clear of the facia to gain access to the rear of the instruments. Before doing any work on the instruments, disconnect the battery. Remove the heater control knobs using a $\frac{1}{16}$ inch (1.6 mm) Allen key. Take out the four screws from the corners of the panel and carefully withdraw it.

12:6 The heater

The heater details are shown in **FIG 12:12** and the arrangement of the air hoses under the facia is shown in **FIG 12:13**.

Removal:

1 Drain the cooling system. Disconnect the heater hoses 31 and 36 from the water valve 34 and engine connection. Put one hose into a container and blow down the other hose to expel the coolant. If any coolant remains then blow through in the reverse direction. Disconnect the hoses from the heater.
2 Working inside the car, remove the facia support bracket and gearbox cover. Remove the passenger's side parcel shelf and, to give more access room, take out the instrument panel. Disconnect the air hoses 18, 38, 43 and 49 from the heater. Slacken the cable securing bolts 42 and 44 to free the control cable.
3 Disconnect the electrical cables to the blower motor. Remove the four bolts 16 that secure the heater to the dash and manoeuvre the unit out of the car.
Replace the unit in the reverse order of removal.

Blower motor:

Before this can be removed the heater unit must be taken out of the car. Separate the halves of the heater box

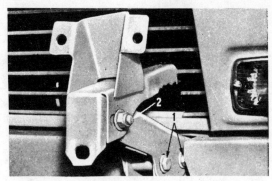

FIG 12:8 GT6 bonnet hinge and adjustments

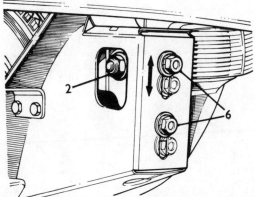

FIG 12:9 Bonnet fixings and adjustment points—GT6 Mk 3

by removing the ten screws that secure them. Use a screwdriver to prise off the metal clip that holds the impeller to the spindle. Take out the four screws that secure the motor.

Replace the motor in the reverse order of removal. If the motor is defective it must be renewed as it is a sealed unit and cannot be repaired.

Water valve:

If the water valve 34 is defective it must be renewed as no repair is possible. Disconnect the hose 31 and release the control cable. Unscrew the unit from the engine.

Replace the unit in the reverse order of removal, using Hermatite on the threads. Secure the control cable back in place with the water valve in the 'Off' position and the control on full 'Cold'.

Vents:

The facia fresh air vent is shown in **FIG 12:14**. Free it by disconnecting the air hose and slackening the knurled nuts 1. Rotate the clamp 3 until its slots align with the retaining pins 4 and the clamp can be pulled off.

Stale air is extracted through the louvres on either side of the tail gate so take care not to block these with parcels or luggage. Flap valves are fitted in these vents to prevent a reverse flow of air.

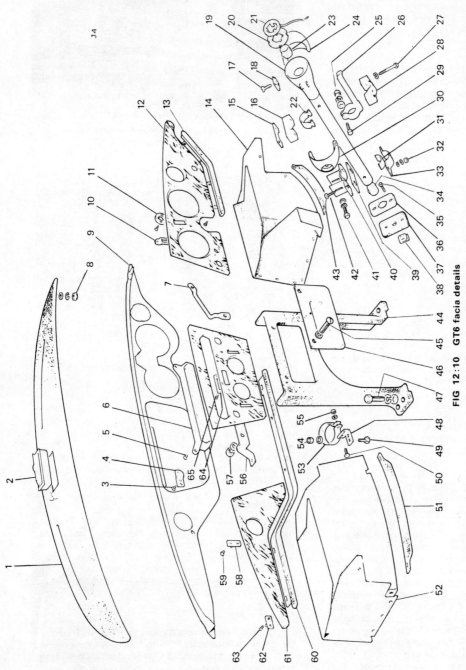

FIG 12:10 GT6 facia details

Key to Fig 12:10 1 Crash pad 2 Ash tray 3 Attachment plate 4 Attachment plate woodscrew 5 Heater control escutcheon 6 Heater control escutcheon woodscrew
7 Steering column to facia tie bar 8 Crash pad to deck nut 9 Facia panel assembly 10 Hazard light switch retainer plate 11 Screen washer plate washer
12 Righthand veneered facing 13 Lower facia padding 14 Driver's side parcel tray assembly 15 Tapped plate 16 Steering column upper clamp 17 Self-tapping
screw (escutcheon to column cowl) 18 Fix nut (escutcheon to column cowl) 19 Steering column cowl 20 Slip ring insulator 21 Slip ring 22 Column clamp spring
23 Bearing assembly 24 Flasher and lighting switch escutcheon 25 Harness cover attachment nut 26 Harness cover 27 Upper and lower clamp attachment bolt
28 Upper column clamp 29 Harness cover attachment bolt 30 Flasher assembly 31 Support bracket felt strip 32 Support bracket clamp nut
33 Support bracket clamp 34 Bearing assembly 35 Self-tapping screw 36 Retainer plate 37 Rubber sealing pad 38 Spire nut 39 Support bracket felt strip
40 Support bracket assembly 41 Support bracket setscrew 42 Clamp to support bracket bolt 43 Parcel tray support assembly 44 Gearbox support bracket
45 Support bracket to facia setscrew 46 Radio aperture coverplate 47 Support bracket to floor bolt 48 Bracket-foot level vent 49 Bracket attachment setscrew
50 Clamp ring attachment setscrew 51 Parcel tray support assembly 52 Passenger's side parcel tray assembly 53 Clamping ring 54 Vent bracket attachment nut
55 Vent bracket attachment nut 56 Parcel tray support bracket 57 Support bracket Nyloc nut 58 Attachment plate 59 Attachment plate woodscrew
60 Lower facia padding assembly 61 Passenger's side veneered facing 62 Attachment plate 63 Attachment plate woodscrew 64 Switch retainer plate
65 Switch plate to facia woodscrew

PART II VITESSE

12:7 The doors

The door details are shown in **FIG 12:15** and the attachment of the components in **FIG 12:16**.

The door is removed and replaced on the car using the same method as the door on the GT6 (see **Section 12:3**) and the door striker plate is also adjusted in the same manner.

Trim panel:

The attachments are shown in **FIG 12:17** and the method of removing the door handles in the inset.

FIG 12:11   Parcel shelf attachments

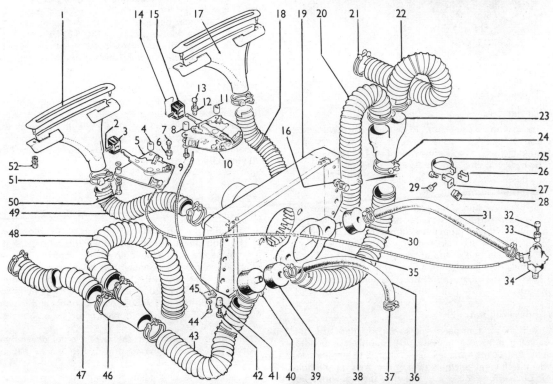

FIG 12:12   GT6 heater details

Key to Figs 12:12 and 12:13   1 Demister outlet capping
2 Knob grubscrew   3 Knob assembly
4 Control lever spacer   5 Water valve control lever
6 Trunnion cable attachment   7 Cable attachment screw
8 Control lever spacer   9 Lever control attachment setscrew
10 Ventilator and heater motor lever control   11 Control
lever spacer   12 Trunnion (cable attachment)
13 Screw (cable attachment)   14 Pull boost label
15 Knob assembly   16 Heater attachment setscrew
17 Demister nozzle   18 Hose demister   19 Heater unit
assembly   20 Hose Y-piece to foot level vent
21 Hose clip   22 Hose Y-piece to facia level vent   23 Y-piece
24 Hose clip   25 Clip Y-piece retainer   26 Fix nut
27 Bracket Y-piece clip   28 Fix nut
29 Bracket attachment setscrew 30 Inlet and outlet pipes seal
31 Hose water valve to heater   32 Screw (cable to water valve)
33 Trunnion (cable to water valve)   34 Water control valve
35 Heater blower seal   36 Water return hose
37 Hose clip   38 Heater to Y-piece hose
39 Inlet and outlet pipes seal   40 Hose clip
41 Trunnion (cable attachment)   42 Screw (cable attachment)
43 Heater to Y-piece hose   44 Cable clamp attachment setscrew   45 Cable clamp   46 Y-piece

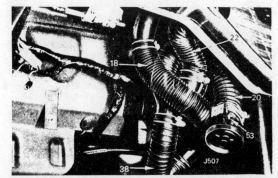

FIG 12:13   Arrangement of air hoses under facia

47 Hose Y-piece to foot level vent   48 Hose Y-piece to foot
level vent   49 Demister hose   50 Lever control attachment
setscrew   51 Hose clip   52 Demister nozzle attachment
nut   53 Nut

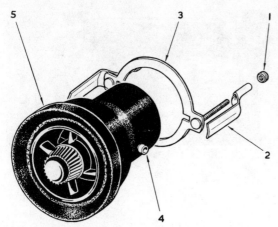

FIG 12:14   GT6 fresh air vent details

Weatherstrip:

Remove the weatherstrip 86 by using a screwdriver to press the securing clips downwards. The weatherstrip is refitted by using a tool as shown in **FIG 12:18** to pull the clips back into place on the flange.

Glass-run channel:

Remove the trim panel and wind the glass up to the fully closed position, with the handle loosely refitted. Remove the rubber grommet 82, from the end face of the door just above the lock, and take out the exposed bolt. Pull the lower end of the channel 64 forward to free it from the tension wire 70. Lower the channel into the bottom of the door and remove it through the lower aperture.

Window regulator:

Remove the trim panel and lower the glass until the operating arms are accessible through the aperture. Remove the clips 4 and leather washers 2 to free the arms from the channel assembly 88. Lift the glass up and hold it in place with a soft wedge. Remove the regulator pivot 3 and its associated nut and washers. Free the front quarter light vent and raise it 2 inches (see later). Remove the four screws 99 and manoeuvre the regulator unit out of the door.

Replace the unit in the reverse order of removal, but noting that the screw 98 also secures the forward end of the tension wire.

Door glass:

Remove the trim panel, glass run channel and inner weatherstrip. Lower the glass and disconnect the regulator arms from the glass channel. Lift the quarter vent up 2 inches after removing the two bolts 95, screw 94 and the two cross-headed screws accessible through the circular apertures in the door. Tilt the glass as required and manoeuvre it out of the door. The quarter light ventilator can be removed after the door glass has been taken out.

Replace the parts in the reverse order of removal.

Remote control:

Remove the trim panel. Refit the door handle and retain it in the door open position. Free the link arm from the lock 62 by removing the spring clip 58 and waved washer 59. Take out the three screws 97 and remove the remote control unit 61 from the door.

Replace the unit in the reverse order of removal.

Door lock:

Remove the trim panel and disconnect the remote control link from the lock 62. Remove the three counter-sunk screws 93 which secure the dovetail and lock to the end face of the door. Remove the screw that secures the lock to the inner panel of the door and manoeuvre the lock out of the door as shown in **FIG 12:19**.

Refit the lock in the reverse order of removal, making sure that the plastic weather sheet is in its correct place.

Exterior handle:

This is secured to the door by two bolts, one of which is accessible at the rear of the door, the other being inside the door. The adjusting screw 65 should be set so that there is a $\frac{1}{16}$ inch (1.6 mm) gap between it and the lock operating lever. **Check this gap visually and not by trying the button.**

12:8 The bonnet

Removal:

1 Disconnect the battery. Disconnect the horn and lighting cables at the snap connectors situated at the top centre of the grille. With the bonnet still open disconnect the bonnet stay from its wheel arch attachment. Lower the bonnet to the closed position.
2 Refer to **FIG 12:20**. Remove the overriders by taking out the bolts 4 and 7. Support the bonnet and remove the bolts 5 and 6. The bonnet can now be lifted off from the car.

Replace the bonnet in the reverse order of removal, noting that adjustments are provided to ensure that the bonnet is a correct fit.

Front height:

Raise or lower the bonnet with the bolts 5 and 6 partially tight until clearance between the vertical edges of the bonnet and doors are parallel and even. Tighten the bolts in this position.

Rear height:

Refer to **FIG 12:21**. Adjust the position of the rubber bumper 1 until the height is correct. Adjust the locking plate 3 until the locks operate smoothly but still firmly secure the bonnet.

Horizontal adjustment:

Refer to **FIG 12:20**. Slacken the locknuts 2 and turn the sleeve nuts 1 as required until the gap between the rear edge of the bonnet and scuttle is parallel at $\frac{3}{16}$ inch (5 mm). Retighten the locknuts 2 in this position.

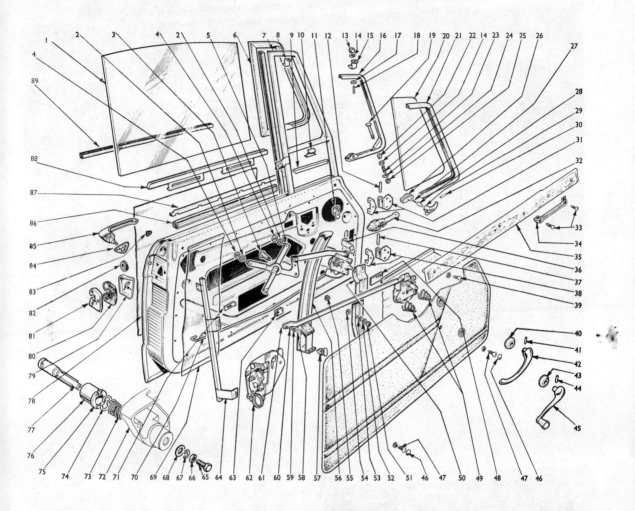

FIG 12:15   Vitesse door details

Key to Figs 12:15, 12:16 and 12:17   1 Door glass   2 Leather washer   3 Regulator mounting pivot   4 Retainer clip
5 Window regulator assembly   6 Weatherstrip   7 Outer frame   8 Top pivot outer bracket   9 Waist forward, inner finisher
10 Catch plate   11 Vent support bracket   12 Door hinge pin   13 Thick washer   14 Thin washer   15 Top pivot inner bracket
16 Inner frame assembly   17 Thin washer   18 Semi-tubular rivet   19 Bottom pivot shaft assembly   20 Vent glass
21 Glazing strip   22 Spacing piece   23 Spring   24 Tabwasher   25 Nut   26 Bracket assembly handle   27 Spring
28 Push button   29 Locking handle   30 Locking pin   31 Door hinge   32 Door check link assembly   33 Screw
34 Door pull handle   35 Veneer capping   36 Vent support assembly bracket   37 Door hinge pin   38 Door hinge
39 Veneer capping screw   40 Inside handle escutcheon   41 Handle fixing pin   42 Remote control handle
43 Inside handle escutcheon   44 Handle fixing pin   45 Window regulator handle   46 Door trim cap   47 Door trim screw
48 Felt pad   49 Regulator spring   50 Regulator pivot reinforcement   51 Nut   52 Lockwasher   53 Plain washer
54 Plain thin washer   55 Special washer   56 Anti-drum stiffener assembly   57 Trim panel to door clip   58 Clip
59 Waved washer   60 Plain washer   61 Remote control mechanism   62 Cam lock assembly   63 tie rod attachment clip
64 Glass assembly channel   65 Lock adjusting bolt   66 Lock adjusting nut   67 E-clip securing push button in handle
68 Rubber washer   69 Weather curtain   70 Bottom glass channel tie rod   71 Window regulator stop bracket
72 Outside door handle body   73 Button return spring   74 E-clip locking handle only   75 Locator plunger
76 Push button, locking handle only   77 Locking plunger barrel, locking handle only   78 Door assembly
79 Cam lock dove tail plate   80 Cam lock striker rubber sealing   81 Cam lock striker assembly   82 Rubber grommet
83 Small seating washer   84 Large seating washer   85 Outside door handle assembly   86 Sealing strip, waist, door inner
87 Sealing strip, waist, door outer   88 Window regulator channel assembly   89 Glazing channel strip

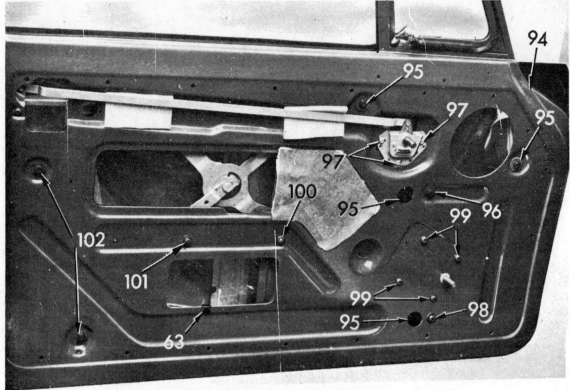

FIG 12:16 Vitesse door component attachments

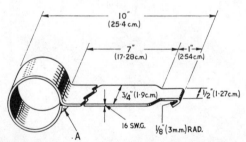

FIG 12:18 Tool for refitting weatherstrip clips on Vitesse models

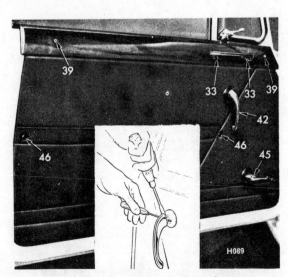

FIG 12:17 Vitesse trim panel attachments

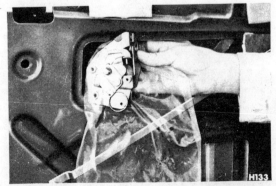

FIG 12:19 Removing/refitting Vitesse door lock

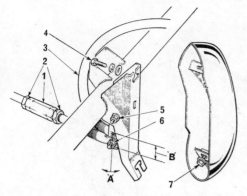

FIG 12:20 Vitesse bonnet hinges and adjustment points

FIG 12:21 Vitesse bonnet height adjusters

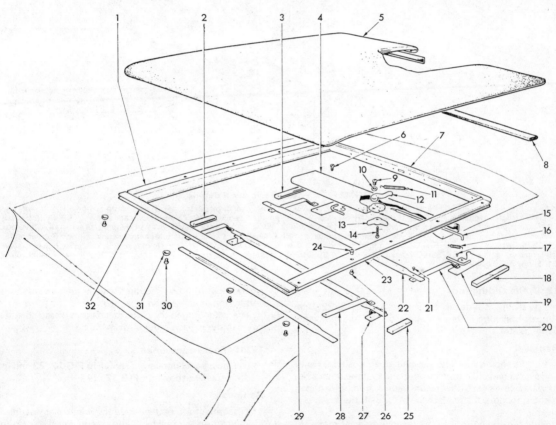

FIG 12:22 Vitesse sliding roof details

Key to Fig 12:22 1 Side rail 2 Intermediate slide 3 Front slide 4 Intermediate listing rail assembly 5 Sliding roof cover assembly 6 Front coverplate screw 7 Front angle assembly 8 Front rubber strip 9 Hook to cam screw 10 Hook to cam washer 11 Tension spring 12 Locking hook 13 Handle 14 Handle to control box screw 15 Pushrod 16 Front slide spring 17 Rivet 18 Front slide 19 Front side assembly 20 Lifting spring 21 Listing rail rivet 22 Listing rail 23 Side rail 24 Side rail to roof sleeve 25 Intermediate slide 26 Side rail to roof screw 27 Intermediate listing rail assembly 28 Lifting spring 29 Listing rail 30 Rear coverplate setscrew 31 Washer 32 Rear rail

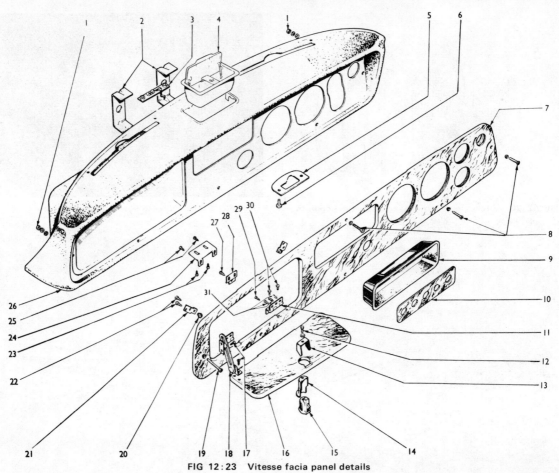

FIG 12 : 23   Vitesse facia panel details

Key to Fig 12:23   1 Panel attachment nut   2 Switch panel saddle bracket   3 Facia light switch   4 Ash tray   5 Light switch coverplate   6 Light switch Nylon stud   7 Veneered panel   8 Panel attachment screw   9 Switch panel   10 Finisher plate   11 Glove box hinge   12 Lock clamp screw   13 Lock clamp   14 Finger pull   15 Glove box lock   16 Glove box lid   17 Link attachment screw   18 Check link   19 Facia attachment screw   20 Rubber buffer   21 Buffer bracket   22 Bracket attachment screw   23 Tie bracket screw   24 Tie bracket   25 Tie bracket screw   26 Trimmed facia   27 Striker bracket screw   28 Striker bracket   29 Hinge to lid screw   30 Hinge to panel screw   31 Hinge to lid screw

12 : 9 The sliding roof

The sliding roof details are shown in **FIG 12 : 22**. Use Ambersil Silicone Formula 1 spray on the runners if the action is stiff.

Removal :

Put the sliding roof into the half-open position. Hold one side to prevent it from moving and pull the other side forwards to release the nylon sliders from the metal runners. Remove the four screws 30 and lift the assembly clear.

Refit the sliding roof in the reverse order of removal. The holes in the fabric for the screws 30 are elongated so that the fabric can be positioned and tensioned for the best appearance.

Catch mechanism :

Remove the sliding roof from the car. Pull the ends of the front listing rail clear of the fabric and pull the fabric

clear of the front box section. Remove the two screws 6 and lift the metal section clear.

After attending to the catch mechanism reassemble the cover in the reverse order of dismantling.

12 : 10 Facia components

The facia panel details are shown in **FIG 12 : 23** and its attachments are shown in **FIG 12 : 24**.

Removal :

1 Disconnect the battery. Free the wiring harness from the clip on the bulkhead and disconnect the leads to stop lamp switch, wiper motor and steering column switches.

2 Free the control cables from the carburetter, water valve and heater distribution box. Disconnect the hoses from the demister vents, and the screen washer plastic pipes from the pump. Disconnect the drive cables from the tachometer and speedometer.

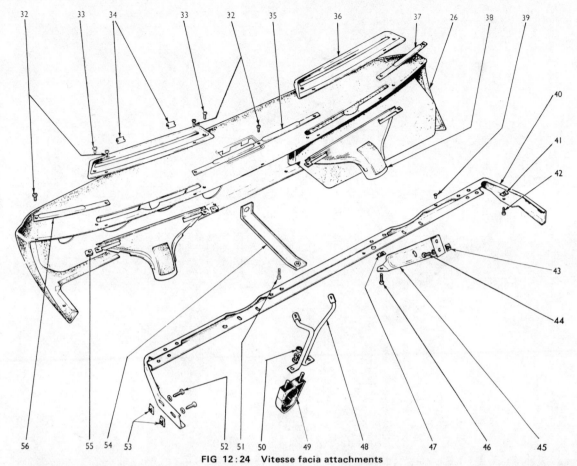

FIG 12:24　Vitesse facia attachments

Key to Fig 12:24　　32 Facia attachment screw　　33 Demister finisher attachment screw　　34 Demister finisher attachment clips
35 Top edge centre finisher　　36 Demister vent finisher　　37 Top edge lefthand finisher　　38 Demister vent　　39 Pop rivet
40 Facial rail　　41 Fix nut　　42 Facia to rail screw　　43 Fix nut　　44 Bracket to bulkhead screw　　45 Support bracket
46 Bracket to facia screw　　47 Fix nut　　48 Steering column support bracket　　49 Steering column clamp　　50 Nut
51 Choke bracket attachment screw　　52 Facia rail to dash side bolts　　53 Fix nuts　　54 Choke support bracket
56 Top edge righthand finisher

3　Remove the steering column as described in **Chapter 9, Section 9:7.**

4　Free the facia rail support 45 and choke support bracket 54 from the bulkhead. Remove the seven screws 32 from along the facia top. Remove the four screws 52 securing the facia rail 40 to the dash sides. Withdraw the facia and disconnect the remainder of the electrical connections.

Refit the facia in the reverse order of dismantling. After the facia has been refitted, take the car for a road test and check the correct functioning of all the instruments and controls.

Instruments and controls:

The instruments are secured to the facia by bridge pieces and knurled nuts which are accessible from the back of the instrument panel.

The heater air control connection to the facia is shown in **FIG 12:25.** This type of connection is typical for

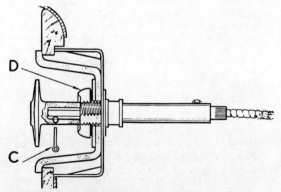

FIG 12:25　Vitesse heater cable attachment (typical of most control attachments)

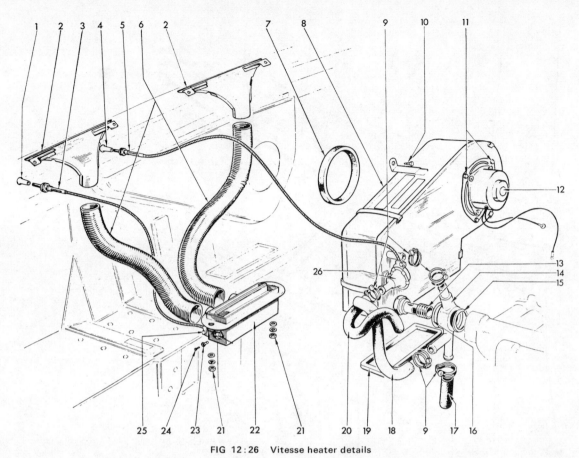

FIG 12:26   Vitesse heater details

Key to Fig 12:26   1 Control knob   2 Demister duct   3 Air distribution control cable   4 Control knob   5 Temperature control cable   6 Demister hoses   7 Sealing rubber   8 Heater unit   9 Hose clips   10 Spire screw   11 Blower motor attachment screw   12 Heater blower   13 Banjo bolt   14 Adaptor   15 Washer   16 Washer   17 Bottom hose 18 Adaptor/heater unit hose   19 Seal   20 Adaptor/water valve hose   21 Nuts   22 Air distribution box   23 Trunnion 24 Securing bolt   25 Securing bracket   26 Water valve

control knobs and some switches. Use a suitable pin C to press in the spring-loaded plunger on the spindle and slide off the control knob. Undo the chromium-plated bezel D and the control cable or switch can be pulled out of the back of the facia panel.

The facia rail and veneered panel can be removed from the facia assembly after the assembly has been removed from the car and the instruments and controls taken off.

12:11 The heater

The heater details are shown in **FIG 12:26**.

Removal:

1 Disconnect the battery and drain the cooling system. Remove the water hoses 18 and 20. Release the temperature control cable 5 from the water valve 26 and disconnect the electrical cables from the blower motor 12. Take out the screw 10 securing the heater

top bracket. Release the choke cable from the rear carburetter.

2 Working from inside the car, remove the nuts and washers 21. The distribution box 22 can be removed after disconnecting the control cable 3 and the demister 6 from it.

3 Lift the heater unit out from in front of the bulkhead.

The unit is replaced in the reverse order of dismantling. Before refitting the heater unit, liberally smear the contact faces of the seals 7 and 19 with Seelastik SR.51. Reconnect the control cable 3 to the distribution box 22 with the control knob 1 pressed fully in and the lever on the distribution box pressed fully forwards.

Water valve:

This is a sealed unit and must be renewed if it is defective. Disconnect the hose 20 and the control cable 5 from the valve. Remove the two nuts and washers securing the valve to the heater and pull off the valve, taking care not to displace the rubber sealing ring. Refit the valve in the reverse order of removal. Connect the cable to the valve loosely. Push the control knob fully in and turn the valve lever fully clockwise. Secure the cable 5 in this position.

Blower motor:

Disconnect the battery and the blower motor leads. Remove the three screws 11 and withdraw the blower motor from the heater. Slacken the nut securing the impeller to the motor spindle and draw off the impeller. The nut tightens the contracting collet so there is no need to fully remove the nut. If the motor is found to be defective it must be renewed as it is a sealed unit and cannot be repaired. Refit the motor in the reverse order of removal.

12:12 Modifications

It should be noted that an occasional rear seat can be fitted to GT6 Mk 2 models. The parts required are obtainable in Stanpart Kit No. 575292/9.

Locks for the bonnet catches are available as a kit. These require the drilling and cutting of one shaped hole beside each catch and once fitted, the bonnet catches can be locked closed with a key.

On later models the windscreen surround has been included in the bulkhead assembly which has the effect of increasing the overall windscreen depth by 2 inches. The design of the rear quarter light also has been modified.

In place of the outside door handle shown in **FIG 12:3** a new flush fitting type was introduced for 1971. This also necessitated a slight alteration in the interior trim.

NOTES

APPENDIX

TECHNICAL DATA

Engine   Emission controlled engine   Fuel system
Ignition system   Cooling system   Clutch
Gearbox and overdrive   Rear axle and suspension
Front suspension and steering   Brakes   Electrical
Weights and dimensions   Capacities   Tyres
Torque wrench settings

SPECIAL TOOLS

RUNNING-IN

STANDARD MEASURE AND METRIC EQUIVALENTS

FRACTIONAL AND METRIC EQUIVALENTS

WIRING DIAGRAMS

HINTS ON MAINTENANCE AND OVERHAUL

GLOSSARY OF TERMS

INDEX

NOTES

TECHNICAL DATA

Dimensions are given in inches; figures in brackets are in millimetres

ENGINE

Type	6-cylinder, OHV, water-cooled
Compression ratio	
GT6 Mk 2, GT6 Plus	9.25:1 or 9.5:1
Vitesse Mk 2	9.25:1
Cubic capacity	1998 cc (122 cu ins)
Nominal bore	2.94 (74.7)
Stroke	2.992 (76.0)
Firing order	1–5–3–6–2–4
Crankshaft	
End float	.006 to .008 (.152 to .203) but may be allowed to reach .014 (.356)
Thrust washers:	
Standard	.091 (2.311)
Oversize	.096 to .098 (2.436 to 2.487)
Main bearings	
Journal diameter	2.0005 to 2.001 (50.813 to 50.825)
Undersize bearings	—.010, —.020, —.030 (.254, .508, .762)
Big-end bearings	
Crankpin diameter	1.875 to 1.8755 (47.625 to 47.638)
Undersize bearings	—.010, —.020, —.030 (.254, .508, .762)
Cylinder block	
Standard bore grades	see under Pistons
Bore for oversize pistons	2.9614 to 2.9609 (73.685 to 73.683)
Liners	When bore is too large for oversize piston
Part No.	130815
Cylinder bore for fitting	3.063 to 3.062 (77.8 to 77.775)
Cylinder bore finish	45 to 60 micro-inches CLA
Maximum bore wear	.010 (.254) at top of bore across thrust axis
Connecting rod bend and twist	.0015 (.038) maximum in length of gudgeon pin
Pistons	
Oversize	+.020 (+.508)
Piston and bore grades	

Grade	F	G	H
Bore	2.9408 to 2.9405 (74.696 to 74.689)	2.9412 to 2.9409 (74.706 to 74.699)	2.9416 to 2.9513 (74.717 to 74.709)
Piston top diameter (B)	2.9370 to 2.9366 (74.600 to 74.590)	2.9374 to 2.9370 (74.610 to 74.600)	2.9378 to 2.9374 (74.620 to 74.610)
Piston bottom diameter (A)	2.9388 to 2.9384 (74.646 to 74.635)	2.9392 to 2.9388 (74.656 to 74.646)	2.9396 to 2.9392 (74.666 to 74.656)

Piston ring grooves:	
Compression ring	.0797 to .0807 (2.024 to 2.050)
Oil control ring	.1573 to .1583 (3.995 to 4.023)
Piston rings	
Top ring	Plain compression ring
Centre ring	Taper-faced compression ring
Bottom ring	Oil control ring
Ring gap (fitted)	.008 to .013 (.203 to .327)
Oversize rings	+.010, +.020, +.030

Ring thickness:
Compression ... ... .077 to .0787 (1.956 to 1.999)
Oil control .. .. .1553 to .1563 (3.945 to 3.970)
Ring clearance in piston
Compression ... ... .0019 to .0035 (.048 to .089)
Oil control ... ... .0007 to .0027 (.0178 to .068)

Camshaft
Journal diameter .. .. 1.8402 to 1.8407 (46.741 to 46.754)
Bore in block ... ... 1.8433 to 1.8448 (46.820 to 46.858)
End float ... ... .004 to .008 (.102 to .203)

Cam followers
Diameter ... ... .8000 to .7996 (20.32 to 20.310)
Bore in block ... ... .8009 to .8002 (20.343 to 20.325)

Valves
Head diameter, early cars:
Inlet... ... ... 1.301 to 1.305 (33.045 to 33.147)
Exhaust ... ... 1.176 to 1.180 (29.870 to 29.792)
Head diameter, later cars:
Inlet... ... ... 1.441 to 1.445 (36.6 to 36.7)
Exhaust ... ... 1.256 to 1.260 (31.9 to 32.0)
Exhaust, Mk 3 intermittent from engine
KE21546 ... ... 1.193 to 1.187 (30.3 to 30.4)
Stem diameter:
Inlet... ... ... .3107 to .3112 (7.891 to 7.905)
Exhaust ... ... .310 to .3105 (7.874 to 7.887)

Valve springs ... ...   Close coils adjacent to cylinder head
Free length:
Inner 1.56 (39.624)
Outer 1.57 (39.878)
Free length, single springs:
Up to engine No. 10,001 ... ... 1.59 (40.386)
From engine No. 10,001 ... ... 1.52 (38.608)

Valve guides
Length 2.72 (69.078)
Bore ... ... .312 to .313 (7.924 to 7.950)
Outside diameter ... ... .501 to .502 (12.725 to 12.750)
Protrusion ... ... .749 to .751 (19.025 to 19.075)

Valve timing
Inlet opens ... ... 18 deg. BTDC (25 deg. for 1971)
Inlet closes ... ... 58 deg. ABDC (65 deg. for 1971)
Exhaust opens... ... ... 58 deg. BBDC (65 deg. for 1971)
Exhaust closes... ... ... 18 deg. ATDC (25 deg. for 1971)
Rocker clearance ... ... .040 (1.0) for setting valve timing only
Rocker clearance ... ... .010 (.254) cold

Lubrication
Oil pump ... ...   Hobourn Eaton, high-capacity,
                                 eccentric lobe
Clearance between rotors ... ... .010 (.254) maximum
Clearance between outer rotor and body ... .010 (.254) maximum
End float of rotors ... ... .004 (.102) maximum
Oil filter ... ...   Purolator, AC Delco, or Tecalmit full-
                                 flow, replaceable element
Relief valve spring:
Free length ... .: 1.55 (39.37)
Fitted length 1.25 (31.75)
Fitted load ... ... 14.5 lb (6.58 kg)

EMISSION CONTROLLED ENGINE

This is basically similar to the standard engine with the following differences:

Compression ratio	...	...	...	...	8.5:1
Exhaust valves ...	...	...	...	...	Stellite faced
Valve timing	...	...	...	...	Using different camshaft
Inlet opens	...	...	...	...	10 deg. BTDC
Inlet closes	...	...	...	...	50 deg. ABDC
Exhaust opens	...	...	...	...	50 deg. BBDC
Exhaust closes	...	...	...	...	10 deg. ATDC

FUEL SYSTEM

Fuel pump	...	...	...	...	AC mechanically operated
Carburetters					
Type:					
GT6 Mk 2 and 3 and Vitesse Mk 2 ...		...			Twin Stromberg 150CD
GT6 (emission controlled) ...		...			Twin Stromberg 150CDSE
GT6 Mk 3 (USA) ...		...			Twin Stromberg 150CDSEV
Needles:					
Stromberg 150CD ...		...	...	...	6AC
Stromberg 150CDSE	...	...	...	...	B5AJ
Stromberg 150CD (1971) ...		...	...		B5BT
Stromberg 150CDSE (1972–73)	...	...			B5CF
Stromberg 150CDSEV	...	...	...		B5CF
Idling speed					
Stromberg 150CD ...		...	...	...	600 to 650 rev/min
Stromberg 150CDSE ...		...	...		800 to 850 rev/min
Emission control data					
Hydrocarbon emission		...	...	...	Not to exceed 350 parts per million
Carbon monoxide emission		...	...	...	Not to exceed 2 per cent by volume
Idle CO emission	...	...	...	...	2.5 to 3.5 per cent at idling with engine warm
Air/fuel ratio ...		...	...	...	13.5:1 at idling with engine warm

IGNITION SYSTEM

Firing order	...	...	...	...	1–5–3–6–2–4
Sparking plugs					
Standard	...	...	...	...	Champion N.9Y (or Lodge HNY)
Emission controlled	...	...	...	...	Champion UN.12Y
Gap ...		...	...	...	.025 (.64)
Ignition timing					
Standard	...	...	...	...	10 deg. BTDC
GT6 Mk 3 ...		...	...	...	6 deg. BTDC static
GT6 Mk 3 (USA) ...		...	...		12 deg. BTDC static
GT6 Mk 3 (USA emission control)		...			6 deg. BTDC static
					4 deg. ATDC at idle
Ignition coil					
Type, early cars	...	...	...	...	Lucas HA12
early GT6	...	...	...	...	Lucas 16C6
late GT6 Mk 3 ...		...	...	...	Lucas 15C6
Distributor					
Vitesse...	...	...	...	...	Lucas 22D6
GT6 (standard)	...	...	...	...	Delco Remy D200
GT6 (emission controlled)	...	...	...		Delco Remy D204
Rotation	...	...	...	...	Anticlockwise, viewed on rotor

	Lucas	*Delco Remy*
Contact gap	.014 to .016 (.36 to .41)	.015 (.38)

| Contact spring tension | ... | ... | ... | 18 to 24 ozs | 17 to 21 ozs |
| Capacitor ... | ... | ... | ... | .20 mfd | .18 to .23 mfd |

COOLING SYSTEM

Cooling fan ... ... Crankshaft mounted
GT6 Mk 2 ... ... Eight-bladed, 12½ inch diameter
GT6 Mk 3 ... ... Seven-bladed 12½ inch diameter
All other models ... ... Six-bladed, 12½ diameter
Pressure
GT6 Mk 3 ... ... 13 lb/sq inch (.91 kg/sq cm)
Others ... ... 7 lb/sq inch (.49 kg/sq cm)
Antifreeze ... ... To specification BSI.3151 or 3152. For
   quantity see Chapter 4

Thermostat
Part No. 140970
Opening temperature ... ... 79.5 to 83.5°C (175 to 183°F)
Fully open ... ... 93.5 to 96°C (200 to 205°F)

CLUTCH

Type
GT6 ... ... Borg and Beck 8½ inch diameter
   DS No. BB.8/235
Vitesse ... ... Borg and Beck DS No. BB.8/236
Adjustment ... ... Self-adjusting, hydrostatic operation
Driven plate
Type ... ... Belleville washer
Springs ... ... 6, White/Light Green
Lining:
   GT6 ... ... Wound yarn WR7
   Vitesse ... ... Raybestos 1133C
Fluid ... ... Castrol Girling Crimson Clutch and
   Brake Fluid to specification SAE.70
   R3

GEARBOX AND OVERDRIVE

Type
Gearbox ... ... Four forward and one reverse ratio,
   synchromesh engagement on all four
   forward speeds.
Overdrive (optional extra) ... ... Laycock de Normanville
Ratios
Overdrive ... ... .802:1

Gearbox	Top	Third	Second	First	Reverse
	1.0:1	1.25:1	1.78:1	2.65:1	3.10:1

Overdrive operating pressure ... ... 540 to 560 lb/sq in
   (35.853 to 37.259 kg/sq cm)

Gearbox thrust washers
Countershaft front ... ... .123 to .125 (3.124 to 3.175)
Countershaft rear ... ... .066 to .068 (1.676 to 1.727)
Second/third gear ... ... .152 to .154 (3.861 to 3.912)
Second/third gear alternative ... ... .161 to .163 (4.089 to 4.139)
First gear ... ... .122 to .124 (3.099 to 3.149)
Centre ballrace-circlip:

Part No.	Thickness
143289	.091 to .093 (2.311 to 2.362)
143290	.094 to .096 (2.387 to 2.438)
143291	.097 to .099 (2.464 to 2.514)
143292	.100 to .102 (2.540 to 2.591)

Rear axle

Type ... ... Hypoid bevel gears. Final drive through inboard universal joint and outboard Rotoflex coupling

Ratio

GT6 (standard) 3.27:1
GT6 (with overdrive) 3.89:1
Vitesse ... ... 3.89:1 on all models

Camber

Unladen:
Vitesse Mk 2 Saloon ... ... 2 ± 1 deg. positive
Vitesse Mk 2 Convertible ... ... $2\frac{1}{4} \pm 1$ deg. positive
GT6 Mk 2, GT6 Plus and early GT6 ... 0 ± 1 deg.
GT6 Mk 3 from KF20,001 ... ... 1 ± 1 deg. negative
Laden ... ... All seats occupied (not rear on convertible)

Vitesse Mk 2 Saloon ... ... $2 \pm \frac{1}{2}$ deg. negative
Vitesse Mk 2 Convertible ... ... $\frac{1}{2} \pm \frac{1}{2}$ deg. positive
GT6 Mk 2 and GT6 Plus ... ... $2 \pm \frac{1}{2}$ deg. negative
GT6 Mk 3 ... ... $3\frac{1}{4} \pm 1$ deg. negative

Wheel alignment

GT6 Mk 3 ... ... $\frac{1}{32}$ to $\frac{3}{32}$ toe-out
Others ... ... $0 \pm \frac{1}{32}$
Laden:
All Vitesse and early GT6 ... ... $0 \pm \frac{1}{32}$ (0 ± .79)
GT6 from No. KF20,001 ... ... $\frac{1}{16}$ to $\frac{1}{8}$ (1.6 to 3.0) toe-in
GT6 up to KF20,001 ... ... 0 to $\frac{1}{16}$ toe-in

Road spring

	GT6	Vitesse	GT6 Mk 3
Part No.	308499	308485	313148
Number of blades	6	11	5
Blade thickness	.234 (5.943)	.203 (5.159)	.343 (8.729)

Camber

Unladen:
Vitesse ... ... $3\frac{1}{4} \pm 1$ deg. positive
GT6 ... ... $2\frac{3}{4} \pm 1$ deg. positive
Laden ... ... $2 \pm \frac{1}{2}$ deg. positive (all models)

Castor

Unladen:
Vitesse Mk 2 Saloon ... ... $2\frac{3}{4} \pm 1$ deg. positive
Vitesse Mk 2 Convertible ... ... 4 ± 1 deg. positive
GT6 Mk 2 and GT6 Plus ... ... $3\frac{1}{2} \pm 1$ deg. positive
Laden ... ... $4 \pm \frac{1}{2}$ deg. positive

Steering axis inclination (KPI)

Unladen:
Vitesse ... ... $5\frac{1}{2} \pm 1$ deg. positive
GT6 ... ... 6 ± 1 deg. positive
Laden ... ... $6\frac{3}{4} \pm \frac{3}{4}$ deg. positive (all models)

Front wheel alignment

Unladen ... ... $\frac{1}{16}$ to $\frac{1}{8}$ (1.6 to 3.0) toe-in
Laden ... ... 0 to $\frac{1}{16}$ (0 to 1.6) toe-in

Steering

Type ... ... Rack and pinion, with collapsible steering column
Lock ... ... Controlled by dimension of steering unit

Turns from lock to lock:						
GT6...	...	...	...	...	...	$4\frac{1}{4}$
Vitesse	...	...	...	...	...	$4\frac{3}{8}$
Shims for pinion	...	...	...	...	...	.004 (.102) and .010 (.254)
Shims for inner ball joints	...	...	...	...	...	.002 (.05) and .010 (.254)

Road spring

						GT6	Vitesse
Part No.	...	...	...	...	...	212425	209009
Wire diameter ...	...	...	...	...	...	$.45 \pm .002$	$.47 \pm .002$
						$(11.43 \pm .05)$	$(11.94 \pm .05)$
Number of working coils	...	...	...	...	...	$9\frac{1}{2}$	10
Free length	...	...	...	...	...	12.46 (316.5)	12.49 (317.3)
Fitted length	...	...	...	...	...	$8.06 \pm .09$	$8.18 \pm .09$
						(204.7 ± 2.3)	(207.75 ± 2.3)
Fitted load	...	...	...	...	...	880 lb (399.2 kg)	940 lb (426.5 kg)

Maximum back lock	...	...	...	...	...	50 deg. 30 min
Maximum front lock	...	...	...	...	...	48 deg. (note 20 deg. back lock gives 20 deg. front lock)
Front hub end float	...	...	...	...	...	.003 to .005 (.08 to .13)

BRAKES

Type	...	...	...	...	...	Hydraulic operated, front disc brakes drum rear brakes
						Tandem master cylinder fitted to USA models
Fluid	...	...	...	...	...	Castrol Girling Crimson Clutch and Brake Fluid to specification SAE.70 R3

Front disc brakes

Type	...	...	...	...	...	9.7 inch (246.4 mm) disc
Swept area	...	...	...	...	...	197 sq in (1270.97 sq cm)
Adjustment	...	...	...	...	...	Self-adjusting

Rear drum brakes

Type	...	...	...	...	...	8 x $1\frac{1}{4}$ (203 x 31.75) leading and trailing shoe
Swept area	...	...	...	...	...	63 sq in (406.45 sq cm)
Adjustment	...	...	...	...	...	One point per brake (also sets handbrake)

ELECTRICAL

The electrical system is negatively earthed and some components are polarity sensitive.

Battery

Type

GT6	...	...	...	...	...	Exide Auto-Fil 6.XNAZ9R (or Exide Supreme)
Vitesse	...	...	...	...	...	Exide Auto-Fil 6.VTAZ9BR (or Lucas D9)

				6.XNAZ9R	6.VTAZ9BR	D9
Capacity 20 hr rate	...	...		56 amp/hr	39 amp/hr	40 amp/hr
Plates per cell	...	...		9	9	9
Normal charge	...	...		6 amps	4 amps	3.5 amps
Size (approx)	...	...		$6\frac{3}{4}$ x 10 x $8\frac{3}{4}$	$5\frac{1}{2}$ x $9\frac{1}{2}$ x $8\frac{1}{8}$	$5\frac{1}{2}$ x $9\frac{1}{2}$ x $8\frac{1}{8}$

Generator (Vitesse models)

Type	...	...	...	...	...	Lucas C40L
Maximum output (cold)	...	...	...	...	25 amp at 13.5 volts on .54 ohm load at 2275 generator rev/min (1660 engine rev/min)

Brush tension ...	...	...	...	...	17 to 32 oz
Minimum brush length		...	...	...	$\frac{9}{32}$ inch
Brush grade ...	...	...	...	...	H.100 (preformed)
Field winding resistance		...	...	...	$5.9 \pm .3$ ohm
Minimum commutator diameter			...	...	1.430 inch

Generator control box

Type ...	...	...	...	...	...	Lucas RB.340
Cut-in voltage ...		...	...	...	...	12.7 to 13.3 volts
Drop-off voltage		...	...	...	...	9.5 to 11 volts
Current regulator setting			...	...	...	24 to 26 amps (on load)
Open circuit settings ...			...	...	...	

Ambient temperature	Voltage
10°C (50°F)	14.9 to 15.5
20°C (68°F)	14.7 to 15.3
30°C (86°F)	14.5 to 15.1
40°C (104°F)	14.3 to 14.9

Alternator (GT6 models)

Type ...	...	...	...	...	Lucas 15ACR	16ACR
Output ...	...	...	...	...	28 amp	34 amp
Engine speed ...	...	...	...	...	2450 rev/min	2450 rev/min
Brush minimum length		...	...	...	.2 (5) protruding free	

Starter motor

Type ...	...	...	...	...	...	Lucas M35G, four pole, four brush series wound
Brush tension ...	...	...	...	...	30 to 34 ozs
Minimum brush length		...	...	...	$\frac{5}{16}$ (8.0)
Minimum commutator diameter		...	...	$1\frac{9}{32}$

Performance data

Armature speed Rev/min	Torque lbs ft	Current Amps	Supply Volts
Locked	8.2	370	7.5 to 7.9
1000	5	270	8.6 to 9.0
8000 to 11500	No load	60 Maximum	12

Starter solenoid

Type ...	...	...	...	...	...	Lucas 4ST
Pull in voltage ...		...	...	...	...	4 to 9 volts
Release voltage		...	...	...	...	0 to 2.5 volts
Winding resistance		...	...	...	...	2.3 to 2.8 ohms
Operation ...	...	...	...	...	...	Electric, but can be manual

Windscreen wiper (Vitesse)

Type ...	...	...	...	...	...	Lucas DR3A, shunt wound, single speed
Lighting running current		...	...	...	3.4 amps max (after 60 seconds from cold)
Light running speed ...		...	...	...	45 to 50 rev/min (after 60 seconds)
Brush pressure (new) ...		...	...	...	4.0 to 6.0 ozs (against commutator)
Field winding resistance		...	...	...	8.0 to 9.5 ohms at 15.5°C
Maximum force to move cable rack		...	...	6 lb (2.7 kg)

Windscreen wiper (GT6)

| Type ... | ... | ... | ... | ... | ... | Lucas 14W, two speed, permanent magnet |

Light running current:

| Low-speed ... | ... | ... | ... | ... | 1.5 amp |
| High-speed ... | ... | ... | ... | ... | 2.0 amp |

Light running speed:

Low-speed ...	...	...	...	...	46 to 52 rev/min
High-speed ...	...	...	...	...	60 to 70 rev/min
Armature end float	...	...	...	...	.002 to .008
Brush spring pressure		...	...	...	5 to 7 oz (brush bottom aligned with brushbox slot end)

Minimum brush length:

Earth and low-speed		...	...	...	$\frac{3}{16}$
High-speed ...	...	...	...	...	.28 (narrow section worn away)
Maximum force to move cable rack	...		...	...	6 lb (2.7 kg)

Fuses

Fuse box	...	...	...	...	35 amp rated, colour coded white
In-line fuse (Vitesse) ...	...	...	...		25 amp rated, colour coded pink

Turn signal flasher unit

GT6 ...	...	...	...	...	Lucas 8FL 3.6A
Vitesse	...	...	...	...	Lucas FL5

Horns

GT6:

Relay	...	...	...	...	Lucas 6RA
Type	...	...	...	...	Lucas 9H (or Clearhooter)
Operating current	...	...	...	...	7 to 7.5 amp

Vitesse:

Relay	...	...	...	...	None
Type	...	...	...	...	Lucas 9H (or Clearhooter)
Operating current	...	...	...	...	3.5 to 4 amps

Hazard warning flasher

Type ...	...	...	...	...	Signal-stat 180 or Lucas 9FL

Heated backlight (GT6)

Type ...	...	...	...	...	Triplex Hotline
					Triplex Hotline Sundym (tinted)
Operating current	...	...	...	...	10.2 amps

Oil pressure switch

Make ...	...	...	...	...	AC or Smiths
Stanpart No. ...	...	...	...	...	121398
Operating pressure	...	...	...	...	3 to 5 lb/sq in

Voltage stabiliser

Type ...	...	...	...	...	Smith ER 1307/00
Output voltage	...	...	...	...	10 volts

WEIGHTS AND DIMENSIONS

Overall length

Vitesse...	...	...	...	...	12 ft 9 inch (388.5 cm)
GT6 ...	...	...	...	...	12 ft 1 inch (368 cm)
GT6 Mk 3 ...	...	...	...	...	12 ft 5 inch (379 cm)

Overall width

Vitesse...	...	...	...	...	5 ft (152.5 cm)
GT6 ...	...	...	...	...	4 ft 9 inch (145 cm)
GT6 Mk 3 ...	...	...	...	...	4 ft $10\frac{1}{2}$ inch (149 cm)

Height

Vitesse...	...	...	...	...	4 ft $5\frac{3}{4}$ inch (136.5 cm) unladen
GT6 ...	...	...	...	...	3 ft 11 inch (119 cm) unladen

Ground clearance

Vitesse...	...	...	...	...	$6\frac{3}{4}$ inch (170 mm) laden
GT6 ...	...	...	...	...	4 inch (102 mm) laden

Turning circle ...

... ... 25 ft 3 inch (7.7 m)

Weight (approximately)
Dry:

Vitesse	...	...	...	...	$17\frac{1}{4}$ cwt (876 kg)
GT6 ...	...	...	...	...	16 cwt (813 kg)
GT6 Mk 3 ...	...	...	...	...	$17\frac{1}{4}$ cwt (878 kg)

Complete:

Vitesse	...	...	...	...	$18\frac{1}{4}$ cwt (927 kg)
GT6 ...	...	...	...	...	17 cwt (865 kg)
GT6 Mk 3 ...	...	...	...	...	$18\frac{1}{4}$ cwt (921 kg)

Maximum gross

Vitesse ...	...	...	...	...	$24\frac{3}{4}$ cwt (1225 kg)
GT6 ...	...	...	...	...	21 cwt (1067 kg)
GT6 Mk 3 (1971)	...	...	...	...	23 cwt (1161 kg)
(1973)	...	...	...	...	$22\frac{1}{2}$ cwt (1145 kg)

CAPACITIES

	Imperial	US	Metric
Engine (add 1 pint when filter changed) ...	8 Pints	9.6 Pints	4.5 Litres
Gearbox	1.5 Pints	1.8 Pints	.85 Litres
Gearbox and overdrive	2.38 Pints	2.85 Pints	1.35 Litres
Rear axle	1 Pint	1.2 Pints	.57 Litres
Cooling system (complete)	11 Pints	13.2 Pints	6.2 Litres
Fuel tank:			
GT6 (no reserve)	$9\frac{3}{4}$ Galls	11.7 Galls	44.3 Litres
Vitesse (with reserve)	$8\frac{3}{4}$ Galls	10.5 Galls	40 Litres

TYRES

Type

GT6 ...	...	...	...	...	...	Goodyear 155SR.13 G.800
						Dunlop SP68
Vitesse ...	...	...	...	...	...	Goodyear 155SR x 13 G800

Tyre pressures

All models	...	...	...	...	...	24 lb/sq in (1.69 kg/sq cm) front and rear

These pressures are only suitable for the tyres given and speeds of up to 110 mile/hr (175 kilo/hr) and for different tyres or higher speeds the tyre makers' recommendations should always be taken.

Do **not** intermix radial and cross-ply tyres

TORQUE WRENCH SETTINGS

	lb ft	Kgm
Engine		
Carburetter attachment	12 to 14	1.6 to 1.9
Camshaft chainwheel	24 to 26	3.3 to 3.6
Clutch attachment	20	2.8
Connecting rod bolts	38 to 42	5.3 to 5.8
Crankshaft oil retaining cover to block ...	16 to 18	2.2 to 2.5
Crankshaft sealing block to block	12 to 14	1.7 to 1.9
Crankshaft pulley attachment	90 to 100	12.4 to 13.8
Cylinder head nuts	65 to 70	9 to 9.7
Engine plate attachments (all)	18 to 20	2.5 to 2.8
Exhaust pipe to manifold	24 to 26	3.3 to 3.6
Flywheel to crankshaft	42 to 46	5.8 to 6.4
Inlet manifold	14 to 16	1.9 to 2.2
Inlet manifold to exhaust manifold	20 to 22	2.5 to 3.0
Mounting bracket to engine	26 to 28	3.6 to 3.9
Mounting rubber to chassis front	28 to 30	3.9 to 4.1
Mounting rubber to front bracket	26 to 28	3.6 to 3.9
Mounting rubber attachment rear	12 to 14	1.6 to 1.9
Oil pump to block	8 to 10	1.1 to 1.4
Rocker cover	1.5	.3
Rocker oil feed	16 to 18	2.2 to 2.5
Rocker pedestal	24 to 26	3.3 to 3.6
Spark plug	14 to 16	1.9 to 2.2
Sump (fitting)	16 to 18	2.2 to 2.5
Sump (after settling)	Minimum 8	1.1
Timing cover to engine plate	8 to 10	1.1 to 1.4
Timing cover to engine plate (after settling) ...	4	.5
Water pump	18 to 20	2.5 to 2.8
Water pump pulley	14 to 16	1.9 to 2.2
Gearbox		
Bellhousing	24 to 26	3.3 to 3.6
Fulcrum, reverse lever	14 to 16	1.9 to 2.2
Gearlever coupling	8 to 10	1.1 to 1.4
Gearlever to operating shaft	6 to 8	.8 to 1.1
Overdrive adaptor to gearbox	14 to 16	1.9 to 2.2
Overdrive support	18 to 20	2.5 to 2.8
Flange to mainshaft	90 to 100	12.4 to 13.8
Propeller shaft to flange	28 to 30	3.9 to 4.1
Selector fork	8 to 10	1.1 to 1.4
Top cover attachments	8 to 10	1.1 to 1.4
Top cover to extension	12 to 14	1.7 to 1.9
Rear axle		
Front mounting plate to chassis	26 to 28	3.6 to 3.9
Inner axle to drive shaft	32 to 36	4.4 to 5.0
Flange to hypoid pinion	90 to 100	12.4 to 13.8
Rear axle mounting	38 to 42	5.2 to 5.8
Road spring to axle	28 to 30	3.9 to 4.1
Front suspension		
Anti-roll bar U-bolts	3 to 4	.4 to .6
Anti-roll bar stud	12 to 14	1.7 to 1.9
Anti-roll bar link	38 to 42	5.2 to 5.8
Brake disc to hub	32 to 35	4.4 to 4.8
Caliper mounting plate		
$\frac{3}{8}$ UNF	32 to 35	4.4 to 4.8
$\frac{5}{16}$ UNF	18 to 20	2.5 to 2.8
Caliper to plate	50 to 55	6.9 to 7.6

Damper:				
Top attachment	...	...	8 to 10	1.1 to 1.4
Bottom attachment ...	...	...	42 to 46	5.8 to 6.4
Stub axle to vertical link	...	...	90 to 100	12.4 to 13.8

Rear suspension

Wishbone to vertical link	...	...	55 to 60	7.8 to 8.3
Road spring to vertical link	...	...	42 to 46	5.8 to 6.4
Lower wishbone-outer	...	...	55 to 60	7.6 to 8.3
Outer drive shaft to hub	...	...	100 to 110	13.8 to 15.2
Intermediate drive shaft flange	...	...	110 to 110	13.8 to 15.2
Rotoflex coupling bolts	...	...	65 to 70	9.0 to 9.7
Radius arm to bracket ...	...	...	28 to 30	3.9 to 4.1
Radius arm bracket attachment	...	...	55 to 60	7.6 to 8.3
Radius arm bracket to vertical link	...	...	42 to 46	5.8 to 6.4
Damper:				
GT6 top fixing	...	...	55 to 60	7.6 to 8.3
Vitesse top attachment	...	...	40 to 45	5.5 to 6.3
Vitesse link ...	...	...	18 to 20	2.5 to 2.8
Road spring	...	...	28 to 30	3.9 to 4.1
Radius arm locknuts	...	...	42 to 46	5.8 to 6.4

Wheels

Wheel nuts	...	...	38 to 42	5.2 to 5.8
Wire wheel extension attachment	...	...	45	6.2

Steering

Impact clamp ...	...	...	6 to 8	.8 to 1.1
Impact clamp socket screw	...	...	18 to 20	2.5 to 2.8
Steering unit U-bolts ...	...	...	14 to 16	1.9 to 2.2
Steering wheel nut	...	...	28 to 30	3.9 to 4.1

SPECIAL TOOLS

All special tools required for the models covered by this manual are obtainable from:

Messrs. V. L. Churchill & Co. Ltd.,
PO Box No. 3
London Road
DAVENTRY
Northants.
England.

RUNNING-IN

Whenever new parts are fitted to the engine they require careful bedding in. If these parts are submitted to the full load as soon as they are fitted they will not have the opportunity of being properly mated to the other working surface.

Power and performance will suffer, the working life of the engine will be shortened and it will always have a touch of 'roughness' about it if the running-in period is not complied with. New pistons and cylinder liners require full running-in. If only new piston rings or crankshaft bearings (including big-ends) have been fitted the running-in period is not so rigorous but the engine should still be treated with care for the first 1000 miles.

No specified speeds are recommended for running-in, but the engine should not be allowed to labour. Warm it up at a fast idle before driving away (this should be done at all times not just when running-in) and use the minimum choke sufficient to prevent the engine stalling. Avoid using full throttle at slow speeds. The running-in process is progressive but for the first 500 miles full power should not be used. The engine may be allowed to 'rev' fairly fast provided it is not under a heavy load. It is better to change down a gear and let the engine 'rev' fast than to make it 'slog' in a higher gear at lower rev/min. Full power may be used for short periods after the first 500 miles gradually extending the amount of time in full power as the engine becomes more responsive and the mileage reaches 1000 miles. After 1000 miles the engine may be considered to be fully run-in.

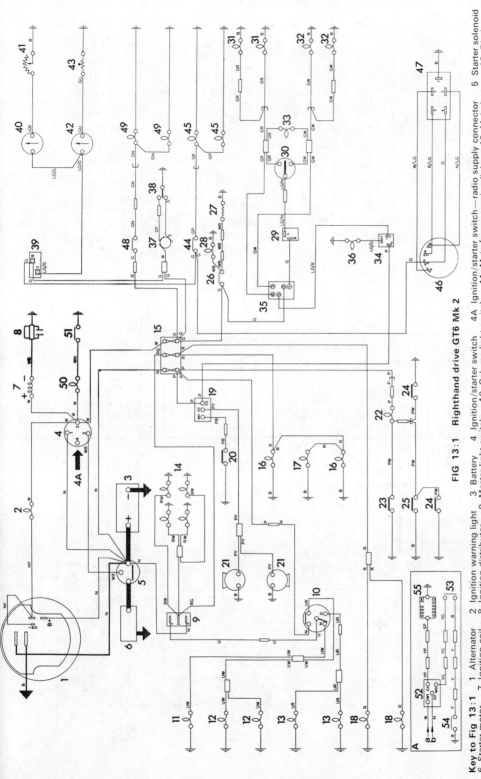

FIG 13:1   Righthand drive GT6 Mk 2

Key to Fig 13:1 1 Alternator 2 Ignition warning light 3 Battery 4 Ignition/starter switch 4A Ignition/starter switch 5 Starter solenoid
6 Starter motor 7 Ignition coil 8 Ignition distributor 9 Master light switch 10 Column light switch 11 Main beam warning light 12 Main beam 13 Dip beam
14 Instrument illumination 15 Fuse assembly 16 Tail lamp 17 Plate illumination lamp 18 Front parking lamp 19 Horn relay 20 Horn push 21 Horn
22 Roof lamp 23 Roof lamp tailgate switch 24 Roof lamp door switch 25 Roof lamp facia switch 26 Heated backlight switch 27 Heated backlight
28 Heated backlight warning light 29 Turn signal flasher unit 30 Turn signal flasher switch 31 Lefthand flasher lamp 32 Righthand flasher lamp
33 Turn signal warning light 34 Hazard flasher unit 35 Hazard switch 36 Hazard warning light 37 Heater motor 38 Heater switch 39 Voltage stabilizer
40 Fuel indicator 41 Fuel tank unit 42 Temperature indicator 43 Temperature transmitter 44 Stop lamp switch 45 Stop lamp 46 Windscreen wiper switch
47 Windscreen wiper motor 48 Reverse lamp switch 49 Reverse lamp 50 Oil pressure warning light 51 Oil pressure switch

A Overdrive (optional extra) 52 Overdrive relay 53 Overdrive column switch 54 Overdrive gearbox switch 55 Overdrive solenoid   (a) From ignition/
starter switch—connector 2   (b) From ignition/starter switch—connector 1   radio supply connector

Cable colour code   N Brown   U Blue   R Red   P Purple   G Green   LG Light Green   W White   Y Yellow   S Slate   B Black   K Pink

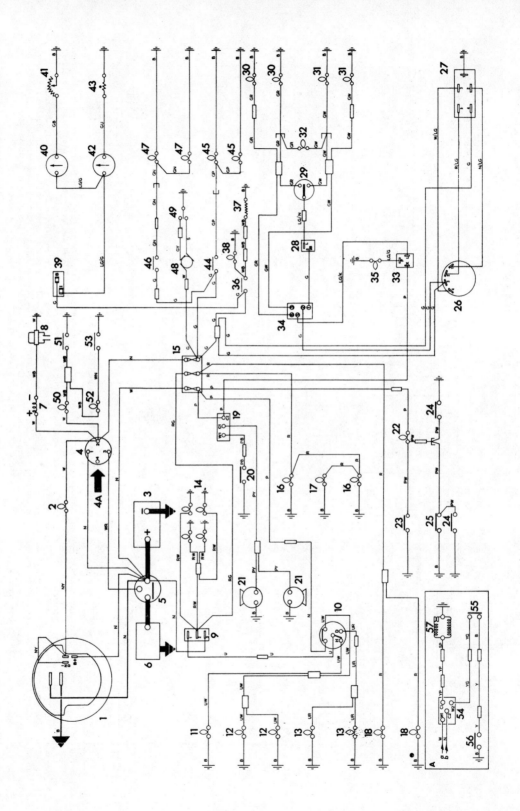

FIG 13 : 2   Lefthand drive GT6 Mk 2 and GT6 Plus

Key to Fig 13 : 2   1 Alternator   2 Ignition warning light   3 Battery   4 Ignition/starter switch   4A Ignition/starter switch—radio supply connector   5 Starter solenoid
6 Starter motor   7 Ignition coil   8 Ignition distributor   9 Master light switch   10 Column light switch   11 Main beam warning light   12 Main beam   13 Dip beam
14 Instrument illumination   15 Fuse assembly   16 Tail lamp   17 Plate illumination lamp   18 Front parking lamp   19 Horn relay   20 Horn push   21 Horn
22 Roof lamp   23 Roof lamp tailgate switch   24 Roof lamp door switch   25 Roof lamp facia switch   26 Windscreen wiper switch   27 Windscreen wiper motor
28 Turn signal flasher unit   29 Turn signal flasher switch   30 Lefthand lamp   31 Righthand flasher lamp   32 Turn signal warning light   33 Hazard flasher unit
34 Hazard switch   35 Hazard warning light   36 Heated backlight switch   37 Heated backlight   38 Heated backlight warning light   39 Voltage stabilizer
40 Fuel indicator   41 Fuel tank unit   42 Temperature indicator   43 Temperature transmitter   44 Stop lamp switch   45 Stop lamp   46 Reverse lamp switch
47 Reverse lamp   48 Heater motor   49 Heater switch   50 Brake line failure warning light   51 Brake line failure switch   52 Oil pressure warning light
53 Oil pressure switch

A Overdrive (optional extra)   54 Overdrive relay   55 Overdrive column switch   56 Overdrive gearbox switch   57 Overdrive solenoid
(a) From ignition/starter switch—connector 2   (b) From ignition/starter switch—connector 1

Cable colour code   N Brown   U Blue   R Red   P Purple   G Green   LG Light Green   W White   Y Yellow   S Slate   B Black   K Pink

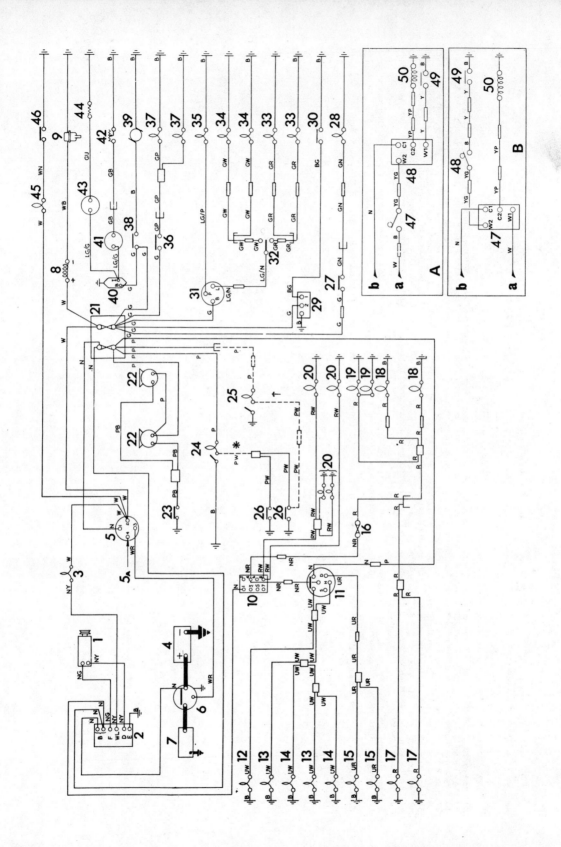

FIG 13:3 All models Vitesse

Key to Fig 13:3
1 Generator
2 Control box
3 Ignition warning light
4 Battery
5 Ignition/starter switch
5A Ignition/starter switch—radio supply position
6 Starter solenoid
7 Starter motor
8 Ignition coil
9 Ignition distributor
10 Master light switch
11 Column light switch
12 Main beam warning light
13 Outer main beam
14 Inner main beam
15 Dip beam
16 Line fuse
17 Front parking lamp
18 Tail lamp
19 Plate illumination lamp
20 Instrument illumination
21 Fuse box
22 Horn
23 Horn push
24 Facia lamp
25 Roof lamp (Saloon only)
26 Door switch
27 Reverse lamp switch
28 Reverse lamp
29 Windscreen wiper motor
30 Windscreen wiper switch
31 Flasher unit
32 Flasher switch
33 Lefthand flasher lamp
34 Righthand flasher lamp
35 Flasher warning light
36 Stop lamp switch
37 Stop lamp
38 Heater switch
39 Heater motor
40 Voltage stabilizer
41 Fuel indicator
42 Fuel tank unit
43 Temperature indicator
44 Temperature transmitter
45 Oil pressure warning light
46 Oil pressure switch
A Overdrive (optional extra)—Early vehicles built before approximately April 1967 only
47 Overdrive column switch
(a) From fuse box
(b) From ignition/starter switch—connector 1
48 Overdrive column switch
49 Overdrive
50 Overdrive solenoid
gearbox switch
B Overdrive (optional extra)—Vehicles built after approximately April 1967 only
47 Overdrive relay
48 Overdrive column switch
49 Overdrive
50 Overdrive solenoid
gearbox switch
(a) From fuse box
(b) From ignition/starter switch—connector 1

Note:
On convertible no roof lamp is fitted—door switches (26) control facia lamp (24). PW wire shown dotted and indicated * is fitted on convertible only. On saloon door switches (26) control roof lamp (25). P and PW wires shown dotted and indicated † are fitted on saloon only.

Cable colour code
N Brown
U Blue
R Red
P Purple
G Green
LG Light Green
W White
Y Yellow
S Slate
B Black
K Pink

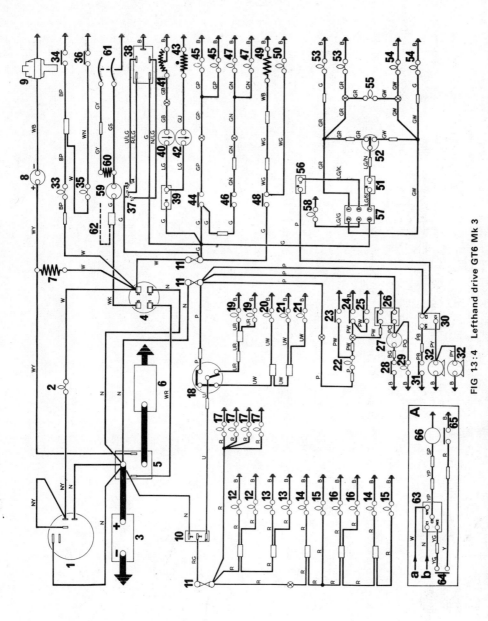

FIG 13:4   Lefthand drive GT6 Mk 3

Key to Fig 13:4   1 Alternator   2 Ignition warning light   3 Battery   4 Ignition/starter switch   5 Starter solenoid   6 Starter motor   7 Ballast resistor   8 Ignition coil, 6-volt   9 Ignition distributor   10 Master light switch   11 Fuse   12 Front parking lamp   13 Front marker lamp   14 Rear marker lamp   15 Tail lamp   16 Plate illumination lamp   17 Instrument illumination   18 Column light switch   19 Dip beam   20 Main beam warning light   21 Main beam   22 Roof lamp   23 Tailgate switch   24 Facia switch   25 Righthand door switch   26 Lefthand door switch   27 Key warning buzzer (USA only)   28 Key switch (USA only)   29 Key courtesy light   30 Horn relay   31 Horn push   32 Horn   33 Brake warning light   34 Brake line failure switch   35 Oil pressure warning light   36 Oil pressure switch   37 Windscreen wiper switch   38 Windscreen wiper motor   39 Voltage stabiliser   40 Fuel indicator   41 Fuel tank unit   42 Temperature indicator   43 Temperature transmitter   44 Stop lamp switch   45 Stop lamp   46 Reverse lamp switch   47 Reverse lamp   48 Heated backlight switch   49 Heated backlight   50 Heated backlight warning light   51 Turn signal flasher unit   52 Turn signal switch   53 Lefthand flasher lamp   54 Righthand flasher lamp   55 Turn signal warning light   56 Radio facility   57 Hazard flasher unit   58 Hazard warning light   59 Heater motor   60 Heater rheostat   61 Heater switch   62 Radio facility

A Overdrive (optional extra)   63 Overdrive relay   64 Overdrive gearlever switch   65 Overdrive gearbox switch   66 Overdrive solenoid   (a) From ignition/starter switch, terminal 3   (b) From ignition/starter switch, terminal 2

166

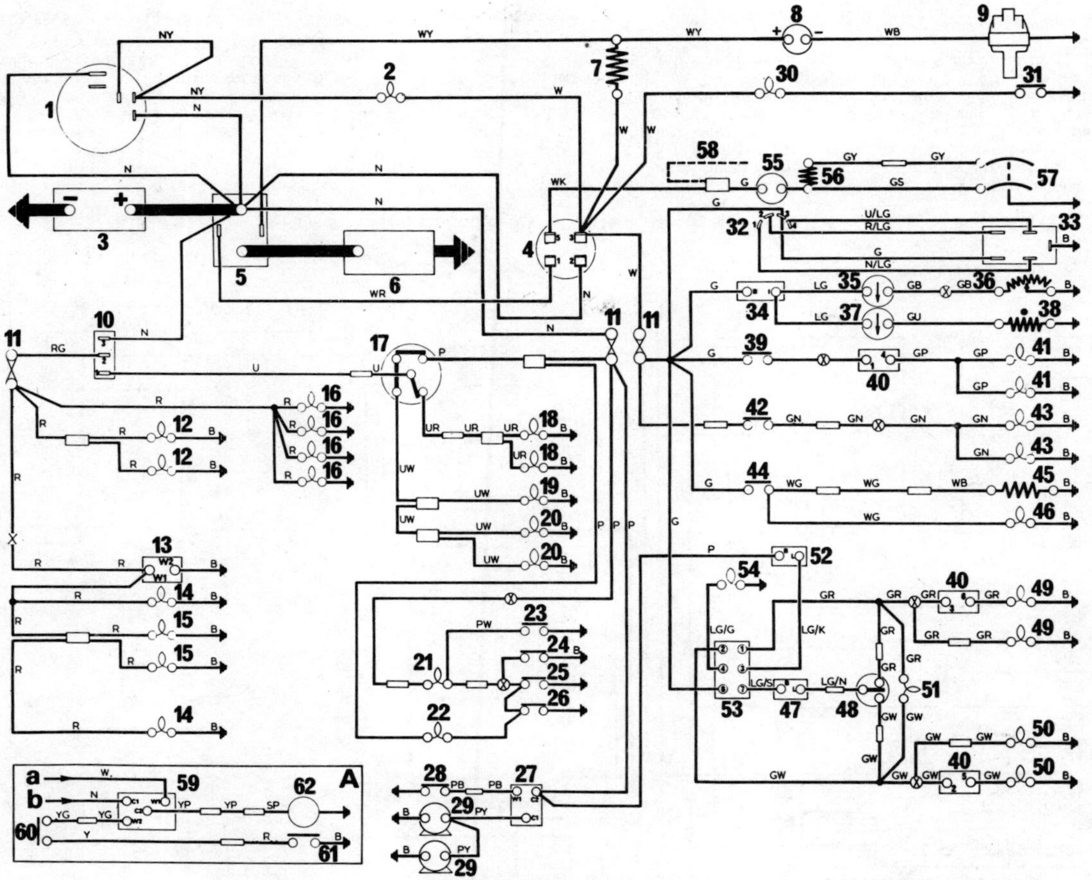

FIG 13:5   Righthand drive GT6 Mk 3—up to No. KE20,000

Key to Fig 13:5   1 Alternator   2 Ignition warning light   3 Battery   4 Ignition/starter switch   5 Starter solenoid   6 Starter motor   7 Ballast resistor   8 Ignition coil, 6-volt   9 Ignition distributor   10 Master light switch   11 Fuse   12 Front parking lamp   13 Night dimming relay winding   14 Tail lamp   15 Plate illumination lamp   16 Instrument illumination   17 Column light switch   18 Dip beam   19 Main beam warning light   20 Main beam   21 Roof lamp   22 Key courtesy light   23 Tailgate switch   24 Lefthand door switch   25 Facia switch   26 Righthand door switch   27 Horn relay   28 Horn push   29 Horn   30 Oil pressure warning light   31 Oil pressure switch   32 Windscreen wiper switch   33 Windscreen wiper motor   34 Voltage stabiliser   35 Fuel indicator   36 Fuel tank unit   37 Temperature indicator   38 Temperature transmitter   39 Stop lamp switch   40 Night dimming relay   41 Stop lamp   42 Reverse lamp   43 Reverse lamp switch   44 Heated backlight switch   45 Heated backlight   46 Heated backlight warning light   47 Turn signal flasher unit   48 Turn signal switch   49 Lefthand flasher lamp   50 Righthand flasher lamp   51 Turn signal warning light   52 Hazard flasher unit   53 Hazard switch   54 Hazard warning light   55 Heater motor   56 Heater rheostat   57 Heater switch   58 Radio facility   59 Overdrive relay   60 Overdrive gearbox switch   61 Overdrive gearlever switch   62 Overdrive solenoid   (a) From ignition/starter switch, terminal 2

A Overdrive (optional extra)   (a) From ignition/starter switch, terminal 3   (b) From ignition/starter switch, terminal 2

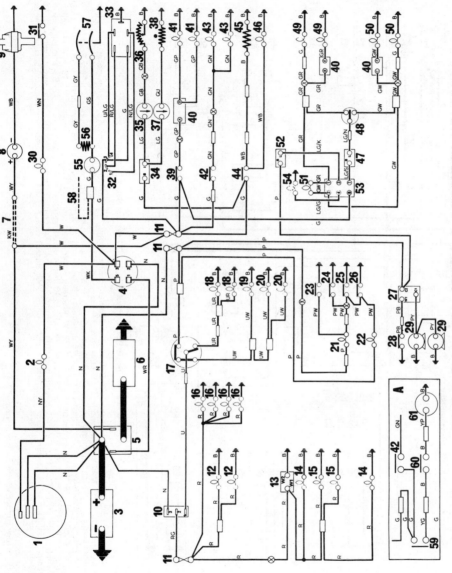

FIG 13:6   Righthand drive GT6 Mk 3—from No. KE20,001

Key to Fig 13:6   1 Alternator   2 Ignition warning light   3 Battery   4 Ignition starter switch   5 Starter solenoid   6 Starter motor   7 Ballast resistor wire   8 Ignition coil, 6-volt   9 Ignition distributor   10 Master light switch   11 Fuse   12 Front parking lamp   13 Night dimming relay winding   14 Tail lamp   15 Plate illumination lamp   16 Instrument illumination   17 Column light switch   18 Dip beam   19 Main beam warning light   20 Main beam   21 Roof lamp   22 Key courtesy light   23 Tailgate switch   24 Lefthand door switch   25 Facia switch   26 Righthand door switch   27 Horn relay   28 Horn push   29 Horn   30 Oil pressure warning light   31 Oil pressure switch   32 Windscreen wiper switch   33 Windscreen wiper motor   34 Voltage stabiliser   35 Fuel indicator   36 Fuel tank unit   37 Temperature indicator   38 Temperature transmitter   39 Stop lamp switch   40 Night dimming relay   41 Turn signal flasher unit   42 Reverse lamp switch   43 Reverse lamp   44 Heated backlight switch   45 Heated backlight   46 Heated backlight warning light   47 Turn signal flasher unit   48 Turn signal switch   49 Lefthand flasher lamp   50 Righthand flasher lamp   51 Turn signal warning light   52 Hazard flasher lamp   53 Hazard switch   54 Hazard warning light   55 Heater motor   56 Heater rheostat   57 Heater switch   58 Radio facility   59 Overdrive gearbox switch   60 Overdrive gearlever switch   61 Overdrive solenoid

A Overdrive (optional extra)   59 Overdrive gearbox switch   60 Overdrive gearlever switch   61 Overdrive solenoid

168

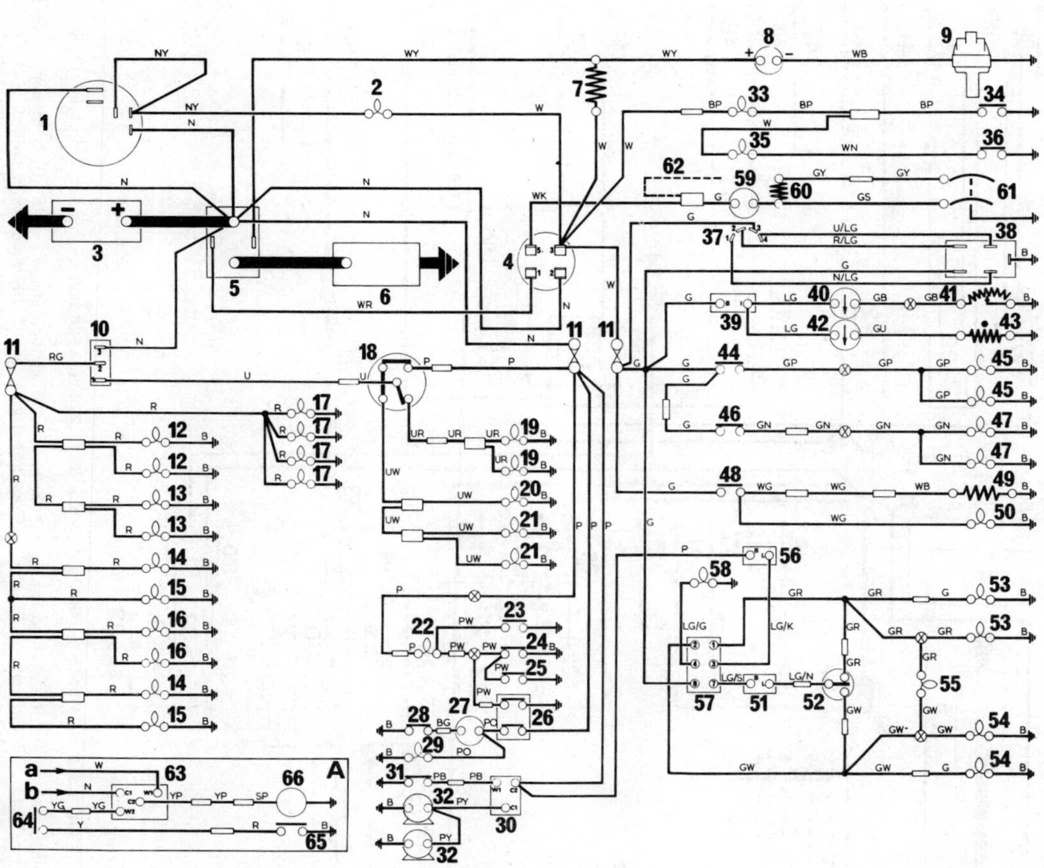

FIG 13:7 GT6 Mk 3, USA only—up to No. KF11,389

Key to Fig 13:7 1 Alternator   2 Ignition warning light   3 Battery   4 Ignition/starter switch   5 Starter solenoid   6 Starter motor   7 Ballast resistor   8 Ignition coil, 6-volt   9 Ignition distributor   10 Master light switch   11 Fuse   12 Front parking lamp   13 Front marker lamp   14 Rear marker lamp   15 Tail lamp   16 Plate illumination lamp   17 Instrument illumination   18 Column light switch   19 Dip beam   20 Main beam warning light   21 Main beam   22 Roof lamp   23 Tailgate switch   24 Facia switch   25 Righthand door switch   26 Lefthand door switch   27 Key warning buzzer   28 Key switch   29 Key courtesy light   30 Horn relay   31 Horn push   32 Horn   33 Brake warning light   34 Brake line failure switch   35 Oil pressure warning light   36 Oil pressure switch   37 Windscreen wiper switch   38 Windscreen wiper motor   39 Voltage stabiliser   40 Fuel indicator   41 Fuel tank unit   42 Temperature indicator   43 Temperature transmitter   44 Stop lamp   45 Stop lamp   46 Reverse lamp switch   47 Reverse lamp   48 Heated backlight switch   49 Heated backlight   50 Heated backlight warning light   51 Turn signal flasher unit   52 Turn signal switch   53 Lefthand flasher lamp   54 Righthand flasher lamp   55 Turn signal warning light   56 Hazard flasher unit   57 Hazard switch   58 Hazard warning light   59 Heater motor   60 Heater rheostat   61 Heater switch   62 Radio facility   63 Overdrive relay   64 Overdrive gearbox switch   65 Overdrive gearlever switch   66 Overdrive solenoid

A Overdrive (optional extra)   63 Overdrive relay   64 Overdrive gearbox switch, terminal 2   65 Overdrive gearlever switch, terminal 3   (b) From ignition/starter switch, terminal 2   (a) From ignition/starter switch, terminal 2

T/GT6

169

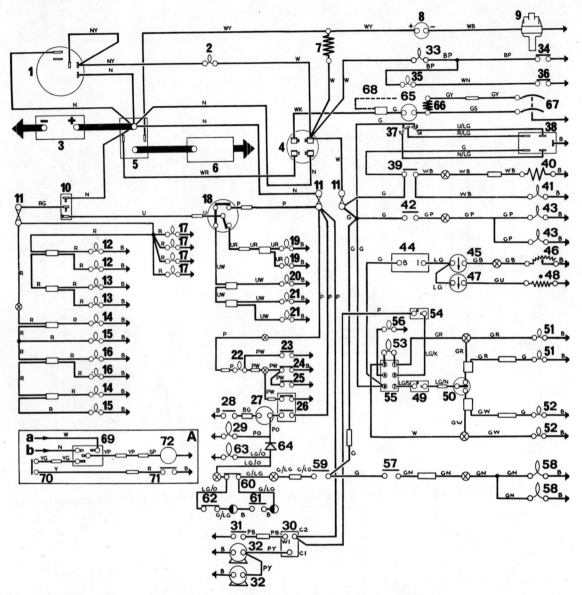

FIG 13:8 GT6 Mk 3, USA only—No. KF11,390 to KF20,000

Key to Fig 13:8 1 Alternator   2 Ignition warning light   3 Battery   4 Ignition/starter switch   5 Starter solenoid
6 Starter motor   7 Ballast resistor   8 Ignition coil, 6-volt   9 Ignition distributor   10 Master light switch   11 Fuse
12 Front parking lamp   13 Front marker lamp   14 Rear marker lamp   15 Tail lamp   16 Plate illumination lamp
17 Instrument illumination   18 Column light switch   19 Dip beam   20 Main beam warning light   21 Main beam   22 Roof
lamp   23 Tailgate switch   24 Facia switch   25 Righthand door switch   26 Lefthand door switch   27 Key warning buzzer
28 Key switch   29 Key light   30 Horn relay   31 Horn push   32 Horn   33 Brake warning light   34 Brake line failure
switch   35 Oil pressure warning light   36 Oil pressure switch   37 Windscreen wiper switch   38 Windscreen wiper motor
39 Heated backlight switch   40 Heated backlight   41 Heated backlight warning light   42 Stop lamp switch   43 Stop lamp
44 Voltage stabiliser   45 Fuel indicator   46 Fuel tank unit   47 Temperature indicator   48 Temperature transmitter   49 Turn
signal flasher unit   50 Turn signal switch   51 Lefthand flasher lamp   52 Righthand flasher lamp   53 Turn signal warning
light   54 Hazard flasher unit   55 Hazard switch   56 Hazard warning light   57 Reverse lamp switch   58 Reverse lamp
59 Seat belt gearbox switch   60 Driver's belt switch   61 Passenger's seat switch   62 Passenger's belt switch   63 Seat belt
warning light   64 Diode   65 Heater motor   66 Heater rheostat   67 Heater switch   68 Radio facility
A Overdrive (optional extra)   69 Overdrive relay   70 Overdrive gearbox switch   71 Overdrive gearlever switch
72 Overdrive solenoid   (a) From ignition/starter switch, terminal 3   (b) From ignition/starter switch, terminal 2

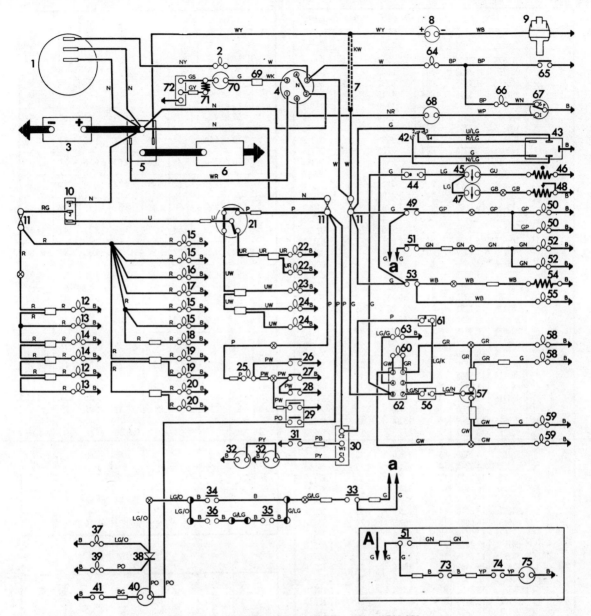

FIG 13:9 GT6 Mk 3, USA only—from No. KF20,001

Key to Fig 13:9   1 Alternator   2 Ignition warning light   3 Battery   4 Ignition/starter switch   5 Starter solenoid
6 Starter motor   7 Ballast resistor wire   8 Ignition coil, 6-volt   9 Ignition distributor   10 Master light switch   11 Fuse
12 Rear marker lamp   13 Tail lamp   14 Plate illumination lamp   15 Instrument illumination   16 Hazard switch identification
light   17 Wipe/wash switch identification light   18 Heater control identification light   19 Front parking lamp   20 Front
marker lamp   21 Column light switch   22 Dip beam   23 Main beam warning light   24 Main beam   25 Roof lamp
26 Tailgate switch   27 Facia switch   28 Righthand door switch   29 Lefthand door switch   30 Horn relay   31 Horn push
32 Horn   33 Belt warning gearbox switch   34 Driver's belt switch   35 Passenger's seat switch   36 Passenger's belt
switch   37 Fasten belts warning light   38 Diode   39 Key light   40 Buzzer   41 Key switch   42 Windscreen wiper switch
43 Windscreen wiper motor   44 Voltage stabiliser   45 Temperature indicator   46 Temperature transmitter   47 Fuel indicator
48 Fuel tank unit   49 Stop lamp switch   50 Stop lamp   51 Reverse lamp switch   52 Reverse lamp   53 Heated backlight
switch   54 Heated backlight   55 Heated backlight warning light   56 Turn signal flasher unit   57 Turn signal switch
58 Lefthand flasher lamp   59 Righthand flasher lamp   60 Turn signal warning light   61 Hazard flasher unit   62 Hazard
switch   63 Hazard warning light   64 Brake warning light   65 Brake line failure switch   66 Oil pressure warning light
67 Oil pressure switch   68 Anti-run-on valve   69 Radio facility   70 Heater motor   71 Heater rheostat   72 Heater switch

A Overdrive (optional extra)   73 Overdrive gearlever switch   74 Overdrive gearbox switch   75 Overdrive solenoid

Inches		Decimals	Milli-metres	Inches to Millimetres		Millimetres to Inches	
				Inches	mm	mm	Inches
	1/64	.015625	.3969	.001	.0254	.01	.00039
1/32		.03125	.7937	.002	.0508	.02	.00079
	3/64	.046875	1.1906	.003	.0762	.03	.00118
1/16		.0625	1.5875	.004	.1016	.04	.00157
	5/64	.078125	1.9844	.005	.1270	.05	.00197
3/32		.09375	2.3812	.006	.1524	.06	.00236
	7/64	.109375	2.7781	.007	.1778	.07	.00276
1/8		.125	3.1750	.008	.2032	.08	.00315
	9/64	.140625	3.5719	.009	.2286	.09	.00354
5/32		.15625	3.9687	.01	.254	.1	.00394
	11/64	.171875	4.3656	.02	.508	.2	.00787
3/16		.1875	4.7625	.03	.762	.3	.01181
	13/64	.203125	5·1594	.04	1.016	.4	.01575
7/32		.21875	5.5562	.05	1.270	.5	.01969
	15/64	.234375	5.9531	.06	1.524	.6	.02362
1/4		.25	6.3500	.07	1.778	.7	.02756
	17/64	.265625	6.7469	.08	2.032	.8	.03150
9/32		.28125	7.1437	.09	2.286	.9	.03543
	19/64	.296875	7.5406	.1	2.54	1	.03937
5/16		.3125	7.9375	.2	5.08	2	.07874
	21/64	.328125	8.3344	.3	7.62	3	.11811
11/32		.34375	8.7312	.4	10.16	4	.15748
	23/64	.359375	9.1281	.5	12.70	5	.19685
3/8		.375	9.5250	.6	15.24	6	.23622
	25/64	.390625	9.9219	.7	17.78	7	.27559
13/32		.40625	10.3187	.8	20.32	8	.31496
	27/64	.421875	10.7156	.9	22.86	9	.35433
7/16		.4375	11.1125	1	25.4	10	.39370
	29/64	.453125	11.5094	2	50.8	11	.43307
15/32		.46875	11.9062	3	76.2	12	.47244
	31/64	.484375	12.3031	4	101.6	13	.51181
1/2		.5	12.7000	5	127.0	14	.55118
	33/64	.515625	13.0969	6	152.4	15	.59055
17/32		.53125	13.4937	7	177.8	16	.62992
	35/64	.546875	13.8906	8	203.2	17	.66929
9/16		.5625	14.2875	9	228.6	18	.70866
	37/64	.578125	14.6844	10	254.0	19	.74803
19/32		.59375	15.0812	11	279.4	20	.78740
	39/64	.609375	15.4781	12	304.8	21	.82677
5/8		.625	15.8750	13	330.2	22	.86614
	41/64	.640625	16.2719	14	355.6	23	.90551
21/32		.65625	16.6687	15	381.0	24	.94488
	43/64	.671875	17.0656	16	406.4	25	.98425
11/16		.6875	17.4625	17	431.8	26	1.02362
	45/64	.703125	17.8594	18	457.2	27	1.06299
23/32		.71875	18.2562	19	482.6	28	1.10236
	47/64	.734375	18.6531	20	508.0	29	1.14173
3/4		.75	19.0500	21	533.4	30	1.18110
	49/64	.765625	19.4469	22	558.8	31	1.22047
25/32		.78125	19.8437	23	584.2	32	1.25984
	51/64	.796875	20.2406	24	609.6	33	1.29921
13/16		.8125	20.6375	25	635.0	34	1.33858
	53/64	.828125	21.0344	26	660.4	35	1.37795
27/32		.84375	21.4312	27	685.8	36	1.41732
	55/64	.859375	21.8281	28	711.2	37	1.4567
7/8		.875	22.2250	29	736.6	38	1.4961
	57/64	.890625	22.6219	30	762.0	39	1.5354
29/32		.90625	23.0187	31	787.4	40	1.5748
	59/64	.921875	23.4156	32	812.8	41	1.6142
15/16		.9375	23.8125	33	838.2	42	1.6535
	61/64	.953125	24.2094	34	863.6	43	1.6929
31/32		.96875	24.6062	35	889.0	44	1.7323
	63/64	.984375	25.0031	36	914.4	45	1.7717

UNITS	Pints to Litres	Gallons to Litres	Litres to Pints	Litres to Gallons	Miles to Kilometres	Kilometres to Miles	Lbs. per sq. In. to Kg. per sq. Cm.	Kg. per sq. Cm. to Lbs. per sq. In.
1	.57	4.55	1.76	.22	1.61	.62	.07	14.22
2	1.14	9.09	3.52	.44	3.22	1.24	.14	28.50
3	1.70	13.64	5.28	.66	4.83	1.86	.21	42.67
4	2.27	18.18	7.04	.88	6.44	2.49	.28	56.89
5	2.84	22.73	8.80	1.10	8.05	3.11	.35	71.12
6	3.41	27.28	10.56	1.32	9.66	3.73	.42	85.34
7	3.98	31.82	12.32	1.54	11.27	4.35	.49	99.56
8	4.55	36.37	14.08	1.76	12.88	4.97	.56	113.79
9		40.91	15.84	1.98	14.48	5.59	.63	128.00
10		45.46	17.60	2.20	16.09	6.21	.70	142.23
20				4.40	32.19	12.43	1.41	284.47
30				6.60	48.28	18.64	2.11	426.70
40				8.80	64.37	24.85		
50					80.47	31.07		
60					96.56	37.28		
70					112.65	43.50		
80					128.75	49.71		
90					144.84	55.92		
100					160.93	62.14		

UNITS	Lb ft to kgm	Kgm to lb ft	UNITS	Lb ft to kgm	Kgm to lb ft
1	.138	7.233	7	.967	50.631
2	.276	14.466	8	1.106	57.864
3	.414	21.699	9	1.244	65.097
4	.553	28.932	10	1.382	72.330
5	.691	36.165	20	2.765	144.660
6	.829	43.398	30	4.147	216.990

HINTS ON MAINTENANCE AND OVERHAUL

There are few things more rewarding than the restoration of a vehicle's original peak of efficiency and smooth performance.

The following notes are intended to help the owner to reach that state of perfection. Providing that he possesses the basic manual skills he should have no difficulty in performing most of the operations detailed in this manual. It must be stressed, however, that where recommended in the manual, highly-skilled operations ought to be entrusted to experts, who have the necessary equipment, to carry out the work satisfactorily.

Quality of workmanship:

The hazardous driving conditions on the roads to-day demand that vehicles should be as nearly perfect, mechanically, as possible. It is therefore most important that amateur work be carried out with care, bearing in mind the often inadequate working conditions, and also the inferior tools which may have to be used. It is easy to counsel perfection in all things, and we recognize that it may be setting an impossibly high standard. We do, however, suggest that every care should be taken to ensure that a vehicle is as safe to take on the road as it is humanly possible to make it.

Safe working conditions:

Even though a vehicle may be stationary, it is still potentially dangerous if certain sensible precautions are not taken when working on it while it is supported on jacks or blocks. It is indeed preferable not to use jacks alone, but to supplement them with carefully placed blocks, so that there will be plenty of support if the car rolls off the jacks during a strenuous manoeuvre. Axle stands are an excellent way of providing a rigid base which is not readily disturbed. Piles of bricks are a dangerous substitute. Be careful not to get under heavy loads on lifting tackle, the load could fall. It is preferable not to work alone when lifting an engine, or when working underneath a vehicle which is supported well off the ground. To be trapped, particularly under the vehicle, may have unpleasant results if help is not quickly forthcoming. Make some provision, however humble, to deal with fires. Always disconnect a battery if there is a likelihood of electrical shorts. These may start a fire if there is leaking fuel about. This applies particularly to leads which can carry a heavy current, like those in the starter circuit. While on the subject of electricity, we must also stress the danger of using equipment which is run off the mains and which has no earth or has faulty wiring or connections. So many workshops have damp floors, and electrical shocks are of such a nature that it is sometimes impossible to let go of a live lead or piece of equipment due to the muscular spasms which take place.

Work demanding special care:

This involves the servicing of braking, steering and suspension systems. On the road, failure of the braking system may be disastrous. Make quite sure that there can be no possibility of failure through the bursting of rusty brake pipes or rotten hoses, nor to a sudden loss of pressure due to defective seals or valves.

Problems:

The chief problems which may face an operator are:
1 External dirt.
2 Difficulty in undoing tight fixings
3 Dismantling unfamiliar mechanisms.
4 Deciding in what respect parts are defective.
5 Confusion about the correct order for reassembly.
6 Adjusting running clearances.
7 Road testing.
8 Final tuning.

Practical suggestion to solve the problems:

1 Preliminary cleaning of large parts—engines, transmissions, steering, suspensions, etc.,—should be carried out before removal from the car. Where road dirt and mud alone are present, wash clean with a high-pressure water jet, brushing to remove stubborn adhesions, and allow to drain and dry. Where oil or grease is also present, wash down with a proprietary compound (Gunk, Teepol etc.,) applying with a stiff brush—an old paint brush is suitable—into all crevices. Cover the distributor and ignition coils with a polythene bag and then apply a strong water jet to clear the loosened deposits. Allow to drain and dry. The assemblies will then be sufficiently clean to remove and transfer to the bench for the next stage.

On the bench, further cleaning can be carried out, first wiping the parts as free as possible from grease with old newspaper. Avoid using rag or cotton waste which can leave clogging fibres behind. Any remaining grease can be removed with a brush dipped in paraffin. If necessary, traces of paraffin can be removed by carbon tetrachloride. Avoid using paraffin or petrol in large quantities for cleaning in enclosed areas, such as garages, on account of the high fire risk.

When all exteriors have been cleaned, and not before, dismantling can be commenced. This ensures that dirt will not enter into interiors and orifices revealed by dismantling. In the next phases, where components have to be cleaned, use carbon tetrachloride in preference to petrol and keep the containers covered except when in use. After the components have been cleaned, plug small holes with tapered hard wood plugs cut to size and blank off larger orifices with grease-proof paper and masking tape. Do not use soft wood plugs or matchsticks as they may break.

2 It is not advisable to hammer on the end of a screw thread, but if it must be done, first screw on a nut to protect the thread, and use a lead hammer. This applies particularly to the removal of tapered cotters. Nuts and bolts seem to 'grow' together, especially in exhaust systems. If penetrating oil does not work, try the judicious application of heat, but be careful of starting a fire. Asbestos sheet or cloth is useful to isolate heat.

Tight bushes or pieces of tail-pipe rusted into a silencer can be removed by splitting them with an open-ended hacksaw. Tight screws can sometimes be started by a tap from a hammer on the end of a suitable screwdriver. Many tight fittings will yield to the judicious use of a hammer, but it must be a soft-faced hammer if damage is to be avoided, use a heavy block on the opposite side to absorb shock. Any parts of the steering system which have been damaged should be renewed, as attempts to repair them may lead to cracking and subsequent failure, and steering ball joints should be disconnected using a recommended tool to prevent damage.

3 If often happens that an owner is baffled when trying to dismantle an unfamiliar piece of equipment. So many modern devices are pressed together or assembled by spinning-over flanges, that they must be sawn apart. The intention is that the whole assembly must be renewed. However, parts which appear to be in one piece to the naked eye, may reveal close-fitting joint lines when inspected with a magnifying glass, and, this may provide the necessary clue to dismantling. Left-handed screw threads are used where rotational forces would tend to unscrew a right handed screw thread.

Be very careful when dismantling mechanisms which may come apart suddenly. Work in an enclosed space where the parts will be contained, and drape a piece of cloth over the device if springs are likely to fly in all directions. Mark everything which might be reassembled in the wrong position, scratched symbols may be used on unstressed parts, or a sequence of tiny dots from a centre punch can be useful. Stressed parts should never be scratched or centre-popped as this may lead to cracking under working conditions. Store parts which look alike in the correct order for reassembly. Never rely upon memory to assist in the assembly of complicated mechanisms, especially when they will be dismantled for a long time, but make notes, and drawings to supplement the diagrams in the manual, and put labels on detached wires. Rust stains may indicate unlubricated wear. This can sometimes be seen round the outside edge of a bearing cup in a universal joint. Look for bright rubbing marks on parts which normally should not make heavy contact. These might prove that something is bent or running out of truth. For example, there might be bright marks on one side of a piston, at the top near the ring grooves, and others at the bottom of the skirt on the other side. This could well be the clue to a bent connecting rod. Suspected cracks can be proved by heating the component in a light oil to approximately 100°C, removing, drying off, and dusting with french chalk, if a crack is present the oil retained in the crack will stain the french chalk.

4 In determining wear, and the degree, against the permissible limits set in the manual, accurate measurement can only be achieved by the use of a micrometer. In many cases, the wear is given to the fourth place of decimals; that is in ten-thousandths of an inch. This can be read by the vernier scale on the barrel of a good micrometer. Bore diameters are more difficult to determine. If, however, the matching shaft is accurately measured, the degree of play in the bore can be felt as a guide to its suitability. In other cases, the shank of a twist drill of known diameter is a handy check.

Many methods have been devised for determining the clearance between bearing surfaces. To-day the best and simplest is by the use of Plastigage, obtainable from most garages. A thin plastic thread is laid between the two surfaces and the bearing is tightened, flattening the thread. On removal, the width of the thread is compared with a scale supplied with the thread and the clearance is read off directly. Sometimes joint faces leak persistently, even after gasket renewal. The fault will then be traceable to distortion, dirt or burrs. Studs which are screwed into soft metal frequently raise burrs at the point of entry. A quick cure for this is to chamfer the edge of the hole in the part which fits over the stud.

5 **Always check a replacement part with the original one before it is fitted.**

If parts are not marked, and the order for reassembly is not known, a little detective work will help. Look for marks which are due to wear to see if they can be mated. Joint faces may not be identical due to manufacturing errors, and parts which overlap may be stained, giving a clue to the correct position. Most fixings leave identifying marks especially if they were painted over on assembly. It is then easier to decide whether a nut, for instance, has a plain, a spring, or a shakeproof washer under it. All running surfaces become 'bedded' together after long spells of work and tiny imperfections on one part will be found to have left corresponding marks on the other. This is particularly true of shafts and bearings and even a score on a cylinder wall will show on the piston.

6 Checking end float or rocker clearances by feeler gauge may not always give accurate results because of wear. For instance, the rocker tip which bears on a valve stem may be deeply pitted, in which case the feeler will simply be bridging a depression. Thrust washers may also wear depressions in opposing faces to make accurate measurement difficult. End float is then easier to check by using a dial gauge. It is common practice to adjust end play in bearing assemblies, like front hubs with taper rollers, by doing up the axle nut until the hub becomes stiff to turn and then backing it off a little. Do not use this method with ballbearing hubs as the assembly is often preloaded by tightening the axle nut to its fullest extent. If the splitpin hole will not line up, file the base of the nut a little.

Steering assemblies often wear in the straight-ahead position. If any part is adjusted, make sure that it remains free when moved from lock to lock. Do not be surprised if an assembly like a steering gearbox, which is known to be carefully adjusted outside the car, becomes stiff when it is bolted in place. This will be due to distortion of the case by the pull of the mounting bolts, particularly if the mounting points are not all touching together. This problem may be met in other equipment and is cured by careful attention to the alignment of mounting points.

When a spanner is stamped with a size and A/F it means that the dimension is the width between the jaws and has no connection with ANF, which is the designation for the American National Fine thread. Coarse threads like Whitworth are rarely used on cars to-day except for studs which screw into soft aluminium or cast iron. For this reason it might be found that the top end of a cylinder head stud has a fine thread and the lower end a coarse thread to screw into the cylinder block. If the car has mainly UNF threads then it is likely that any coarse threads will be UNC, which are not the same as Whitworth. Small sizes have the same number of threads in Whitworth and UNC, but in the $\frac{1}{2}$ inch size for example, there are twelve threads to the inch in the former and thirteen in the latter.

7 After a major overhaul, particularly if a great deal of work has been done on the braking, steering and suspension systems, it is advisable to approach the problem of testing with care. If the braking system has been overhauled, apply heavy pressure to the brake pedal and get a second operator to check every possible source of leakage. The brakes may work extremely well, but a leak could cause complete failure after a few miles.

Do not fit the hub caps until every wheel nut has been checked for tightness, and make sure the tyre pressures are correct. Check the levels of coolant, lubricants and hydraulic fluids. Being satisfied that all is well, take the car on the road and test the brakes at once. Check the steering and the action of the handbrake. Do all this at moderate speeds on quiet roads, and make sure there is no other vehicle behind you when you try a rapid stop.

Finally, remember that many parts settle down after a time, so check for tightness of all fixings after the car has been on the road for a hundred miles or so.

8 It is useless to tune an engine which has not reached its normal running temperature. In the same way, the tune of an engine which is stiff after a rebore will be different when the engine is again running free. Remember too, that rocker clearances on pushrod operated valve gear will change when the cylinder head nuts are tightened after an initial period of running with a new head gasket.

Trouble may not always be due to what seems the obvious cause. Ignition, carburation and mechanical condition are interdependent and spitting back through the carburetter, which might be attributed to a weak mixture, can be caused by a sticking inlet valve.

For one final hint on tuning, never adjust more than one thing at a time or it will be impossible to tell which adjustment produced the desired result.

GLOSSARY OF TERMS

Allen key — Cranked wrench of hexagonal section for use with socket head screws.

Alternator — Electrical generator producing alternating current. Rectified to direct current for battery charging.

Ambient temperature — Surrounding atmospheric temperature.

Annulus — Used in engineering to indicate the outer ring gear of an epicyclic gear train.

Armature — The shaft carrying the windings, which rotates in the magnetic field of a generator or starter motor. That part of a solenoid or relay which is activated by the magnetic field.

Axial — In line with, or pertaining to, an axis.

Backlash — Play in meshing gears.

Balance lever — A bar where force applied at the centre is equally divided between connections at the ends.

Banjo axle — Axle casing with large diameter housing for the crownwheel and differential.

Bendix pinion — A self-engaging and self-disengaging drive on a starter motor shaft.

Bevel pinion — A conical shaped gearwheel, designed to mesh with a similar gear with an axis usually at 90 deg. to its own.

bhp — Brake horse power, measured on a dynamometer.

bmep — Brake mean effective pressure. Average pressure on a piston during the working stroke.

Brake cylinder — Cylinder with hydraulically operated piston(s) acting on brake shoes or pad(s).

Brake regulator — Control valve fitted in hydraulic braking system which limits brake pressure to rear brakes during heavy braking to prevent rear wheel locking.

Camber — Angle at which a wheel is tilted from the vertical.

Capacitor — Modern term for an electrical condenser. Part of distributor assembly, connected across contact breaker points, acts as an interference suppressor.

Castellated — Top face of a nut, slotted across the flats, to take a locking splitpin.

Castor — Angle at which the kingpin or swivel pin is tilted when viewed from the side.

cc — Cubic centimetres. Engine capacity is arrived at by multiplying the area of the bore in sq cm by the stroke in cm by the number of cylinders.

Clevis — U-shaped forked connector used with a clevis pin, usually at handbrake connections.

Collet — A type of collar, usually split and located in a groove in a shaft, and held in place by a retainer. The arrangement used to retain the spring(s) on a valve stem in most cases.

Commutator — Rotating segmented current distributor between armature windings and brushes in generator or motor.

Compression ratio — The ratio, or quantitative relation, of the total volume (piston at bottom of stroke) to the unswept volume (piston at top of stroke) in an engine cylinder.

Condenser — See capacitor.

Core plug — Plug for blanking off a manufacturing hole in a casting.

Crownwheel — Large bevel gear in rear axle, driven by a bevel pinion attached to the propeller shaft. Sometimes called a 'ring gear'.

'C'-spanner — Like a 'C' with a handle. For use on screwed collars without flats, but with slots or holes.

Damper — Modern term for shock-absorber, used in vehicle suspension systems to damp out spring oscillations.

Depression — The lowering of atmospheric pressure as in the inlet manifold and carburetter.

Dowel — Close tolerance pin, peg, tube, or bolt, which accurately locates mating parts.

Drag link — Rod connecting steering box drop arm (pitman arm) to nearest front wheel steering arm in certain types of steering systems.

Dry liner — Thinwall tube pressed into cylinder bore

Dry sump — Lubrication system where all oil is scavenged from the sump, and returned to a separate tank.

Dynamo — See Generator.

Electrode — Terminal, part of an electrical component, such as the points or 'Electrodes' of a sparking plug.

Electrolyte — In lead-acid car batteries a solution of sulphuric acid and distilled water.

End float — The axial movement between associated parts, end play.

EP — Extreme pressure. In lubricants, special grades for heavily loaded bearing surfaces, such as gear teeth in a gearbox, or crownwheel and pinion in a rear axle.

Fade	Of brakes. Reduced efficiency due to overheating.
Field coils	Windings on the polepieces of motors and generators.
Fillets	Narrow finishing strips usually applied to interior bodywork.
First motion shaft	Input shaft from clutch to gearbox.
Fullflow filter	Filters in which all the oil is pumped to the engine. If the element becomes clogged, a bypass valve operates to pass unfiltered oil to the engine.
FWD	Front wheel drive.
Gear pump	Two meshing gears in a close fitting casing. Oil is carried from the inlet round the outside of both gears in the spaces between the gear teeth and casing to the outlet, the meshing gear teeth prevent oil passing back to the inlet, and the oil is forced through the outlet port.
Generator	Modern term for 'Dynamo'. When rotated produces electrical current.
Grommet	A ring of protective or sealing material. Can be used to protect pipes or leads passing through bulkheads.
Grubscrew	Fully threaded headless screw with screwdriver slot. Used for locking, or alignment purposes.
Gudgeon pin	Shaft which connects a piston to its connecting rod. Sometimes called 'wrist pin', or 'piston pin'.
Halfshaft	One of a pair transmitting drive from the differential.
Helical	In spiral form. The teeth of helical gears are cut at a spiral angle to the side faces of the gearwheel.
Hot spot	Hot area that assists vapourisation of fuel on its way to cylinders. Often provided by close contact between inlet and exhaust manifolds.
HT	High Tension. Applied to electrical current produced by the ignition coil for the sparking plugs.
Hydrometer	A device for checking specific gravity of liquids. Used to check specific gravity of electrolyte.
Hypoid bevel gears	A form of bevel gear used in the rear axle drive gears. The bevel pinion meshes below the centre line of the crownwheel, giving a lower propeller shaft line.
Idler	A device for passing on movement. A free running gear between driving and driven gears. A lever transmitting track rod movement to a side rod in steering gear.
Impeller	A centrifugal pumping element. Used in water pumps to stimulate flow.
Journals	Those parts of a shaft that are in contact with the bearings.
Kingpin	The main vertical pin which carries the front wheel spindle, and permits steering movement. May be called 'steering pin' or 'swivel pin'.
Layshaft	The shaft which carries the laygear in the gearbox. The laygear is driven by the first motion shaft and drives the third motion shaft according to the gear selected. Sometimes called the 'countershaft' or 'second motion shaft.'
lb ft	A measure of twist or torque. A pull of 10 lb at a radius of 1 ft is a torque of 10 lb ft.
lb/sq in	Pounds per square inch.
Little-end	The small, or piston end of a connecting rod. Sometimes called the 'small-end'.
LT	Low Tension. The current output from the battery.
Mandrel	Accurately manufactured bar or rod used for test or centring purposes.
Manifold	A pipe, duct, or chamber, with several branches.
Needle rollers	Bearing rollers with a length many times their diameter.
Oil bath	Reservoir which lubricates parts by immersion. In air filters, a separate oil supply for wetting a wire mesh element to hold the dust.
Oil wetted	In air filters, a wire mesh element lightly oiled to trap and hold airborne dust.
Overlap	Period during which inlet and exhaust valves are open together.
Panhard rod	Bar connected between fixed point on chassis and another on axle to control sideways movement.
Pawl	Pivoted catch which engages in the teeth of a ratchet to permit movement in one direction only.
Peg spanner	Tool with pegs, or pins, to engage in holes or slots in the part to be turned.
Pendant pedals	Pedals with levers that are pivoted at the top end.
Phillips screwdriver	A cross-point screwdriver for use with the cross-slotted heads of Phillips screws.
Pinion	A small gear, usually in relation to another gear.
Piston-type damper	Shock absorber in which damping is controlled by a piston working in a closed oil-filled cylinder.
Preloading	Preset static pressure on ball or roller bearings not due to working loads.
Radial	Radiating from a centre, like the spokes of a wheel.

Radius rod	Pivoted arm confining movement of a part to an arc of fixed radius.
Ratchet	Toothed wheel or rack which can move in one direction only, movement in the other being prevented by a pawl.
Ring gear	A gear tooth ring attached to outer periphery of flywheel. Starter pinion engages with it during starting.
Runout	Amount by which rotating part is out of true.
Semi-floating axle	Outer end of rear axle halfshaft is carried on bearing inside axle casing. Wheel hub is secured to end of shaft.
Servo	A hydraulic or pneumatic system for assisting, or, augmenting a physical effort. See 'Vacuum Servo'.
Setscrew	One which is threaded for the full length of the shank.
Shackle	A coupling link, used in the form of two parallel pins connected by side plates to secure the end of the master suspension spring and absorb the effects of deflection.
Shell bearing	Thinwalled steel shell lined with anti-friction metal. Usually semi-circular and used in pairs for main and big-end bearings.
Shock absorber	See 'Damper'.
Silentbloc	Rubber bush bonded to inner and outer metal sleeves.
Socket-head screw	Screw with hexagonal socket for an Allen key.
Solenoid	A coil of wire creating a magnetic field when electric current passes through it. Used with a soft iron core to operate contacts or a mechanical device.
Spur gear	A gear with teeth cut axially across the periphery.
Stub axle	Short axle fixed at one end only.
Tachometer	An instrument for accurate measurement of rotating speed. Usually indicates in revolutions per minute.
TDC	Top Dead Centre. The highest point reached by a piston in a cylinder, with the crank and connecting rod in line.
Thermostat	Automatic device for regulating temperature. Used in vehicle coolant systems to open a valve which restricts circulation at low temperature.
Third motion shaft	Output shaft of gearbox.
Threequarter floating axle	Outer end of rear axle halfshaft flanged and bolted to wheel hub, which runs on bearing mounted on outside of axle casing. Vehicle weight is not carried by the axle shaft.
Thrust bearing or washer	Used to reduce friction in rotating parts subject to axial loads.
Torque	Turning or twisting effort. See 'lb ft'.
Track rod	The bar(s) across the vehicle which connect the steering arms and maintain the front wheels in their correct alignment.
UJ	Universal joint. A coupling between shafts which permits angular movement.
UNF	Unified National Fine screw thread.
Vacuum servo	Device used in brake system, using difference between atmospheric pressure and inlet manifold depression to operate a piston which acts to augment brake pressure as required. See 'Servo'.
Venturi	A restriction or 'choke' in a tube, as in a carburetter, used to increase velocity to obtain a reduction in pressure.
Vernier	A sliding scale for obtaining fractional readings of the graduations of an adjacent scale.
Welch plug	A domed thin metal disc which is partially flattened to lock in a recess. Used to plug core holes in castings.
Wet liner	Removable cylinder barrel, sealed against coolant leakage, where the coolant is in direct contact with the outer surface.
Wet sump	A reservoir attached to the crankcase to hold the lubricating oil.

INDEX

A

Acceleration pump	29
Air cleaners	36
Alternator checks	120
Alternator diodes	121
Antifreeze	54
Anti-roll bar	87
Armatures	115

B

Ball joints	90
Battery testing	114
Beam-setting, headlamps	125
Bearings, big-end	21
Bearings, electric motor	115
Bearings, main	23
Belt tension	52
Bleeding the brakes	109
Bleeding the clutch	60
Bonnet, GT	134
Bonnet, Vitesse	138
Brake adjustments	101
Brake disc	103
Brake drum	104
Brake master cylinder, standard	58
Brake master cylinder, tandem	108
Brake servo	110
Brushgear	115

C

Cables, handbrake	108
Cable rack, windscreen wiper	123
Caliper maintenance	103
Cam followers	13
Camshaft	18
Camshaft driving chain	16
Capacities	157
Capacitor, distributor	46
Carburetter adjustments, emission control	35
Carburetter adjustments, standard	32
Carburetter needle sizes	151
Carburetter operation	29
Carburetter servicing, emission control	33
Carburetter servicing, standard	29
Clutch master cylinder	58
Clutch driven plate	61
Clutch removal	19
Clutch release mechanism	61
Clutch slave cylinder	60
Commutators	115
Compression ratio	149
Condenser (see Capacitor)	
Connecting rods	22
Contacts, generator control box	117
Contacts, distributor	43
Control box, generator	117
Control unit, alternator	120
Crankshaft bearings, big-end	21
Crankshaft bearings, main	23
Crankshaft details	23

D

Cylinder bore	21
Cylinder head nut sequence	16
Cylinder head removal	13
Cylinder head servicing	14

D

Damper, carburetter	27, 29
Damper (shock absorber) front	91
Damper (shock absorber) rear	83
Damper, steering rack	95
Decarbonising	14
Diaphragm, fuel pump	28
Diaphragm, servo	110
Diaphragm, Stromberg carburetter	29
Diaphragm spring, clutch	57
Dimensions	156
Diodes, alternator	121
Disc brake friction pads	102
Disc brake removal	87, 103
Distributor adjustment	41
Distributor drive gear	18
Distributor maintenance	43
Doors and components, GT	132
Doors and components, Vitesse	137
Drum brakes	103

E

Electrolyte, battery	114
Engine description	9
Engine removal	12
Engine reassembly	24
Emission controlled engine	24, 151
Emission control carburetters	33
Emission control data	151
Emission control vacuum system for ignition	41
Emission control valve	36

F

Facia, GT	135
Facia, Vitesse	142
Fan belt	52
Fan blades	16
Field coils	116
Firing order	151
Flasher unit	125
Flywheel and ring-gear	19
Friction linings, clutch	61
Friction linings, drum brakes	103
Friction pads, disc brakes	102
Front hubs, adjustment	89
Front hubs, lubrication	87
Front road spring	91
Front road spring data	154
Front suspension geometry	92
Front suspension sub-assembly	90
Front wheel alignment	96
Fuel filter	28
Fuel gauge	126
Fuel pump	28
Fuses	125

G

Gasket, cylinder head 13
Gaskets, engine 24
Gearbox description 63
Gearbox lubrication 63
Gearbox removal 65
Gear selector mechanism 69
Generator 116
Glossary of terms 176
Grading of pistons 22, 149
Grinding-in valves 15
Gudgeon pins 22

H

Handbrake adjustment 107
Handbrake cables 107
Headlamps 125
Head nut tightening sequence 16
Head removal 13
Heater, GT 135
Heater, Vitesse 144
Heater blower motor, GT 135
Heater blower motor, Vitesse .. 145
Hints on maintenance and overhaul .. 173
Horn adjustment 124
HT leads 49
Hub bearings, front 87
Hub bearings, rear 79
Hydraulic fluid 57, 102
Hydraulic system, brakes 108
Hydraulic system, bleeding 60, 109
Hydraulic pressure differential actuator .. 108
Hydrometer test 114

I

Idling adjustment, emission controlled .. 35
Idling adjustment, standard 32
Idling speeds 151
Ignition faults 45
Ignition leads 49
Ignition timing 48
Impact clamp 98
Instruments, GT 135
Instruments, Vitesse 143

J

Jet, carburetter 29
Jet centralising 32
Jet adjustment, emission control .. 36
Jet adjustment, standard 32

L

Lock, bonnet 145
Lock, door, GT 132
Lock, door, Vitesse 138
Lock, steering 93, 95
Low-tension circuit, ignition 45

M

Main bearings 23
Master cylinder, clutch and standard brakes 58
Master cylinder, tandem brakes 108
Mixture control, carburetters 32, 36

N

Needle, carburetter, emission control .. 33
Needle, carburetter, standard 29, 31
Needle sizes 151
Needle valves 31, 33

O

Oil filter 20
Oil filter, overdrive 74
Oil pump 20
Oil pressure relief valve 20
Oil seals, crankshaft 23
Oil seals, differential 82
Overdrive 70

P

Park position, wipers 123
Pistons, engine 22
Piston, carburetter 29, 31
Piston grades, engine 149
Piston rings 22, 149
Pressure differential warning actuator 108, 110
Propeller shaft 76
Pump, fuel 28
Pump, oil 20
Pump, water 53

R

Rack adjustment 94
Rack lubrication 93
Radiator 52
Radius arm 83
Rear axle drive shaft 76
Rear axle oil leaks 82
Rear dampers 83
Rear brakes 103
Rear brake adjustment 101
Rear road spring 84
Rear road spring data 153
Rear suspension 83
Regulator, control box 117
Regulator, door window, GT 133
Regulator, door window, Vitesse .. 138
Removing engine and gearbox 12
Remote control door lock, GT 134
Remote control door lock, Vitesse .. 138
Rocker gear 16
Rotoflex coupling 79

S

Selector mechanism, gearbox 69
Shock absorbers (see Dampers)
Slave cylinder, clutch 60
Sliding roof 142
Slow-running, emission controlled .. 35
Slow-running, standard 32
Sparking plugs 49
Sparking plug type 151
Specific gravity, battery 114
Sprockets, alignment 16
Springs, road 84, 91

Springs, valve 16
Stator, alternator 122
Starter motor 118
Starter solenoid 119
Steering column 97
Steering unit 93
Stroboscopic ignition timing 48
Synchromesh units 67
Synchronising carburetters, emission control 35
Synchronising carburetters, standard .. 32

T

Temperature gauge 126
Thermostat 54
Timing chain 16
Timing, ignition 48
Timing, valves 17
Torque wrench settings 158
Track, front wheels 96
Tyres and tyre pressures 157

U

Universal joints, transmission 75

V

Vacuum control, ignition 41
Valve clearances 24
Valve data, engine 150
Valve guides 15
Valve seat grinding 15
Valve springs 16
Valve timing 17, 150
Voltage stabiliser 126

W

Water circulation 51
Water drain taps 52
Water filler cap 51
Water pump.. 53
Weights 156
Window glass, backlight and quarter light .. 129
Window glass, door, GT 133
Window glass, door, Vitesse 138
Windscreen 129
Wiper motor 123
Wiper wheelboxes 124
Wiring diagrams 161

NOTES

Alfa Romeo Giulia 1600,
  1750, 2000 1962 on
Aston Martin 1921-58
Auto Union Audi 70, 80,
  Super 90, 1966-72
Audi 100 1969 on
Austin, Morris etc.
  1100 Mk. 1 1962-67
Austin, Morris etc. 1100
  Mk. 2, 3, 1300 Mk. 1, 2, 3
  America 1968 on
Austin A30, A35, A40
  Farina 1951-67
Austin A55 Mk. 2, A60
  1958-69
Austin A99, A110 1959-68
Austin J4 1960 on
Austin Allegro 1973 on
Austin Maxi 1969 on
Austin, Morris 1800
  1964 on
Austin, Morris 2200 1972 on
Austin Kimberley, Tasman
  1970 on
Austin, Morris 1300, 1500
  Nomad 1969 on
BMC 3 (Austin A50, A55
  Mk. 1, Morris Oxford
  2, 3 1954-59)
Austin Healey 100/6,
  3000 1956-68
Austin Healey, MG
  Sprite, Midget 1958 on
Bedford CA Mk. 2 1964-69
Bedford CF Vans 1969 on
Bedford Beagle HA Vans
  1964 on
BMW 1600 1966 on
BMW 1800 1964-71
BMW 2000, 2002 1966 on
Chevrolet Corvair 1960-69
Chevrolet Corvette V8
  1957-65
Chevrolet Corvette V8
  1965 on
Chevrolet Vega 2300
  1970 on
Chrysler Valiant V8
  1965 on
Chrysler Valiant Straight
  Six 1963 on
Citroen DS 19, ID 19
  1955-66
Citroen ID 19, DS 19, 20,
  21 1966 on
Citroen Dyane Ami 1964 on
Daf 31, 32, 33, 44, 55
  1961 on
Datsun Bluebird 610 series
  1972 on
Datsun Cherry 100A, 120A
  1971 on
Datsun 1000, 1200 1968 on
Datsun 1300, 1400, 1600
  1968 on
Datsun 240C 1971 on

Datsun 240Z Sport 1970 on
Fiat 124 1966 on
Fiat 124 Sport 1966 on
Fiat 125 1967-72
Fiat 127 1971 on
Fiat 128 1969 on
Fiat 500 1957 on
Fiat 600, 600D 1955-69
Fiat 850 1964 on
Fiat 1100 1957-69
Fiat 1300, 1500 1961-67
Ford Anglia Prefect 100E
  1953-62
Ford Anglia 105E, Prefect
  107E 1959-67
Ford Capri 1300, 1600 OHV
  1968 on
Ford Capri 1300, 1600,
  2000 OHC 1972 on
Ford Capri 2000 V4, 3000 V6
  1969 on
Ford Classic, Capri
  1961-64
Ford Consul, Zephyr,
  Zodiac, 1, 2 1950-62
Ford Corsair Straight
  Four 1963-65
Ford Corsair V4 1965-68
Ford Corsair V4 2000
  1969-70
Ford Cortina 1962-66
Ford Cortina 1967-68
Ford Cortina 1969-70
Ford Cortina Mk. 3
  1970 on
Ford Escort 1967 on
Ford Falcon 6 1964-70
Ford Falcon XK, XL
  1960-63
Ford Falcon 6 XR/XA
  1966 on
Ford Falcon V8 (U.S.A.)
  1965-71
Ford Falcon V8 (Aust.)
  1966 on
Ford Pinto 1970 on
Ford Maverick 6 1969 on
Ford Maverick V8 1970 on
Ford Mustang 6 1965 on
Ford Mustang V8 1965 on
Ford Thames 10, 12,
  15 cwt 1957-65
Ford Transit V4 1965 on
Ford Zephyr Zodiac Mk. 3
  1962-66
Ford Zephyr Zodiac V4,
  V6, Mk. 4 1966-72
Ford Consul, Granada
  1972 on
Hillman Avenger 1970 on
Hillman Hunter 1966 on
Hillman Imp 1963-68
Hillman Imp 1969 on
Hillman Minx 1 to 5
  1956-65
Hillman Minx 1965-67

Hillman Minx 1966-70
Hillman Super Minx
  1961-65
Jaguar XK120, 140, 150,
  Mk. 7, 8, 9 1948-61
Jaguar 2.4, 3.4, 3.8 Mk.
  1, 2 1955-69
Jaguar 'E' Type 1961-72
Jaguar 'S' Type 420
  1963-68
Jaguar XJ6 1968 on
Jowett Javelin Jupiter
  1947-53
Landrover 1, 2 1948-61
Landrover 2, 2a, 3 1959 on
Mazda 616 1970 on
Mazda 808, 818 1972 on
Mazda 1200, 1300 1969 on
Mazda 1500, 1800 1967 on
Mazda RX-2 1971 on
Mazda R100, RX-3 1970 on
Mercedes-Benz 190b,
  190c, 200 1959-68
Mercedes-Benz 220
  1959-65
Mercedes-Benz 220/8
  1968 on
Mercedes-Benz 230
  1963-68
Mercedes-Benz 250
  1965-67
Mercedes-Benz 250
  1968 on
Mercedes-Benz 280
  1968 on
MG TA to TF 1936-55
MGA MGB 1955-68
MGB 1969 on
Mini 1959 on
Mini Cooper 1961-72
Morgan Four 1936-72
Morris Marina 1971 on
Morris (Aust) Marina
  1972 on
Morris Minor 2, 1000
  1952-71
Morris Oxford 5, 6 1959-71
NSU 1000 1963-72
NSU Prinz 1 to 4 1957-72
Opel Ascona, Manta
  1970 on
Opel GT 1900 1968 on
Opel Kadett, Olympia 993 cc
  1078 cc 1962 on
Opel Kadett, Olympia 1492,
  1698, 1897 cc 1967 on
Opel Rekord C 1966-72
Peugeot 204 1965 on
Peugeot 304 1970 on
Peugeot 404 1960 on
Peugeot 504 1968 on
Porsche 356A, B, C 1957-65
Porsche 911 1964 on
Porsche 912 1965-69
Porsche 914 S 1969 on
Reliant Regal 1952-73

Renault R4, R4L, 4 1961 on
Renault 5 1972 on
Renault 6 1968 on
Renault 8, 10, 1100 1962-71
Renault 12, 1969 on
Renault 15, 17 1971 on
Renault R16 1965 on
Renault Dauphine
  Floride 1957-67
Renault Caravelle 1962-68
Rover 60 to 110 1953-64
Rover 2000 1963-73
Rover 3 Litre 1958-67
Rover 3500, 3500S 1968 on
Saab 95, 96, Sport
  1960-68
Saab 99 1969 on
Saab V4 1966 on
Simca 1000 1961 on
Simca 1100 1967 on
Simca 1300, 1301, 1500,
  1501 1963 on
Skoda One (440, 445, 450)
  1955-70
Sunbeam Rapier Alpine
  1955-65
Toyota Carina, Celica
  1971 on
Toyota Corolla 1100,
  1200 1967 on
Toyota Corona 1500 Mk. 1
  1965-70
Toyota Corona Mk. 2
  1969 on
Triumph TR2, TR3, TR3A
  1952-62
Triumph TR4, TR4A
  1961-67
Triumph TR5, TR250,
  TR6 1967 on
Triumph 1300, 1500
  1965-73
Triumph 2000 Mk. 1, 2.5 PI
  Mk. 1 1963-69
Triumph 2000 Mk' 2, 2.5 PI
  Mk. 2 1969 on
Triumph Dolomite 1972 on
Triumph Herald 1959-68
Triumph Herald 1969-71
Triumph Spitfire, Vitesse
  1962-68
Triumph Spitfire Mk. 3, 4
  1969 on
Triumph GT6, Vitesse
  2 Litre 1969 on
Triumph Stag 1970 on
Triumph Toledo 1970 on
Vauxhall Velox, Cresta
  1957-72
Vauxhall Victor 1, 2, FB
  1957-64
Vauxhall Victor 101
  1964-67
Vauxhall Victor FD 1600,
  2000 1967-72

Continued on following page

THE AUTOBOOK SERIES OF WORKSHOP MANUALS

Vauxhall Victor 3300,
   Ventora 1968-72
Vauxhall Victor FE
   Ventora 1972 on
Vauxhall Viva HA 1963-66
Vauxhall Viva HB 1966-70

Vauxhall Viva, HC Firenza
   1971 on
Volkswagen Beetle 1954-67
Volkswagen Beetle 1968 on
Volkswagen 1500 1961-66

Volkswagen 1600 Fastback
   1965-73
Volkswagen Transporter
   1954-67
Volkswagen Transporter
   1968 on

Volkswagen 411 1968-72
Volvo 120 series 1961-70
Volvo 140 series 1966 on
Volvo 160 series 1968 on
Volvo 1800 1960-73